MY GARDEN AND OTHER ANiMALS

THE ONE SHOW NATURALIST

MIKE DILGER

MY GARDEN AND OTHER ANIMALS

Illustrations by Christina Holvey

Collins

First published in 2012 by Collins
an imprint of HarperCollins*Publishers*
77–85 Fulham Palace Road,
London W6 8JB

www.harpercollins.co.uk

17 16 15 14 13 12
10 9 8 7 6 5 4 3 2 1

Text © Mike Dilger 2012
Illustrations © Christina Holvey 2012

Mike Dilger asserts the moral right to
be identified as the author of this work

A catalogue record of this book is
available from the British Library

ISBN 978-0-00-745770-0

Printed and bound in Great Britain by
Clays Ltd, St Ives plc

MIX
Paper from
responsible sources
FSC® C007454

FSC™ is a non-profit international organisation established to promote
the responsible management of the world's forests. Products carrying the
FSC label are independently certified to assure customers that they come
from forests that are managed to meet the social, economic and
ecological needs of present and future generations,
and other controlled sources.

Find out more about HarperCollins and the environment at
www.harpercollins.co.uk/green

To the three women in my life:
Christina, Mum and Hilary

CONTENTS

JANUARY
THE MOVE

'Potential' was definitely the word that sprang to mind the first time I clapped eyes on our new 'house-and-garden-to-be' in the small rural village of Chew Stoke, eight miles south of Bristol. On my partner Christina's first viewing, the adjectives that sprung to her mind were 'dilapidated', 'overpriced' and 'abandoned'. True, the unprepossessing semi we had just purchased was an ex-council property, hastily built in 1956 to house those displaced by the flooding of 1,200 acres of farmland that would ultimately form the Chew Valley Lake Reservoir. The house had also been sitting empty for the best part of a year, often not one of the best of signs. Don't get me wrong, the property was more than habitable and according to our surveyor had been solidly built and was structurally sound, so at least it would be dry and warm. It was also a house perfectly designed with the phrase 'bog-standard' in mind, and certainly wouldn't be the recipient of any architectural prizes.

From the outside the pebble-dashed facade smeared over concrete-block walls bore more than a passing resemblance to the colour of boiled shite; and with a combination of pine-panelling, hideously dated wallpaper and marigold-coloured walls, the interior offered little improvement. Even though the house was of cheap construction and stuck in a 1970s time warp, we had always declared this to be of little concern, as the real reason behind making the huge financial leap of faith had been the bell-bottom-jeans-shaped garden at the rear.

Surrounded on either side by mature gardens and playing fields, and book-ended with a small wooded bank leading to a stream that also represented the northern boundary of the property, the garden, whilst currently tired, unkempt and unloved, might just be in a position to offer huge promise under the right stewardship.

Along one of the boundaries – which divided the garden from an adjacent playing field – a small peeled-up section of fence and digging-marks in the lawn were a sign of the active presence of badgers. Surely, too, the stream might just play host to passing kingfishers, and the mini-woodland would certainly act as the perfect wildlife corridor for the comings and goings of everything from grey squirrels to great tits. Who wouldn't bet on deer, foxes and woodpeckers making an appearance at some point too?

On our second viewing, endless possibilities as to how I could turn the garden into that mini nature reserve I yearned for began to run through my mind. My mouth followed suit, as I attempted to convince Christina of the simple, fun tasks we would be able to undertake to make the garden even more attractive to wildlife. 'The bottom of the garden is where we should create the meadow, the pond would be next to the garage, we could then remove the alien species from the wooded bank and place the bug hotel in a quiet corner ...' I breathlessly declared in a soliloquy that would have left Hamlet short of a few words. Building up a head of steam, and getting even more carried away, I further stated that if we were successful in purchasing the property, I would personally take in hand the task of re-designing and re-wilding the garden, while maybe Christina could be persuaded to take on the slightly less glamorous task of redeveloping the house ...

Now I hate to characterise our relationship as that of a 'building-castles-in-the-sky' type pitted against a cautious pragmatist, but broadly speaking it's true. So I was in no position to argue when Christina put down a few conditions as to how the division of labour would work even IF we were to make an offer.

While on one hand she thought it churlish to ride roughshod over my naive optimism, she also felt compelled to point out the uncomfortable truth that I was not exactly the most practical of people, and so would have to give serious thought as to whether I would have the technical 'know-how' to carry out such ambitious plans. Not helping my argument was my track record; in my old communal garden in Bristol I had always tended to be a little work-shy when it came to any hard graft, and my 'share' of the gardening chores had usually consisted of little more than filling the bird-feeders. In response, I assured her in no uncertain terms that this time it would be different.

Feeling like I was winning the argument, I also offered an additional sweetener by suggesting that I would of course seek advice immediately if I felt out of my depth and promised I wouldn't attempt anything foolhardy. Still unsure as to whom I was trying most to convince – her or myself – Christina suddenly and uncharacteristically threw caution to the wind, catching me totally off guard, by boldly stating that we should put in an offer without further ado! I could have kissed her … and in fact I did!

If anyone has ever tried to buy and sell property simultaneously they will understand why moving home is apparently right on the heels of death and divorce in that infamous list of 'the most stressful things in life'. Once our offer was accepted the purchase moved through at double-quick time and moving day quickly followed.

It's quite humbling seeing your worldly possessions – which have taken the best part of four decades to accumulate – reduced to a pile of cardboard boxes. This meant that Bill and his removal boys made short work of the flat's contents, as I watched my dwelling of the last ten years reduced to an empty shell in just a couple of hours. Stopping only briefly to help themselves to more tea and the last of the biscuits, they hopped in the van and headed for our new home, leaving Christina and me behind to take the opportunity to say goodbye to a flat that had treated us to so many happy memories, but which we had now also undoubtedly outgrown. Without looking back, we closed the front door on our old lives and headed off to the vendors' estate agents in Chew Stoke for our prize of two small keys, purchased for the mind-boggling sum of £220,000.

We arrived at our new house just a couple of minutes after the removals lorry had pulled up on the drive – *our* drive. The ever-practical Christina proceeded to open up the house and take the lads on a guided tour, pointing out which boxes were to be deposited where, which gave me the chance to excuse myself from the hustle and bustle for just a moment so that I could take in the garden through an entirely new set of eyes. This time it was OUR garden!

Passing through the crude, asbestos-covered outhouse adjoining the kitchen at the back of the property and out of the back door, the functional concrete patio funnelled down to a nondescript path, bisecting a lawn which had definitely seen better days. Dotted randomly around the lawn were a couple of long-neglected rose-standards, a sickly collection of random shrubs which had been planted in all the wrong places (and in the wrong soil type), two different-sized birch trees, two rowan trees positioned far too close together for either to flourish, and a majestic if slightly lop-sided beech tree. The centre of the garden featured a huge and monumentally ugly wooden pergola that had been built in the form of an archway and which quite possibly could have been the only other man-made structure, apart from the Great Wall of China, viewable from outer space.

As I took in the view from the patio, *our* patio, the left-hand boundary was split between next door's mature garden, with the further half running adjacent to a council playing field consisting of a goal post and a small playground for infants. Following down the right-hand side, the small creaky and rusting garden gate, which gave access to the drive at the side of the house, was attached to a short breeze-block wall, which in turn was adjoined to a great, hulking garage, shared with our neighbours. Finally, at the rear of the garage a panelled fence delineated the boundary between our property and that of next door's, giving our garden privacy if nothing else.

Pacing down the garden, the lawn ran in a fairly regimented fashion for some 25 yards in a northwesterly direction, increasing in width from the patio (or hips) down to a tree-covered shady bank (or the ankles), revealing at its base the aforementioned water feature poking out of the bottom of the flares like a pair of grubby feet. From our very first visit, I had envisaged the water course, with the remarkably unprepossessing name of Strode Brook, as the ace in our deck of wildlife cards. Our section of the brook happened to join our property at the head of a large meander, meaning that the water met the garden at an angle before caressing the bank for a 10-yard stretch and retreating away again at a tangent. Inside the bend on the opposite bank was an area that looked like it was attached to a much larger and formal garden, but apart from a carefully mown strip that had been cut to allow access down to the brook, the rest of the land had obviously been left to glorious abandonment – making it great for nature.

In addition to the more formal part of the garden, the bank on our side was in desperate need of attention. Being on the outer bend of the meander, the constant water flow had acted like a huge corrosive brillo pad, and had seriously undercut the bank to such an extent that the small, steep section closest to the playing field looked decidedly unstable. Additionally, the adjacent and much shallower middle section had previously been used as a dumping ground for garden waste, giving the bank more the look of a rubbish dump than a wooded glade.

Dominating the air space above the bank were a sickly-looking and ivy-festooned oak, whose exposed roots crudely protruded out of the steep bank in the precipitous northwesterly corner, and a 60-foot-tall flagpole-straight ash in the centre. Both of these trees were surrounded by overgrown rank hazels and hawthorns, which hadn't been touched for decades, and as a result had run amok in the understory, making an already dark north-facing slope look a

Tolkienesque mini-Mirkwood. To put it bluntly, it was hard to see the wood for the trees!

The wooded bank and brook were partitioned off from the rest of the garden by a 3-foot-high wooden fence, covered in chicken wire, meaning any entry to the wood could only be achieved via a straddle at the height which tends to be awkward for males. Apparently the reason for this fence lay in the fact that the house had belonged to a very senior gentleman by the name of Mr Gregory, who had lived and raised a family here for the best part of 50 years until he was removed against his will, but for his own safety, into an old folks' home nearby. Once an extremely keen gardener, in his latter years he suffered dementia but was still prone to impromptu walkabouts. During one of his mini-excursions down to the river, Mr Gregory had apparently accidentally uncovered a wasps' nest, resulting in him being stung numerous times before tumbling down the bank and into the brook. Unable to haul himself out, apparently Mr Gregory had lain dazed and confused in the water for several hours until his faint cries for help were heard by neighbours.

As I wandered around the garden, with my chest puffed out and a heady mixture of excitement and trepidation welling up, little seemed to have changed since our last viewing, but in other ways everything had changed – the garden was now our responsibility! Contemplating the gravitas of what we had just taken on, my mood was instantly lightened as I spotted the first basal rosettes of primroses, pushing their way up exactly where I had planned the meadow to be! In little more than a month, their flowers would be providing the first boost of nectar for any emerging queen bumblebees that had successfully navigated the perils of hibernation.

As I got to my feet, one of those unforgettable red-letter moments suddenly occurred as a bird began to sing – my first thrush song in 2011. To make the moment even more special, it was not only being sung by my favourite songbird, but the individual in

question had decided to belt out its mellifluous, strident and instantly recognisable song from the top of the oak tree, *our* oak tree, making it *our* song thrush!

When comparing birdsong, many say the nightingale is the finest songster in Britain, but I reckon in full swing the song thrush gives it a damn good run for its money. It's difficult to explain with mere words the astonishing complexity, beauty and power of the song thrush's song. Consisting of over a 100 exquisite, different musical phrases, each is repeated three or four times before the thrush draws breath in prelude to belting out another. It's as though the gaps in between each phrase have evolved to give the song thrush a second to retrospectively admire his artistry. If so, he wasn't the only one. As I stood there, listening to the virtuoso performance, it sounded like the bird was actually serenading me with a welcome song. The song thrush's timing was impeccable, birdsong had never sounded sweeter and, more importantly, it made me feel that everything *would* be all right.

Landing back on Planet Earth with a bump and suddenly painfully aware as to how much had to be done, I wandered back in to find Bill, the Bristolian born and bred removals gaffer, espousing his philosophy to Christina on everything from Formula 1 to the finer points of interior decoration. Despite his West Country chatter constantly reverberating around the bare walls of the house, giving the impression that there was rather more tea drinking going on than what we were actually paying them to do, both Bill and his two henchmen, Derek and, yes, Derek, made light work of unloading the van. Having distributed all the boxes, they paused only briefly to have one more round of tea and biscuits and receive their all-important tip for a job well done before hands were shaken and they were off, leaving us and our boxes to a new life in the country.

The thing that instantly hit me, as I watched the removals van disappear from view, was the sound of silence – I could hear nothing. No trains or planes, no ambulances, no road-drills – nothing. It was a far cry from my old flat in central Bristol where the constant background hum of the city had been something I had taken for granted for far too long. Undoubtedly a townie born and bred, this would be my first attempt at living in the country. It would also be the first ever house I had lived in where I would be able to lie in bed and listen to the sounds of the dawn chorus. How exciting would that be?!

My hypnotic trance of imagining how wonderful it would be to listen to blackcaps before breakfast was suddenly broken by the sight and sound of another van outside trying its best to squeeze past my hurriedly parked car on the pavement. It was only then that I realised in our rush to open up for the removals guys that we had partially blocked the entrance to next door's drive, and the owners of the other half of our semi. Not a good start. Dashing out to both apologise profusely and greet in one fell swoop, I offered the hand of friendship to my new neighbour, a wiry chap in his late forties called Andy, for whom an apology was deemed totally unnecessary and who seemed delighted that the other half of his property would finally be occupied. With big, bucket hands the texture of sandpaper, Andy was patently not someone who whiled away his professional life shuffling papers behind a desk; this was a man with a van, a man with technical ability and therefore someone worth cultivating a friendship with!

Despite being someone who crops up on telly on a regular basis to talk about everything from bumblebees to basking sharks, I'm often genuinely surprised when people recognise me. I suppose it's because I forget that people will make the connection between the similarity of the chap appearing on the goggle-box and the person in the flesh. And while it's very rarely an unpleasant experience when people want to meet you purely because you make regular appearances in the corner of their sitting rooms, it is a feeling, that unless you're Paul McCartney or David Beckham, you never really get used to. So adopting my usual tactic of quickly changing the subject from his opening gambit of 'I saw you on the telly last week',

I was quickly able to find out that not only was Andy a married man with three kids but also jointly ran a small plumbing business – handy indeed!

Apparently our arrival had been the talk of the street for the last couple of weeks, and whether this was down to my minor celebrity status or because anyone moving into a cul-de-sac in a small rural village would get the same level of scrutiny, I wasn't sure. After pleasantries were exchanged, and as Andy patently seemed aware of my wildlife pedigree, he immediately implored me to come and see his garden, with which we shared a boundary for some 15 yards, so he could show me the array of feeders he had installed at various locations. Being a practical fellow, he had built a couple of lovely bespoke wooden feeding tables, rather than choosing the Dilger Way, which is usually to part with the cash at an inflated price instead.

It being a cold, wintery day, the local bird community was indeed piling in to his refuelling stations, and even without my trusty binoculars, in the matter of just a couple of minutes I was able to point out the usual cast of characters including great tit, blue tit, chaffinch, robin and dunnock. What I didn't expect, though, was to see the tell-tale flashing white outer tail feathers of an altogether more unusual garden bird coming down to Andy's offerings.

'Reed bunting!' I suddenly blurted out like a Tourette's Syndrome sufferer, crudely cutting right across the middle of an entirely different discussion about the impressive amount of building work Andy had done to their house. To be fair, Andy also genuinely seemed thrilled by this find, declaring that he had never seen one before, and for me, back once again on the more comfortable subject of garden bird ecology rather than the intricacies of building regulations, I was able to give Andy a brief, impromptu lecture on the life history of the reed bunting.

Seemingly interested in my intricate knowledge of the bird's ecology, and warming to the theme, Andy pointed out where they fed the local fox and then showed me another wildlife feature in their garden, which up until that point I hadn't even noticed.

Nestling behind an ugly *leylandii* and no more than two yards from our communal fence I was delighted to be shown a pond that Andy's wife Lorraine, who apparently adores frogs, had cajoled her husband into digging back in 2007. Despite the feature looking like it needed a clear-out, as I could barely see any standing water for plants, Andy informed me, with immense pride, that both he and Lorraine regularly came down with a cuppa to watch both frogs and newts surfacing for a gulp of air before disappearing back down below to carry on with their aquatic shenanigans.

The reason for my delight at this news was twofold. Firstly it was wonderful that we had neighbours who were singing from the same song-sheet as us, in being keen to embrace the wildlife coming into their garden, rather than doing their level best to shut it out in favour of a sterile and – in my opinion – utterly soulless garden. Secondly, enticing frogs and newts into both our garden and the pond I would be creating later would surely be much easier if they only needed to travel a matter of a few yards across herbaceous border, rather than risk the perilous journey across acres of concrete and decking under the watchful eye of any number of predators.

Thanking Andy for the impromptu tour, and having had my offer of a glass of wine over the next couple of weeks accepted, I took my leave with the perfectly reasonable excuse that I had a house to unpack and shouldn't be giving Christina the impression that I was purposefully shirking my box-emptying duties. I barely had one foot through the door when I heard a small voice behind me. Marjory, as her name turned out, was our neighbour on the other side, and the lady with whom we had joint custody over the drive, although we didn't have a wall in common. Looking, to be honest, a touch unwell, Marjory must have been in her early fifties and was married to a chap called Dennis, who wouldn't be popping out to say hello as he was unwell and vulnerable to the sharp winter chill. It turned out that Marjory was also fighting her own battles with illness and was not keen to linger too long on the doorstep either, so she offered a brief but warm welcome to the street.

I prepared to attack the boxes with gusto, but only after one vital task was carried out. I had to get my priorities right and so immediately put up a couple of my feeders from my old flat into our new garden – we wanted reed buntings too!

As the day-to-day living essentials slowly began to be unpacked we at last began to make some progress in turning the house from a warehouse into some kind of home. Concentrating on the kitchen, so that we would at least be able to eat, and the bedroom, so that we could at least sleep, pots were placed in bare cupboards, cutlery located in empty drawers and the bed reassembled before being made. Pausing only for a cup of tea, poured out of the newly located teapot, our conversation was cut short by a knock at the door.

Having arrived back from work, Andy's wife Lorraine's curiosity had obviously got the better of her as she decided that meeting her new neighbours was something that couldn't wait until the following day. Talking in a thick Bristolian accent, which I have come to adore since moving to this part of the world, this blonde, super-slim mum of three was someone for whom talking was obviously a passion – what a chatterbox! In no time at all, we were all getting on like we had been friends for years, and very kindly she had no qualms in instantly offering her husband's services on hearing our most pressing domestic concern as to why we had no water coming out of any of the hot taps.

With hungry adolescents to feed next door, Lorraine bid us goodnight, and barely had we closed the door when the third neighbour of the day came knocking, also keen to welcome us to the street. Pausing only briefly to contemplate the difference between our warm reception in Chew Stoke and the decidedly chillier welcome I had received on purchasing my previous flat in Bristol, when it had taken weeks for my neighbours just to acknowledge my existence, I invited Stuart in to find a seat amongst the boxes. Stuart, it has to be said, was someone I already knew well, as until recently he had been a TV editor. Hailing from the West Midlands town of Stafford, I had always felt a kindred spirit with Stuart's Black Country roots and especially after we had discovered during one

previous discourse on football that we must have coincidentally been at a number of the same Wolverhampton Wanderers matches as kids.

Whilst helping us drain the rest of a bottle of champagne we had brought with us to celebrate the move, Stu regaled us with all the gossip about those neighbours we hadn't yet had the pleasure of meeting and declared how wonderful it was going to be to have a drinking partner on hand, who was, firstly, not a southerner, secondly, liked talking endlessly about football and, last but not least, was willing to neck a couple of pints every now and then.

Seeing we were visibly tiring from the physical and emotional exertions of the day – and perhaps more pertinently noting the last of the champagne had been drained and we couldn't immediately locate any more alcohol without emptying 15 boxes, Stu left for a nightcap at his own home some 50 yards up the road, but not before giving both of us one more of his 'welcome to the street' hugs.

With a slightly bizarre and utterly forgettable first meal in our new house of grilled sausages and steamed vegetables, and unable to watch TV because it hadn't yet been unpacked, we watched a DVD on my laptop, before going *up* to bed. Yes, we had finally moved out of a flat, and now, being in a proper grown-up house, we had stairs ... and did I also mention we had a garden as well?!

FEBRUARY
SETTLING IN AND KNUCKLING DOWN

For the entire first week in our new house I'm not afraid to admit that the garden hardly got a look-in. Anyone who has ever moved house knows that the list of jobs needing to be done in order to get services up and running can seem endless. In fact, most of the week was spent waiting in various electronic queuing systems as I attempted to persuade everyone from internet providers to satellite installers to actually do what they were supposedly paid to do – help me out!

Having moved in on Monday 31 January, it was the following weekend before we were even able to surface for air and actually carve out some garden time. Finally, as our first Sunday in the house arrived, we hurriedly showered, dressed, excitedly gulped down our porridge and donned warm clothes. At last, a garden day!

Equipped with notebooks, we had decided that the wisest use of time would be to take both a full stock-take of what we actually had in the garden and, importantly, what state it was in, before brutal decisions were to be made as to what was for the chop. To say that in many ways we were starting with a blank slate would have been an understatement. From even the most cursory of glances around the garden it was obvious that many of the shrubs and trees had been neglected for so long they had become so malformed and twisted that to put them out of their misery might be the kindest course of action.

First to come under our scrutiny was a mature but hideously deformed wisteria, sprawled across the central half of the garage wall. The climber gave the impression more of a mangy dog tied to a rusty fence than the stately and regal vine we know it to be when given proper care and attention. Hanging by its own weight a couple of yards away from the wall in some places and virtually nailed to it elsewhere, I don't think I've ever seen a plant more in need of a bit of TLC. After much debate we decided that it might not be a lost cause, but would need a ferocious short back-and-sides and total retraining to be given a fighting chance of making the grade.

The same, however, couldn't be said for two small cherry trees behind the garage, which had been so brutally disfigured by the seemingly totally random action of lopping off of various limbs, and were in such poor condition that they looked half dead. After somewhat less of a debate we decided the best option here would be to remove them entirely and replace them with some healthy new fruit trees.

Another plant that we also had to give the Caligula-style thumbs down was the middle rowan tree, which, sandwiched between another similar-sized rowan and a big beech tree, had, in truth, never really been given enough room to flourish, making it look like the arboreal runt of the litter. Additionally, having been planted right in the middle of the bottom part of the lawn, its foliage would undoubtedly cast a huge shadow over the area I had set aside for the meadow, which as a habitat needed to be both light and airy for the flowers to flourish. Still, cutting down a mature tree is a decision that should never be taken lightly, as the nineteenth-century parson and gardener Canon Henry Ellacombe famously once said, 'A garden without trees scarcely deserves to be called a garden.'

As we were keen to try and make our decisions based on what we thought would best suit the birds and the bees (amongst other groups), we were also mindful of the fact that surely the single most important way to make a garden more wildlife-friendly is to plant a tree. As stated by Ken Thompson in his wonderful wildlife garden-ing book, *No Nettles Required*, the more trees gardens have, the more beetles, bugs, snails, slugs, woodlice, social wasps, leaf-mining insects and moths will be attracted to use them for bed and break-fast, which in turn will prove a magnet for animals from higher up the food chain, such as birds and mammals. In addition, trees provide an extra dimension to gardens, enabling them to house more wildlife, just like we would now be in a position to fit more stuff into our new two-floored/three-bedroom house than in my previous single-bedroom flat.

However, taking everything into consideration, and with heavy hearts, we agreed that the garden would be better served in the long term if the rowan were removed. This same decision was also unfor-tunately extended to a small, sickly birch tree cowering in the shadow of a much larger and beautifully symmetrical birch adjacent to the playing field. A couple of small, nasty alien conifers on the wooded bank would also be for the chop, but these wouldn't be missed for a second.

With other plants, though, our concord would be severely tested. Dotted along the border of the wood, for example, were three or four random shrubs, which in their winter plumage neither of us recognised. Early on in this process, Christina declared herself to be in the 'if in doubt, chop it out' camp, whilst I was a follower of the 'cut in haste, repent at leisure' school of thought, meaning I inevitably took on the roll of defence counsel, arguing that the shrubs should receive a stay of execution until we found out what they were. After much cross-examination, however, the prosecution (Christina) eventually relented and agreed to wait and see how they turned out before making any decisions about their future. I couldn't help feeling, though, that this was just the first of many such battles of wills and that our strong-minded obstinacies would be tested on many more occasions over the next few months.

However, one job we were both keen to see achieved as soon as possible was the removal of Mr Gregory's fence, which stood out as an ugly junction between garden and wooded bank, in contradiction to our preferred natural blending of all the habitats from back door to brook.

Another undertaking we instantly agreed upon would be to clear as much ivy as possible from the oak tree in the northwest corner. On the very first occasion I had viewed the property, I remember being utterly thrilled to find that a mature oak tree was part and parcel of the garden. However, with many of the tree's roots exposed due to the undercutting nature of the brook, the fact that it was festooned from head to toe with ivy and the sheer amount of standing dead wood present, all seemed clearly to indicate that the tree had been struggling for some time.

In terms of an ability to attract wildlife to your garden, no one species can come even close to an English or pedunculate oak, with some naturalists having even likened an individual tree to the status of a nature reserve in its own right. With a staggering 284 different invertebrate species having been identified as living on oak trees, a diverse array of birds and mammals reliant on their acorns, a number of bat species roosting in the hollows and crevices, and great-spotted woodpeckers, nuthatches and treecreepers scouring the wood for food and nesting holes, it's no surprise that even a struggling oak would be one of the garden's real crown jewels.

The other side of the coin, of course, is that ivy has pretty good wildlife credentials too! Not only is ivy our only native, evergreen climber but it also provides the most wonderful late flourish of nectar in November and a ready supply of berries for our winter thrushes too. The latticework that forms as ivy crawls like a malevolent scaffold over other plants can also provide the perfect nooks and crannies for anything from hunting spiders to nesting spotted flycatchers. On this occasion, though, due to the abundance of ivy elsewhere on the bank, and particularly in amongst the hazels, it would have to give way to our not so mighty oak.

Feeling satisfied that we now had a healthy to-do list of hard and soft landscaping tasks, the only other pressing concern would be when to carry out the work. With spring only just around the corner, the time available to carry out tree surgery tasks, which should only really be done during the dormant winter period, was rapidly disappearing. On our walk round, we had already been delighted to spot the first snowdrop shoots emerging, and so the last thing we wanted would be for the sensitive woodland flora and meadow plants to be trampled underfoot at such a vulnerable time. In other words, I would need to find a tree surgeon on Monday morning!

Taking a break from arduous life and death decisions, we were delighted to invite our first non-familial visitors over in the afternoon. Nigel and his wife Cheryle are old friends I originally met through the annual birding fest that is the Rutland Birdfair. Nige, although he is far too modest to admit it, is one of Britain's finest birders and has probably forgotten more about our feathered friends than I will ever know, whilst Cheryle, who claims to be a birding widow, also happens to be much more interested and knowledgeable than she lets on. Much more pertinent to this book, they are also the most wonderful gardeners and Christina and I were both keen to try and emulate elements of what they had managed to achieve in their own gorgeous Sussex garden over the last decade.

Arriving with a house-warming present in the form of a basket of native primroses, we were secretly hoping that rather than coming up with specific suggestions as to what we could put where, they would think it more useful to not allow us to become daunted by the enormous amount of work ahead of us but instead to be encouraging and supportive of our vision ... and they didn't disappoint.

The party of four almost instantly split, so while Cheryle and Christina wandered around the garden excitedly chattering away about building flower-rich herbaceous borders, Nigel and I scrambled around the wooded bank, indulging in one of every birder's favourite games: guessing which birds we could expect to record in the garden over the next year. Kingfishers, grey wagtails and bullfinches were all excitedly discussed in turn as I proudly took Nigel on the first proper guided tour of our soon to be back-garden nature reserve. Our guests couldn't have been better first visitors as they faithfully dished out encouraging words and inspiration in huge dollops.

Being a couple that have to work for a living, it would not be until the following weekend that we would have any opportunity to get stuck into our urgent 'to-do' list, as the evenings were still far too dark to carry out anything meaningful outside after work. However, during this downtime Christina was also able to put her artistic bent to good use by drawing a few basic sketches of the current layout of the garden in her notebook. Onto this plan we were then able to insert potential locations for the various wildlife-friendly features we planned to install later in the year. This enabled us, for example, to trial on paper the best places to dig the herbaceous borders and the pond – two essential components of any self-respecting wildlife garden, and features that would also be added to our garden, hopefully sooner rather than later!

The weekend duly arrived, with a promise of cold and clear weather, or, in other words, perfect conditions for our first practical day in the garden. Initially, prior to bowsaws and loppers being wielded, I wanted to ensure that sufficient numbers of 'before' photos were taken. These would then ensure that people visiting our beautiful swan of a garden would not only be able to marvel at the end product, but also be able to appreciate the full transformation from original ugly duckling too!

Keen to ensure her secateurs saw some action immediately, Christina decided to begin work on our postage-stamp-sized front garden. Having already agreed that tackling both gardens in the first year would have been a bridge too far, we had decided that the much bigger job of the back garden would take priority. There were, however, simple measures that could be carried out in the front to make it look more presentable. So while I snapped away, Christina set to heavily pruning a couple of long-neglected roses and re-training a tired-looking Japanese quince.

When I came round to the front I found Christina armed with secateurs and slowly disappearing behind a pile of severed branches. 'It's going to look a lot worse before it gets better' was her pre-prepared answer to my tremulous question asking why she had really needed to remove so much. Pointing out that she had consulted none other than the mighty Bob Flowerdew, who had written a book on pruning which I had given to her for Christmas some six weeks earlier, I had to concede that on this occasion she knew better than me what she was doing.

Tidying up after Christina is a technique at which admittedly I have had much practice over the last six years, and so while she stood back to admire her handiwork it was left to me to ferry her brash through to the designated dumping zone – a dark corner of the garden behind the garage. This done, I was then keen to encourage her to put those massacring skills to good use in the back garden – we still had a 'to-do' list as long as my arm!

We had decided that, wherever possible, the wooded bank should mostly consist of native species, with the only exceptions being those ornamental aliens that had significant wildlife value. This meant that the two small confers, a *leylandii* cypress (my least favourite garden plant by some distance, for obvious reasons) and a stunted variegated male holly bush, were soon made short change of as I felled them with a bowsaw and Christina lopped the offending articles into more portable pieces. We then combined forces to drag the material over the fence and across to the dumping pile, which was now assuming ever-larger proportions. After all the talking and planning it felt great to at last get physical and stuck in, and the work was made even more enjoyable by the fact that the weather was so cold. As we grafted away whilst building up a sweat in the process we could see our own breath condensing in the cold air right in front of us.

Christina truly had the bit between her teeth, and, having seen off the aliens in a frenzy of lopping, wanted to turn her attentions to the ash tree in the centre of the bank, which she thought made the area look dark and dingy. Having already agreed that the rowan should be removed, to say I was incredibly reluctant to remove another mature native tree would have been an understatement. As the conversation tipped over from a robust difference of opinion into raised voices and then a full-blown argument, the crux became clear. Put simply, the subtext of the disagreement was about nothing less than the future direction of the garden; with Christina in one corner wanting primarily a garden while I wanted it to go down the Nature Reserve route.

The main battle line was going to be the wooded bank, with Christina maintaining it was too messy, and so by removing more vegetation and tidying it up, this would create more light in a dark corner of the garden. I countered that of course woodlands were often a bit dark and messy by their very nature, and therefore it would be better for the wildlife if the bank were to remain largely wild and woolly. I then hammered home my point by arguing that removing the ash tree would break a vital link in the chain, meaning that the continued canopy cover across the bottom of the garden would disappear. This would have the knock-on effect of denying lots of shy woodland birds and mammals the wildlife corridor they needed to move between the gardens. Building up another head of steam, I pointed out that in no way were we in any position to safely remove a mature tree with the tools and experience we had, so it would have to stay. But ever the conciliator, I offered as a compromise my promise that the more formal part of the garden, closer to the house, would be much more manicured and tidy.

While I would define my relationship with Christina as one consisting of reasonably regular arguments, we do make up soon after, and we were both in the act of apologising when interrupted by the sound of Lorraine's voice next door, keen to hear how our first practical morning in the garden was going.

Pleased that our neighbours wanted to take such an interest in our plot, we filled them in on our rationale behind removing the aliens in order both to give more space to the (more cherished) native species and to attempt to open up the woodland a touch more to enable better views of the brook. On hearing the water mentioned, Lorraine's eyes twinkled as she declared how her and Andy had always coveted our river frontage, and then surprised us by revealing that they had previously entertained the idea of trying to purchase the bottom of our garden after Mr Gregory had moved out. Privately of course both Christina and I had 'too late now!' thoughts; but ever the generous souls, I was quick to suggest that any time either needed a watery fix, they both had carte blanche to hop over the fence whenever they felt like it!

Lorraine also hilariously accused us of attempting to steal her garden birds with our now extensive offerings in the form of a stand-up bird table, a sunflower hearts feeder, a Niger feeder and a fat-ball dispenser. It was probably true that in the space of barely a week, and given the superior feed on offer in our garden, many of the birds had already swapped their notoriously fickle allegiances and were now choosing to spend most of their time emptying our feeders rather than theirs.

But joking aside, with our feeders in the centre, Andy and Lorraine's to the left and a small feeding station in Dennis and Marjory's garden immediately to our right, the local resident birds must surely have been some of the best fed in the southwest. Also, in the space of just a couple of weeks since we had moved in, it was not only astonishing how quickly the birds had found the food, but noticeable that we had already recorded a wider range of species at our feeders here than in the previous 10 years at our old garden flat in Bristol. Interestingly, the sheer quantity of birds was also much higher; it was not uncommon for us to peer out of the kitchen window to observe not only that every single perch was taken on all the feeders, but that queuing systems had often formed on the nearby bushes as well. The garden was quite literally alive with birds! This rich variety and abundance instantly brought two thoughts to my mind: firstly, what fun it would be compiling a garden bird list; and secondly, that it wouldn't be too long before this huge concentration of small birds would register on a sparrowhawk's radar!

With Christina away visiting friends overnight, I dragged myself out of bed the following morning for a spot of garden birdwatching, only momentarily undeterred by the miserable weather. One of the slight peculiarities, and immense irritations, of the house meant that there were comparatively few good vantage points from which to actually properly enjoy the garden, a fact we would rectify when we had sufficient cash to build the much-planned rear extension. In the meantime, the current best seat, or stand, in the house was from the landing window, halfway up the stairs.

Looking down, fully expecting a tit and finch-fest, I was aghast to see not a single bird on any of the feeders due to the dominating presence of a whole bunch of greedy grey squirrels. Four of these invaders could be counted, dotted across the garden and monopolising each feeder whilst the birds looked on helplessly from the nearby bushes, too intimidated to compete.

The grey squirrel is an animal that as a naturalist fills me with a whole range of mixed emotions. Brought over from the eastern side of North America and deliberately introduced on some twenty occasions between the late nineteenth and early twentieth centuries, their rapid spread throughout England and Wales has proved the stuff of ecological nightmares. Now numbering as many as 2.5 million, this adaptable and hardy animal has become so widespread in our parks, gardens and woodlands that it is now quite probably the most commonly seen mammal in Britain, and as such is accepted by many as a wholly natural part of our wildlife.

To the neutral, the greys have obvious charm and appeal, and it has to be stated that they didn't actually ask to be brought over to the UK and then become so vilified just for making an unqualified success of their new home. Unfortunately, the cold fact of the matter is that they have undoubtedly had a major impact on our native flora and fauna, which are poorly adapted to withstand their presence. Most well known is the contribution of the grey squirrel to the catastrophic decline of our native red squirrel, so much so that the red squirrel now only flourishes either in large parts of Scotland where the greys are still mostly absent, in a few

grey-squirrel-free offshore islands or in large conifer belts ill-suited to the Yankee invader. Perhaps less understood by the public, though, are both the immense damage that grey squirrels cause to trees and the serious impact on many of our native, breeding woodland birds. Though many have called for their total extermination, this is totally impracticable, and, I'm afraid, irrespective of how we feel about the animal, they are definitely here to stay.

While a small part of me admired their brazen attitude as they reached across from the pergola, like supple athletes, to empty my feeders in double-quick time, the larger part of me was so indignant that I instinctively ran downstairs to shoo them out of the garden, momentarily forgetting I was in little more than my underpants. On seeing my naked flesh and hearing my accompanying 'get out of it!' they hurriedly spun round on their heels and triple-jumped their way back into the woodland at the bottom of the garden, disappearing in a matter of seconds.

I knew that with such a major food source on offer they would be back as soon as the coast was clear. So for the next hour I played a cat-and-mouse game with them, as I watched them quietly creep back into the garden and onto the feeders only for me to rush out and scare them off again (having got dressed in the meantime – of course!). After a while they either got the message that they were not welcome or had had their fill anyway, but no one was more aware than I was that this was little more than tokenism, and that I would ultimately have to adopt some serious anti-squirrel technologies if I didn't want to spend the equivalent of the Greek national debt on bird food. So the 'tree rats' should enjoy the free handouts while they still could! With the squirrels at least temporarily pushed back, this at last gave me my first opportunity to watch the feeders being used by the animals they were designed for.

As the birds slowly returned, I delighted in the most wonderful hour watching blue tits, great tits, robins, chaffinches and greenfinches pile in despite the still awful weather. It's been well known for at least a couple of decades that living with pets can lower blood pressure, lessen anxiety and boost our immunity, but because I can't commit to owning a pet, due to the fact that I'm often away filming, I have to say that watching garden birds comes a very close second. It's hard to explain the level of happiness I gain from watching the birds go about their daily business, but for someone who often spends his life dashing around at 70mph, it was important to take some time out on the hard shoulder every now and again.

I don't claim to have been the only person to have uncovered this elixir of life, as the RSPB recently revealed the astonishing statistic that as many as 40 per cent of British households will feed their garden birds at some point during the year – more evidence of the power of wildlife as one of the best natural anti-depressants on the market.

The rain eventually receded and Christina returned, so we began to make preparations to launch ourselves into the garden for the afternoon's activity: Operation Fence Dismantle. Earlier in the week I had sneakily taken a peek into next door's garage, while they were putting out their recycling, and had noted a far more impressive collection of gardening tools and implements than we had yet been able to muster. Having made a mental note that some of these might come in handy at some point, barely a few days later I was now hoping they could be persuaded to lend us one of their crowbars. Knocking on the door, I fully expected it to be answered by Marjory and so was surprised to meet the tall, gaunt figure of Dennis, the Great Gatsby of our street, and the last of our immediate neighbours I had not yet met.

Though undeniably unwell, in addition to being both an ex-policeman and an utterly charming chap, Dennis also confirmed that he would be more than happy to lend us any of the tools we might need. Because his illness seriously affected his ability to undertake anything but the lightest of duties, he explained that he wasn't in any position to wield tools, and so would be pleased to see them put to good use.

Since Dennis had lived in the house for the best part of 20 years, I was also to discover that he was the most enormous fountain of knowledge about both his and our garden and the adjacent brook.

Both keen gardeners themselves, Dennis and Marjory regularly saw kingfishers whizzing up and down the brook, and in addition to seeing pheasants in the garden had even recorded roe deer on a couple of occasions too! He also tantalisingly revealed that whilst brown trout used to be commonplace in the brook, he hadn't seen them for several years, possibly due to a combination of a couple of unfortunate pollution incidents upstream and a silting up of the stream bed. Trying, in part, to rectify the silt issue, he had even put a few heavy blocks in the water at the bottom of his garden to break up the water flow and perturb the bed, but this was in reality little more than piecemeal and had had little effect.

As the discussion turned to our garden, I excitedly gabbled about both the grand plans and the impressive list of birds we had already attracted to our feeders in the short time since moving in, before turning to the subject of how frustrated I was beginning to get with the bullying tactics of the squirrels. Dennis and Marjory had themselves encountered the same problems, until they had invested in special cage feeders designed to keep the squirrels at bay, and which had seemingly nipped the problem in the bud. Having not encountered anywhere near this level of mammalian feeder disturbance in Bristol, where the squirrels' appearances were usually more novelty than irritation, it was obvious that my old feeders were now patently not up to the job and I would have to invest in some more!

Apparently I was not the first of Dennis's next-door neighbours to have had this issue and he asked if I had heard about Mr Gregory's battle with squirrels. Realising from my quizzical face that patently I hadn't, he recounted how Mr Gregory had so detested their aggressive and domineering tactics that he had taken it upon himself to initiate a shooting and trapping campaign during his last few years in the house, claiming in the process a grand total of 212 squirrel scalps! What made the anecdote even more hilarious was that Lorraine (the neighbour to our other side) positively encouraged the squirrels into her garden and so was mortified to find her furry friends being so ruthlessly wiped out just over the garden fence. This meant that in order not to fall out with his neighbour,

Mr Gregory had limited his operation to either night-time or when Lorraine was out at work – what a character!

Armed with all the correct tools, Christina and I quickly made short work of the fence line, as we firstly removed the wire rabbit-guard stapled to the front, then prised away the wooden rails with the borrowed crowbar and finally wiggled the posts free of their concrete footings. Standing back to admire our handiwork, the garden looked a touch strange without the one obstacle that had prevented the wildlife wandering freely between the wooded bank and the rest of the garden. Importantly, though, the garden and brook had now become one, and it was one more job off the list, too!

Stacking the wood behind the garage, we retreated to the kitchen for Christina to make a quick cuppa and for me to quickly catch up with how the English rugby team was doing against Italy. I had scarcely been given the chance to find out the score before hearing Christina's urgent, shrill voice imploring me to come quickly to the kitchen. Seeing her nose pressed up against the window I followed suit, and was utterly astonished to see a male pheasant strutting around the garden as he cleared up the seed debris dropped by the tits and finches from the feeders, having obviously just strolled in via the new 15-yard wildlife entrance to the garden.

The pheasant is an introduced, and therefore in many purists' eyes, a lesser species. Originally hailing from southeast Russia and Asia, it is thought to have been brought over to Britain by the Normans, and over time has become part and parcel of the British countryside and, in my considered opinion, a wonderful addition to our fauna too. The pheasant is also one of those species character-ised by sexual dimorphism, which means that the sexes look completely different. The female pheasants often tend to be smaller, yellowy-brown and with marked flecking; colours and patterns which enable them to quickly melt into the background when incu-bating their clutch in spring; while the male, with his iridescent copper-coloured body, metallic green head, red facial wattles and ear tufts, could be described as a dandy with an attitude. Fatherhood

is seemingly an alien concept for the male pheasant, as he plays little or no part in the rearing of his chicks. The males are more of the love 'em and leave 'em type, their sole aim being to assemble a harem of two or more females, which they will defend at all costs from other marauding males keen to chance their arm. Until they have been mated, that is, after which the males thoughtlessly abandon the females to their fate.

In our previous Bristol garden I would never have expected to see a pheasant, and even in our new garden I wouldn't have shortened the odds that much at the chance of adding the species to my garden list. With a moment's reflection, though, maybe its appearance shouldn't have been that much of a surprise. For starters, Chew Stoke is a small, rural village set in the countryside, and due to our street being tucked away in the southeastern corner, as the pheasant walks our garden was probably no more than a couple of hundred yards from the nearest arable fields. Hadn't Dennis also said only a couple of hours previously that they did occasionally turn up in his garden too?

I have watched pheasants in the British countryside on thousands of occasions, so what we were looking at, in isolation, wasn't a particularly rare sighting. But watching one on our own lawn, I can officially confirm, was a hundred times better, because it was the most glorious vindication of our policy to break down one of the main barriers to our garden. By making our border porous, the effect had been the equivalent of laying down a green carpet of invitation – with the pheasant, hopefully, being the first of many more animals to accept!

True to my word that I would seek out help for those jobs technically out of my depth, and with time of the essence before spring would be upon us, I had arranged for a tree surgeon to come around and cost up some of the urgent work Christina and I had highlighted on our initial walk around. Rob was a tree surgeon of some repute in the southwest and was proud to report a wide and varied client list, which included our future monarch at his huge Tetbury estate in South Gloucestershire. If he was considered trustworthy enough for Prince Charles's trees then he would certainly suffice for ours! What sold Rob's services to me even more than his royal connections was the fact that Rob was not only born and bred in Chew Stoke, but by an amazing coincidence his parents still lived just around the corner. It was always good, wherever possible, to minimise the carbon footprint by keeping it local!

As his hulking old-school Land-Rover pulled on to the drive, (surely every tree surgeon's chariot of choice), I was unsurprised to see a stocky chap emerging with legs only marginally slimmer than the sizes of mature tree trunks, who offered a handshake that was like having your hand placed in one of those bench-top vice-clamps – and then tightened to an uncomfortable level. While I waited for the blood to return to my hand, we moved straight into the garden, with Rob immediately proving charming and immensely knowledgeable in equal measure as he wandered around our mini-arboretum dispensing pearls of wisdom

Looking at the garden with fresh eyes, it was astonishing to see how in the space of just two short weeks, the garden had well and truly turned its head towards spring. While the male hazel catkins had been out for a while, it was only now that they had matured sufficiently to unleash their smoke-like sprinkles of pollen into the air at the slightest breeze. Some of these tiny packets of genetic material would then be ensured successful pollination by being intercepted in mid-drift by the bright-red erect styles of the tiny female flowers, arising like mini-phoenixes out of the otherwise naked hazel twigs. Daffodil leaves had also begun to emerge from a bewildering variety of locations around the garden, using the early spring rays to ensure sufficient food would be produced, via the miracle of photosynthesis, to produce a flower spike later that season. But botanical pride of place on the walk round easily went to the mini drifts of snowdrops which were scattered along the wooded bank in discrete pearly-white clusters.

The snowdrop curiously is also a plant with a whole host of synonyms, such as 'February fairmaids' or, according to the eighteenth-century poet Thomas Tickell, the wonderfully evocative name of 'vegetable snow'. I personally think that the most intriguing name is 'snow piercer', so named because of the plant's specially hardened leaf-tips, which have evolved to break through frozen ground. Despite some botanists harbouring doubts as to whether the snowdrop is indeed a native British flower, since many seemingly wild colonies may well have begun as garden escapes, what is without doubt is that as the austerity of winter comes to an end, the plant in full bloom is a welcome sign that many more floral delights are only just around the corner.

Looking up at the oak, and contrary to my thinking that the tree was on its last legs, Rob suggested that it would in all probability still outlive me! Having said that, he thought removing the ivy would certainly lighten the load and enable the tree to photosynthesise more easily, giving it a new lease of life. Whilst the beech tree would need no more than a few branches to be removed for safety and aesthetics, he also pointed out considerable damage to one of the main branches that I hadn't previously spotted, which had been caused by those naughty grey squirrels' unfortunate habit of bark-stripping.

Agreeing that the central rowan had always had insufficient space to flourish and did look in poor condition, Rob said that he would do his best to avoid too much damage to my newly demarked meadow whilst bringing it down. His chainsaw, we agreed, would also be taken to the huge rotten pergola in the centre of the lawn, which would have the dual benefit of both removing the garden's biggest eyesore and opening up the meadow to a splash more of sunshine. I love it when a plan comes together!

As I was spending the following week away filming in Scotland, Christina had agreed to take a day's holiday on the Friday to be both tea provider and photographer when Rob returned, this time with both chainsaw and colleagues to carry out the work. Catching the last flight back to Bristol, I arrived too late to see all the changes before nightfall and so had a frustrating wait until the following day before I was able to assess their handiwork.

Rushing out at first light with a coffee to inspect their efforts, I was flabbergasted at the difference. Just the removal of the rowan and the pergola alone had transformed the would-be meadow into one where light could penetrate. Apparently working from the top down to minimise damage to the ground flora, the rowan had been dismantled in less than an hour and had transmogrified into a neat pile of logs. Likewise the monstrous carbuncle that was the pergola had been turned into a neatly stacked pile of weathered timber – surely I would be able to find a multitude of uses for all that lovely wood? Other features permanently erased from the garden included the small birch tree cowering behind its bigger brother in the corner by the playing field and one of the two terribly disfigured cherry trees. Showing some artistic licence with the chainsaw, the other cherry tree had been thoughtfully converted to a bird table, with the table top having been fashioned out of a spliced section of the rowan's trunk.

By systematically severing all the huge climbing stems and stripping the majority of the foliage out of the canopy, the oak was finally free of the ivy's suffocating grip, and looked like it would now be able to breathe properly for the first time in a couple of decades. The beech had also been carefully pruned to both give it a good shape and to ensure not too many branches would fall into Marjory and Dennis's garden. Finally, Rob had made sure that, wherever possible, trampling of all the lovely spring bulbs had been kept to a minimum – spring could now commence!

One of the little treats that we had long been planning, but until now had not found the time to carry out, was a mini-investigation of the surrounding land both upstream and downstream of our section of the brook. So, donning our wellingtons, Christina and I slithered down the bank and into the water for our very first exploratory paddle. As the water tinkled around our boots at a depth of no more than six inches, the first impression we were able to gain from this totally different perspective was how much lower the level of the water actually was below the bottom of the garden. Being a full three yards below the meadow meant that a storm of biblical proportions would have to occur before our property was in any danger of flooding. The downside of this disparity in height, however, also meant that, as the bank faced north, natural light would always be thin on the ground. It wasn't until we were able to stand back and inspect the bank from this hitherto unseen angle that we realised how dark and dingy our little wood really was.

In fact, so dark was the steepest section of the bank below the oak tree that the only vibrant sign of life emanating from the gloom was provided by discrete clusters of the shade-loving hart's-tongue fern, arising out of the bare earth like resplendent green shuttle-cocks. With their strap-shaped leaves, which supposedly resemble a female deer's tongue, this perennial evergreen is one of those plants that is always capable of brightening up the shadiest of wood-land floors, so we were delighted it had chosen to take up residence on our bank too.

Being south-facing, the opposite bank, albeit distinctly shaded by the trees and shrubs from our bank, inevitably had more floral potential. In addition to the hart's-tongue fern and the ubiquitous groundcover of ivy, I was a touch envious to encounter the first leaves of ramsons, or wild garlic, beginning to emerge above ground. Immediately recognisable in early spring by the sweet-and-sour cloying smell of its leaves and then later in the season by the drifts of white flowers as the plant monopolises huge areas, this was one woodland specialist I was hoping would also grace our side of the bank too.

Electing to explore downstream first, we had barely walked past the bottom of Marjory and Dennis's garden before we heard a bird call we knew instantly. 'Kingfisher!' we both shouted in unison, as our ears caught its shrill characteristic whistle.

Aware of my interest in birds, I have lost track of the number of times that novice birdwatchers have asked me for any tips or advice as to how they might finally track down a sighting of a kingfisher. My response to this question is always the same; learning and recognising the call of this noisy and pugnacious little bird means it will often telegraph its arrival, giving you a moment's preparation time to catch a glimpse as it whizzes past.

Sure enough, no more than a second after hearing the call, Christina spotted a blue bullet powering upstream towards us. Shocked at seeing our two huge looming presences standing in the middle of the brook, or its flight path, the bird veered away and took a short cut across the inner bend of the meander. Going at such speed, the kingfisher had to bank to make the turning, meaning we were treated to the most wonderful sighting of its orange underside before it righted itself and joined the brook again some 10 yards further upstream.

It was a thrilling encounter and an exciting moment as we realised that not only could we add kingfisher to our garden list, but having survived the harsh winter it might well be here all season. Breeding kingfishers at the bottom of our ex-council house garden – how good did that sound? I don't mind telling you that at that moment I also performed a little spontaneous and aquatic jig of delight!

Buoyed by this wonderful find, we were soon brought back down to earth further downstream by the realisation that the brook, in addition to great wildlife, contained a disturbingly large amount of rubbish, both snagged in the water and littering the banks. Everything from plastic bottles to a fly-tipped pram and a bus-stop sign had somehow managed to find their way into the brook. Another job had just been added to our to-do list.

In some spots the brook was much more sluggish and deeper than at the bottom of our garden and so we had to either take a detour along the bank or move through the water very slowly to ensure it didn't breach our wellington tops. Large sections of both banks seemed to be either attached to gardens or were just a tangled mess without an immediately identifiable owner. Scrambling up one area of bank, no more than a hundred yards from our garden, was a section dominated by alder trees at the water's edge, where we were delighted to find a large and obviously very active badger sett. Occupying a little ridge which ran parallel with the stream, the sett consisted of at least half a dozen entrances, most of which were devoid of leaf litter, a sure-fire sign of recent use. Additionally, two of these entrances were so large that Christina could probably have joined the badgers down below, had she felt that way inclined, and there was evidence of fresh digging within the last 24 hours. Obviously the incumbents had just carried out their spring clean!

Retracing our steps back to the house and following the brook upstream, the bank on the south side soon flattened out to a small, wooded plateau littered with beer cans. Wondering how these had found their way here, it was not until a quick scout around that we realised that the playing field, which partly ran adjacent to our garden, also had a gate in the 6-foot-high fence, giving quick and easy access to the river bank – so this was where the local adolescents came for a clandestine lager or two! On the opposite side of the brook, the water had gouged out a steep sandy bank some 6 feet high, which seemed perfect for a nesting kingfisher. On closer inspection, my instinct had patently been right as we soon uncovered a couple of long-discarded and now partially collapsed holes that were probably indicative of breeding attempts from previous seasons. I made a mental note that I simply had to bring a four-pack back down here later in the year to spend an evening watching the kingfishers – if we were lucky enough to have them breed in the same bank again.

With many other gardens backing onto the brook, it also gave us the perfect opportunity for a nose around, or a kingfisher's-eye view, of all of our waterside neighbours. As you would expect, the gardens were a mixed bunch, with some beautifully laid-out, whilst others were in a ramshackle state and obviously hadn't been touched for years. Peering over the bank, we were amazed to see one large garden with a model railway running the whole way around its perimeter – how utterly bizarre!

With March rapidly approaching, the next urgent job on the ever-growing to-do list was to get some nest boxes in the garden, as the resident blue tits, great tits and robins would probably already have begun prospecting potential nest sites for the oncoming breeding season. If I were to collect house points for effort in attracting birds to our garden, then I would be awarded one point for every different species spotted actually feeding in the garden, but would be granted an immediate 10 house points for every pair which success-fully raises a brood. For any self-respecting garden naturalist, play-ing host to nesting birds in your garden should really be the greatest accolade, as it says that you are getting much more right than wrong in your attempt to make your garden the ultimate wildlife-friendly destination.

In an ideal world, I would love to have handmade all my own nest boxes, as it is incredibly easy and instructions can be found on the internet. However, as time was of the essence, we decided that we would have to splash the cash. Anyone who has ever purchased a nest box knows that they come in innumerable shapes and sizes, so after much debate down at our local garden centre about the merits of each design, we went for four of the classic boxes as favoured by blue and great tits, three open nest boxes as preferred by robins and spotted flycatchers, and a large box fraternised by jackdaws or tawny owls. On reaching the tills with our trolley full to the brim, I was left with the distinct feeling that creating this haven of wildlife – if done properly – would not only need time and effort but possibly a large proportion of our expendable income too!

With the sun streaming through our bedroom window, it was obvious that the morning after our mercy dash to the garden centre would be beautifully cold and crisp – in fact the perfect day for putting up nest boxes. Having run out of milk for our 'pre-erecting nest boxes coffee', I offered to walk round to the local store to grab a couple of pints whilst Christina sorted out breakfast. Enjoying the warming effect of the low winter sun on my face, I must have gone no more than 50 yards from the house when I heard the unmistakable sound of a male chaffinch belting out his mating song – which in an instant signalled the immediate cessation of winter and beginning of spring.

My *RSPB Handbook of British Birds* describes the chaffinch's song as 'a short, fast and rather dry descending series of trills that accelerates and ends with a flourish', which I suppose is a reasonable interpretation of an unremarkable song. But the description does nothing to explain the huge symbolism of what the song represents, as I always look upon it as signifying the gateway to my favourite season. The song operates like a drum-roll for spring to let us know that the bumblebees and butterflies are about to emerge, bud burst will begin and the breeding season can swing into action.

We had decided that the first place to erect one of the boxes would be on the oak trunk, which had just been liberated from its ivy stranglehold. Marking the northwest boundary of our property, the previous owners had erected a steel fence which butted up to the tree and then topped it off with a barbed-wire strand which had been crudely nailed straight into the oak's trunk.

Keen to remove this impediment to the tree's health before we put up the nest box, I attacked the fencing staples with my pliers, momentarily forgetting that I was right on the edge of the precipice created by the brook. As I reached round to remove the last staple, my foot slipped on the mud, causing me to lose my balance, and a split-second later I was careering off the edge bound for the water below – and to think, I'm ashamed to admit, that I had stifled a laugh when I heard about Mr Gregory's unscheduled visit to the same brook a few years earlier! Also aware of the fact that my ridiculously expensive camera was still around my shoulder, I closed my eyes and prepared for a big splash, no small amount of pain on hitting the water and the instigation of a large insurance claim to replace my soon-to-be-ruined camera. Thump! I opened my eyes to find that I hadn't hit the water at all, as I had straddled one of the huge oak roots protruding from the bank. Despite the fact that the tree had saved both me and my photography kit, I didn't get away scot-free, as I had pulled a groin muscle, slightly bruised my err … undercarriage and cut a couple of fingers. Nevertheless, it was a lucky escape.

Elsewhere in the garden, Christina hadn't been aware of my fall until she turned round on hearing my pathetic cries for help as I came out of my momentary daze and realised I was struggling to get either up or down. On peering over the edge of the bank Christina wasn't sure whether to be worried for me or laugh her socks off at my ridiculous predicament. After passing the camera to her, which had fortunately not been damaged by my tumble, I was eventually able to scramble back up the bank, and recount what had happened, feeling somewhat embarrassed and chastened by the whole experience.

Deciding that because of my sore groin it would probably be easier if Christina put up the tree nest boxes, leaving her klutz of a boyfriend to hold the ladder and pass up the tools, we set about finishing the job. Starting with the tit boxes first, we elected to attach one each to the trunks of the oak and the birch whilst embedding the other two in the centre of the hazel stands. Two of the open nest boxes were nailed at differing heights to the playing field fence line whilst the other was placed on the dividing fence between our garden and Marjory and Dennis's.

The only problem we encountered for the rest of the morning was in our attempt to put up the large nest box. We were struggling to find a place to put it where it would have a chance of being used, without endangering our lives in the process. After a half-hearted attempt to put the box some 15 feet up in the beech tree, using a combination of our ladder and then a bit of tree-climbing, we decided, after my experience a few hours earlier, that it was probably a touch too ambitious and dangerous, and so left the nest box in the garage for another breeding season. Because the nest box was of the open-fronted variety, I was also fearful that if anything did try to nest in there, the chicks would have been an easy target for those opportunistic squirrels.

We planned to spend some time in our postage-stamp-sized front garden in the afternoon, so I went in to prepare lunch, only for Christina to dash in minutes later urging me back out into the garden. As I looked down the garden you could have blown me over with a feather as we watched a prospecting blue tit stick its head back out of the nest box on the birch tree, scarcely more than an hour after we had put it up. Talk about an instant response!

MARCH
SPRINGING INTO ACTION

Although it may seem glamorous from the outside, a career in television can in reality involve working long days, spending many nights living out of a suitcase and substantial periods away from home and loved ones. In my case, it also brought the new and totally unexpected feeling of missing the garden. In the space of just over a month, I had already spent more time in our new garden than the entire previous decade in my old Bristol garden. So as I arrived back at 1am on 3 March after a long trip away filming bats down caves, I felt like I was coming home in more ways than one, and experienced rising excitement at the thought of seeing both Christina and how the garden had changed over the last few days.

Pulling up outside the house, I had barely got out of the taxi before the garden gloriously delivered, as I picked up the unmistakable hoot of a male tawny owl calling from somewhere down by the stream. Perhaps the most surprising thing, in retrospect, was that I hadn't already heard a tawny owl up to that point. After all, I was now living in the country, and the patchwork mosaic of woodland and mature gardens along Strode Brook in many ways represented the ideal habitat for this most adaptable of species. Still, better late than never, I thought, as I dragged my sleep-deprived body and over-sized bags into the house, hoping on just this one occasion that the hooting wouldn't keep me awake!

Due to another filming commitment later the same day, to track down Cornish grey seals, on waking up my first thought was to maximise any spare time in the garden. I was also delighted to discover that while I had been away the substantial order I had placed from a company specialising in bird food and feeders had arrived and awaited my attention on the patio. To someone who gets the most ridiculous satisfaction from feeding his garden birds, the pile of birding paraphernalia just waiting to be unwrapped and distributed around the garden made me feel like my birthday and Christmas had just been rolled into one!

In addition to sacks full of sunflower hearts, peanuts and bird-table mix, I had also ordered a couple of bird feeders especially designed to thwart even the most determined of squirrels. Design number one incorporated a feeder mounted on a pole, with all six feeding ports cleverly encased in a cylindrical mesh cage. This ring of steel would enable tits and finches to pass through but not squirrels or equally domineering wood pigeons. The second design was a regulation hanging feeder but with a Perspex dome attachment, which when placed like a bell immediately above the feeder would prevent the squirrels clambering onto it from the branch above. The key to the successful implementation of this design is that the feeder must be placed high enough to ensure the squirrels can't jump up to it from the ground, but also far enough away from any other branches to prevent them leaping across, and crucially underneath the dome, from another vantage point.

Not wanting to deny the buntings, chaffinches or robins the opportunity to join in the food-fest, I had also ordered a ground feeding table, complete with an anti-squirrel guard in the form of a mesh-rectangle which covered the table and was then secured to the lawn via pegs. Having stashed all the food in rodent-proof bins in the garage, I then set about taking down my old feeders and replacing them with my lovely new acquisitions. The bell feeder was hung about 6 feet from one of the lower branches of the remaining rowan tree, whilst the caged feeder with accompanying pole was stuck into the lawn close to our shared fence with Andy and

Lorraine, in order to entice the birds away from their feeding table and onto to our feeders. Let the battle for (sunflower) hearts and minds begin!

Taking a tour around to admire what was becoming an utterly irresistible garden, I couldn't help but notice that the natural flora, particularly around the meadow, was already subtly beginning to change. Despite the still occasional appearance of ground frosts in the morning, things had patently become far too tropical for the snowdrops, which were definitely looking past their best. However, without doubt one of the most exciting aspects of botany is that, for most of the year, as one flower fades another species will often quickly take centre stage by moving into bloom, and in this case that plant was the primrose.

From the Spanish *prima rosa*, or the 'first rose of spring', the primrose's name can be somewhat misleading, as of course it's not related to the rose but is a member of the primrose family itself. If I were to choose my top ten favourite British wild flowers, then the primrose would comfortably sail into the top five. It is not just about the flowers, which I have always thought emanate from the leafy basal rosette like a large dollop of clotted cream, but, just like the chaffinch's song, it represents a gateway to my favourite season of the year: spring. With the species name *vulgaris*, translated as 'common', this plant is paradoxically nowhere near as abundant as it used to be. Overpicking and a loss of suitable habitat are the prime reasons behind this plant's disappearance from large swathes of our countryside. That would not be the case in this garden, though, as the primroses would be removed over my dead body. They were there for us and the wildlife to enjoy.

Christina joined me for an hour's work in the garden, before I had to disappear away again in the evening, and we rolled up our sleeves and got stuck into the front garden, as the border in front of the house, having now been weeded, prepared and fertilised, was at last ready to be planted up. We had planned for the border to be filled with a combination of plants from a variety of sources: those which had sneakily been dug up from our previous garden and brought with us, as well as recently purchased perennials and some shrubs from our new garden which could still be saved. Being the artistic type, Christina wanted to trial the potted plants at varying locations around the border, to try and work out what would look best where. 'Having spent so much time, effort and money on these plants, it would be a shame not to create a lovely mixture of colour, texture and pattern.' One thing I have learnt over the years with my wonderful girlfriend is not to even attempt to assert my opinion when it comes down to who has the last say on colour or positioning schemes – she just does this kind of thing better. The result of this game of Chinese 'plant' chequers meant that, as the light began to fade, the only plants we had managed to put in the ground that afternoon were a couple of large hydrangeas carefully positioned to cover the gas meter, and a climbing honeysuckle that would eventually mask the ugly cables emanating from our newly installed satellite dish.

As we began to pack up, my thoughts had already turned away from arranging flower borders to my paid work and the pre-departure checklist for filming down in Cornwall. BLACKBIRD! I couldn't believe my ears, for the first blackbird of spring was singing from somewhere down the road. A scan of the most obvious vantage points quickly revealed the silhouette of a male in mid-performance on the TV aerial of Number Six, with a salmon-pink sunset as a backdrop to make the moment even more special.

In a recent poll by the National Trust to find the nation's favourite songbird, the humble blackbird trounced all the opposition with a whopping 45 per cent of all votes cast. In summary, this is a song that means an awful lot to an awful lot of people. I've personally always felt that the song has a beautiful, melancholic sound to it, and if I were to indulge myself further by giving the bird an accent, then it would have to be that lazy but mellow drawl easily encountered in any of the southern states of the USA: 'Y'all come back now yer hear!' it seemed to be singing to us!

The impact of this most natural of symphonies on our brains cannot be overestimated. Recent studies have shown that the psychological impact of birdsong can affect anything from our mood to our levels of attention and creativity. I have no idea how researchers are able to calibrate these effects, but as the blackbird belted out its virtuoso performance, while Christina and I listened enraptured with our arms around each other, all I know is that it made us both feel content.

The weekend finally brought a break to my hectic work schedule, meaning it would also free up some time to indulge in my two new favourite activities: watching the wildlife coming and going in our garden, and planting lots of lovely plants. Taking up my preferred perching point by the landing stairs window, and with the two essentials for any early morning birding session – my binoculars and a cup of coffee – I was particularly keen to see how the new feeders were being received. I had barely taken my first sip of coffee before a flash of pink and an even tinier flash of blue betrayed the presence of a pair of jays playing hide and seek through the hazels on the wooded bank.

Historically an arboreal bird most at home in the wooded countryside, the jay is one species which has seemingly developed much more catholic tastes over the last few decades. As a result of extensive planting schemes in many urban and suburban areas, combined with the fact that urban pollution levels are now at their lowest levels since before the Industrial Revolution our towns and cities are now a much more attractive proposition to birds like the jay. In fact, so prevalent have they become in Bristol's suburbs, for example, that I considered jays to be relatively common visitors to the diminutive urban garden attached to my previous flat. Despite having made the bold decision to come and live alongside us, the jay has still retained that nervous and skittish demeanour and none of the cockiness or swagger of, say, house sparrows or wood pigeons. This introverted nature means that the jay will always be one of those birds that leaves you wanting more, and such was the case here, as the pair all too briefly melted away into the undergrowth.

Nevertheless, I was particularly pleased officially to add this bird to the garden list, as it was the one species that Christina had seen in the garden the week before, but I hadn't yet managed to catch up with. Knowing that I wouldn't have been happy until I had seen them for myself, Christina had enjoyed exploiting this fact by winding me up, or in birding parlance 'gripping me off'. 'How can you have the audacity to actually call yourself a birder when you haven't even managed to see as common a bird as a jay in your own back garden?'

In a number of ways, even more pleasing than the brief appearance of the jays were the large numbers of greenfinches which were constantly crowding around the bell feeder in the rowan tree. The greenfinch is a garden bird familiar to even those with little more than a passing interest in our feathered friends, but it is also a species that since 2005 has been so heavily targeted by a parasite-induced disease called trichomonosis that populations are thought to have plummeted by as much as a third in those areas affected by outbreaks. Living in the bird's upper digestive tract, this dastardly parasite's action is to slowly block the bird's throat so it is unable to swallow food, ultimately causing a long, lingering death by starvation. While the parasite can't survive for long outside the host, it can unfortunately be easily transmitted between birds via saliva, which will always accumulate at communal feeders and drinking areas. This tragically means that the disease cruelly targets those garden owners who ironically care most about their birds by regularly feeding them.

So prevalent has this disease become in the southwest over the last few years that, for me, seeing what was a once abundant bird has now become a notable event. But as I watched the constant flickering of yellow and green around the feeder, I was struck with the thought that maybe our new garden could just conceivably be located in a healthy enclave, meaning we might be spared the ravages of this pernicious disease. I could only hope that this refreshing sighting was one that I would continue to enjoy.

Whilst scanning through the hordes of greenfinch, my gaze latched onto a pair of somewhat more uncommon finches, in the form of a couple of siskin. So excited was I at this find, that my 'birding Tourette's' kicked in once again, causing me to suddenly shout, 'Siskin!' involuntarily to nobody in particular, and certainly not to Christina, who was still doing a fine impression of someone keen to spend the whole day in bed. This smaller cousin of the greenfinch has a curious distribution in Britain, with most individuals preferring to breed in Welsh, Scottish and northern English coniferous forests, before electing to spend their winter holidays in the milder climes of southern England. Having never before seen siskin in any Bristol urban garden since moving to the southwest in 1999, this was one of those winter visitors I was secretly hoping would at some point have turned up in our new garden before disappearing back up north for the breeding season.

I hate to be sexist when talking about birds, but I'm afraid that the male siskin is just so much more attractive than his washed-out female counterpart. Adult males will generally undertake a complete moult between July and November, but it takes until early the following spring for the pale feather tips to abrade sufficiently for the gorgeous back cap and bib to be revealed – and boy, this specimen was looking pretty dapper right now!

Of course the cast of garden characters wouldn't be complete without the presence of a Panto Villain, played so ably as ever by the grey squirrels. Unlike the entire month of February, where they had been given free rein to bully and monopolise the feeding stations whenever they felt hungry, free and easy hand-outs were now proving somewhat more difficult to procure thanks to the addition of my two new feeders. I must also admit to having given myself a childish chuckle of delight on seeing two different squirrels unsuccessfully trying to clamber up the pole on which the caged feeder had been mounted. Like most campaigns it wasn't going all my own way, as I watched what looked to be a still juvenile squirrel, having squeezed through the anti-squirrel bars covering the ground feeder, busily filling his cheeks with food intended for others. Still, I couldn't deny

that a better balance between the birds and squirrels had now been achieved.

Christina having surfaced, after a quick breakfast on the patio we set about our designated task of finishing the planting up of the herbaceous border in the front garden. Having decided on a floral arrangement that she would be happy with, trowels were wielded as planting began. It being very early in the season, a lot of our recently purchased plants were still pretty small, which meant that they were cheap to buy and easy to plant, so it was hardly arduous work as we happily plonked in twos and threes each of foxgloves, lupins, Jacob's ladders and penstemons. Having soon exhausted our supply of recent purchases, we then moved on to the more established lavenders, salvias and fuchsias which we had potted up from our old flat and brought with us. Anyone who has ever put in plants knows that it is hardly rocket science, so after a sufficient-sized hole had been dug, it was furnished with a few granules of slow-release plant-food (nick-named 'Magic Balls' in our household), before the plant was inverted, pot removed and then placed in its carefully excavated hole. An optional extra of a small amount of mulch was then added to give it a good start.

Not for the first time, while watching Christina plant away I was taken aback by how quickly her green fingers had developed. True, her father and uncle were fine gardeners in their own right, so there must have been a genetic element to the instinctual way she seemed to have with plants. But it was not just how she handled them; she had not only managed to pick up the Latin names of many of the plants in double-quick time, but many of their specific and quirky needs too. I love it when a hidden talent surfaces.

We had decided beforehand that plants for the garden would be chosen with three criteria in mind. Firstly, and most importantly for Christina, they needed to look good; whether through imposing foliage or impressive sprays of flowers was of secondary concern. The second point, and the most important factor for me, was that the plants purchased (wherever possible) should be high nectar and pollen producers, to ensure a bountiful selection of invertebrate pollinators which would in turn attract predators such as spiders, birds and insectivorous mammals. Thirdly, neither of us wanted the effort of having to deal with any delicate, wilting types that were considered high maintenance, so only those plants robust enough to withstand the rough and tumble nature of life in our garden would be represented. As we stood back to see our handiwork, it had to be said that the border currently looked far from the finished article, with the discrete clusters of chlorophyll surrounded by a sea of soil. But before we knew it, the days would soon begin both to lengthen and become warmer, triggering the plants into a sustained period of growth, culminating in a riot of colour as the flowers opened up for passing trade.

Having planned to spend the afternoon shopping for various garden-related paraphernalia, we were just at the point of packing up tools when my eagle-eyed partner noticed a bird whose identity she was unsure of soaring way above the garden, causing me to sprint inside to get my binoculars for a better look. On closer inspection my initial guess was correct, as I was able to confirm that we were watching a male displaying sparrowhawk!

Birds of prey, or raptors, can often be incredibly tough to identify for novice and expert alike, as many look superficially similar and are rarely seen at close quarters. But when a sparrowhawk is clearly seen out in the open, its relatively small size and distinctive 'flap, flap, sail' way of flying are usually enough to ensure a confident identification. Having said that, the only time when the sparrowhawk deviates from this more usual way of flying tends to be in early spring when love is in the air. Usually conducted above the nest site, the spring courtship flight sees the male flapping his wings much more slowly than normal, almost as if in an exaggerated fashion, which is then often combined with a narrowing of the tail and a sticking out of the pale undertail-covert feathers. This slow-flapping flight, if the observer is lucky, will then conclude with a breathtaking series of peregrine-esque stoops designed both to demarcate his territory and impress his potential mate.

As we watched what must have been our resident male spar-rowhawk go through this skydancing routine, and irrespective of what his prospective mate thought, he certainly impressed us. If the pair did indeed settle down locally, and I for one hoped they would, then both male and female would also over the breeding season be making a slightly different impression with all the tits and finches currently flocking to my garden for food too!

Without doubt one of the best features that any self-respecting wildlife gardener should find room for is a compost heap. Obviously this makes getting rid of household vegetable and garden waste a piece of cake, rather than going to the extra effort of sending it off for somebody else to make a profit from or, worse still, using it as land-fill. There is also something amazing about the miracle of decomposition; a process whereby potato peelings, banana skins and apple cores can be broken down, only to be reconstituted back into the most wonderful fertilizer with which to feed your herba-ceous borders.

We too were keen on making our own compost rather than spending our hard-earned cash on bags of it from the local garden centre, but the other reason why I wanted one was because they are hugely important wildlife habitats in their own right. All manner of animals are drawn to compost heaps because all that warm, rotting plant material provides a habitat which is mostly absent from gardens.

Ask most knowledgeable gardeners which animals are most commonly associated with compost heaps and hopefully the major-ity would respond with the answer – reptiles. This heat-loving group simply adores the warmth and protection offered, evidenced by an urban wildlife survey recently conducted around Bristol which revealed that those gardens with a compost heap were twice as likely to play host to resident slow-worms as those without. Compost heaps are also pretty much the only place in a garden (unless you have a huge pond) where you have any chance of catching up with a grass snake, as this is often where females choose to incubate and hatch their eggs. In fact, on the two occasions I have been lucky enough to have seen this wonderful and enigmatic snake in a garden setting, it had converted the heap to a home.

While not every garden compost heap will be able to double up as a natural vivarium, all heaps can be guaranteed to attract a much wider array of invertebrates, such as beetles and woodlice, than would otherwise be found in a sterile, tidy garden where a compost heap would be considered an unsightly eyesore. So, with all this in mind, and aware of the fact that the wood from the dismantling of both the fence and pergola was still sitting there just begging to be used, I had decided that in the spirit of recycling I would try to use the timber to build a couple of compost bins.

Of course, on the surface this grand plan seemed a quite brilliant way to improve the wildlife potential of the garden without either spending much money or wasting any more of the world's timber resources, but the biggest obstacle to the successful completion of this task was that, in a nutshell, I'm terribly unpractical. As all the Dilgers hail from an academic background, it's safe to say that, like my mother, father and two brothers, the practical or technical genes seem largely to have skipped a couple of generations, and like the rest of my family I'm much better at talking the talk, rather than walking the walk! In many ways what makes this even more hilarious is that I'm actually considered the most practical one, simply because of my ability to wire a plug or use a drill to mount a picture – we are that bad! A plug or a picture was one thing, but would I have the ability to cope with building something as technically demanding as a couple of compost bins? Well, we would have to see.

Having found a timber design for compost bins from an old Geoff Hamilton gardening book and having been promised the loan of an electric saw from Christina's father (did he realise what he was promising?), the only bit of kit I now needed to begin the big build was a work bench, hence the visit that afternoon to our local DIY supermarket. As a person who has only recently realised the difference between a plum-bob and a plum-duff, I have always felt a touch intimidated going into these large DIY stores, where the staff have a habit of making you feel terribly inadequate, by perversely responding to your tentative question with another question they know you'll struggle to answer. However, today was different as I knew exactly what I wanted; I was after that iconic tool of the trade which has done more to convey rugged manliness than any beer, aftershave or pair of jeans could ever do ... I was after a Black & Decker Workmate!

Unaware that there was more than one design of Workmate, but not wanting to enquire further about the precise technical differences of each model without sounding stupid either, I did what I usually do in this situation, which is to go for the middle of the range. Christina, who incidentally does come from both practical and academic stock and so would have been a useful sounding board with my workbench dilemma, had taken herself off to the gardening section to feed her plant-buying addiction and so was unavailable for a quick consultation. Nevertheless, I felt both confident and ever so slightly thrilled at the fun I would have with my new purchase ... 'Mike Dilger, naturalist, broadcaster and compost bin builder'!

The following day should have brought the promise of more fun and frolics in the garden for both of us, but instead it started off with a big argument. Like all disagreements it had begun with something small; with us arguing as to where the pond would be located, but this had merely been the stalking horse for a much larger bone of contention, namely what we actually wanted the garden to represent.

In our sketched plan we had effectively decided to divide the garden in two, with the half closer to the house representing the more cultivated and formal part of the garden, while the other half alongside the wooded bank would be left more *au naturel* with a screen of apple trees marking the border between the two sections and effectively operating as green curtains through to the secret nature reserve.

While we agreed that a pond was something we both wanted, the only issue was whether I would lose a large chunk of my meadow for the pond to be situated in the nature reserve, or whether Christina would have to sacrifice a site closer to the house which she had earmarked as a potential seating area. The crux of my argument consisted of why we would go to all the considerable effort of digging a pond if we couldn't even observe what would be attracted to the feature due to it being hidden behind the trees, while Christina countered that the area where I wanted to locate the pond was one of the very few positions which would also comfortably accommodate a table and chairs in the sun.

Once again, our beloved birds abruptly ended the argument, as above our shouting match I suddenly heard a siskin in the birch tree above our heads! The argument stopped instantly as we both fully understood this was not a moment to be squandered, but one to be savoured. I suppose the siskin's song is like a cross between the wheezy greenfinch song and the chaotic, staccato rhythm of a sedge warbler, and to someone like me, whose favourite aspect of natural history has to be birdsong, it was a very special moment. Unlike the blackbirds and chaffinch which had already begun singing to hold territories, this siskin would soon be leaving our garden to raise a family elsewhere and so I suspect was probably just putting in a bit of practice in order to hit the ground running on his chosen breeding ground up in Scotland or Scandinavia.

Deciding that a compromise could easily be worked out, we elected instead to use our time more usefully by making a cuppa and enjoying the garden rather than arguing about it, so the rest of the morning was spent sitting on the patio with our coats and coffee, as we watched early spring unfurl across our garden. Although the siskin had by that time left to practise elsewhere, the sun coming out had patently given other birds sufficient stimulus to join in the throng, and so in quick succession we were also treated to a chorus of dunnock, great tit and chaffinch all competing for both air space and territory in and around our garden.

Despite early spring undeniably having already begun, food was obviously still thin on the ground in the wider countryside as greenfinch, chaffinch and siskin were still fraternising the feeders in large numbers. In addition to the normal suspects, three reed buntings were happily feeding away on my ground feeder, having decided that they weren't quite ready to desert the lush oasis of our garden for the reed beds just yet. Continuing the raptor theme from the previous day, we were also thrilled to spot three buzzards wheeling away on the thermals some 200 feet above the garden whilst making their mewing 'peee-uu' display call. Now vying with the sparrowhawk as Britain's commonest bird of prey, the buzzard was a bird I never saw as a child due to draconian persecution tactics, but thanks to the complete protection of all birds of prey, it has made a sterling comeback and seemed a particularly regular fixture amongst the West Country's cast of wild characters.

Watching wildlife is one of those lovely hobbies which rewards the time and effort you put in, and as we sat there being warmed by the sun's rays, in addition to all the birds going about their business, another somewhat smaller creature that had just emerged from hibernation was also buzzing about. At this time of the year, bumblebees are easy to sex as it is only the queens who are equipped to survive the perils of winter, the rest of her colony having perished in the first frosts of the previous autumn. In a life cycle that beggars belief, the queen, having already been fertilised by the previous year's males, then stores the sperm throughout winter. Upon emerging from hibernation the following spring, her first priority is to immediately replenish the body fats lost during the winter with the pollen and nectar from any suitable early-flowering plants. Using this food to develop her ovaries, it is only then that she will be in a position to fertilise the eggs. With the eggs ready to be laid, her next task is to find a suitable location for the nest to initiate her new colony, explaining why many people in early spring report bumblebees seemingly behaving erratically as they investigate nooks and crannies in walls and holes in lawns. All the queens are doing is looking for somewhere to set up home.

We leapt up to take a closer look, and we could clearly see her crawling around the bottom of the wisteria looking for a mouse-hole or any suitable cavity, and that she was a buff-tailed bumblebee (*Bombus terrestris*), one of the commonest of our bumblebees and also one of the earliest to emerge from hibernation. Bumblebees in Britain have had a tough time over the last 30 years, with two species having become extinct and around half the remaining species being recorded as in serious decline. Unfortunately it is no coincidence that during this period large swathes of our countryside have fundamentally changed from being places teeming with wildlife, to sterile monocultures with little space for the wild flowers and their attendant insects. However, throughout this dark, depressing period of environmental degradation, a ray of light has been created by gardens. Due to the extended flowering seasons gardeners often create and the bountiful sources of nectar and pollen on offer from all the different blooms, gardens have taken on the mantle of becoming extremely important habitats for these beleaguered insects. How appropriate then that our first bumblebee sighting of the year should be in the garden. Our planned trip to the garden centre that afternoon would now also need to include the purchase of a few more early-flowering, bee-friendly plants, as a garden can't be called wildlife-friendly, unless it is full of the sound of buzzing bumbles!

Due to work commitments it was not until the following Friday that I was presented with any further opportunity to get my hands dirty in the garden. I downed my breakfast even faster than usual before bidding goodbye to Christina, who was off to work, for the whole day had been earmarked for a particularly manly job – commencing compost bin construction! But even before I would be able to start the measuring and sawing, the first task would be to actually build the Workmate, as it was only available for purchase in flat-pack form.

One of the prime reasons why historically I have tried to avoid shops like IKEA is that I hate building flat-packed furniture from instructions. To someone like me for whom DIY is a dirty acronym, the accompanying instructions can be the stuff of nightmares; these awful leaflets always assume dangerous levels of competence, are invariably poorly written and often contain diagrams that seem to bear no resemblance to the product you have just purchased. Despite the instructions being more of a hindrance than a help (Black & Decker please note), it was not until lunchtime – yes, a full three hours later – that at last I was ready to begin sawing up the timber.

Despite Mr Hamilton's design initially looking complicated, it was easier to follow than I had expected, and with Christina's father's circular saw cutting through the timber like a hot knife through butter, I was soon giving the wood from the pergola and fence a second lease of life as precisely measured planks. With it being such a lovely, clear day my top half was soon stripped down to nothing more than a T-shirt as a result of the exertion – what a manly occupation compost-bin building was! Geoff's design had incorporated wooden planks both on the back and either side, with small, vertical wooden battens at the front that would keep in place removable slats, which could then be slid out when the compost either needed to be turned or was ready to be removed and then used on our, as yet, nonexistent flower beds. The roof would then simply consist of a large piece of marine plywood to be purchased at a later date. The thinking behind the building of two bins was that it enabled one bin to be maturing while the other one was being filled with household waste and garden trimmings.

Standing back after a couple of hours, I was stunned with my progress. I had turned a large pile of partly rotten timber into a neat stack of perfectly sawn planks, and without any incidents either! I had also achieved something in my own mind of much more significance – I had put to bed my silly notion that I simply wasn't up to anything more difficult than the simplest of practical tasks. There was also a huge feel-good factor associated with re-using and recycling rather than my usual course of action, which would have been to throw away the old timber then solve the 'conundrum' by buying something pre-constructed in a Thai sweatshop. Making my own was cheaper, better on the environment, would probably function better than anything I could have purchased in a store and had proved fun to build too. The only downside was that because the noise of the saw had driven everything elsewhere for the day, it had been the one occasion where I had neither seen nor heard any wildlife of note. I was sure they'd be back the following day, though.

There was only so much that could be achieved with two pairs of hands at such a crucial time of the year, so Christina had asked her family in Bath if they fancied turning up in force to help out on the Sunday. Kindly accepting our offer of a free lunch in return for a day's labour, the work crew had agreed to arrive by mid-morning, giving Christina and I time to scribble down a quick list as to who would do what and, equally crucially, who would work with whom.

Three main jobs were targeted; these were primarily tasks which really had to be undertaken in winter so could not be delayed any further, but they were also activities that could be completed with a day's hard graft. Firstly Christina and her technically minded father Graham would tackle the most technically demanding job of putting up trellis along the fascia of the garage and re-training the old wisteria and clematis back to some degree of order after their years of neglect. Christina's sister Katy and her boyfriend Andy would be given what we considered to be the most fun job, which involved the planting of three apple trees and a damson purchased from Simon at the excellent local Chew Valley tree nursery. And finally Christina's brother Jon and I would get stuck into the most physically demanding task of digging a trench along the fence line between our garden and Marjory and Dennis's, into which we would be planting a combination of native whips, with the ultimate aim of producing a mixed-species hedgerow.

The team didn't just bring manpower with them, but the weather too, as their arrival heralded the disappearance of the early morning fog to reveal wall-to-wall blue sky, with little or no wind to upset the status quo. Cracking straight on after a quick cuppa to admire the new sofa Christina and I had just bought (it was not *just* about the garden), the posse split up into their respective teams, to receive instructions where necessary, before tooling up and getting stuck in. Given the physical aspect of all the jobs, it wasn't long before all team members were peeling off fleeces and coats as the mantra 'cast no clout, fore May be out!' was also cast aside. Most importantly of all, it was delightful to see how much everyone was enjoying the work – clearly audible in between the grunts created by the swinging of the pick-axe or the whine from the drill was the laughter from chirpy banter. There was also a fair amount of spade-leaning too as each group took regular breaks to check up on the progress elsewhere.

The jobs were nevertheless far from plain-sailing, as what we thought initially might have been the most straightforward task ended up being the most problematic when Andy suddenly hit concrete while digging the hole for the first apple tree. Andy's misfortune had been to hit the subterranean concrete foundation of the furthest washing-line pole from the house. On evaluating the problem, three options seemed immediately available – plant the tree in the smaller hole regardless of the block; move the tree to a different location; or keep the tree where we originally wanted it by removing the concrete. Option one was quickly discarded as we decided that planting the tree next to the block would have severely restricted its root system, and the second option soon proved equally untenable as moving the sapling would have placed it far too close to the other apple trees, ultimately giving them insufficient space in which to thrive. The only feasible option left was also the most exhausting one – the block would have to come out.

Having taken Andy a mere 20 minutes to dig the initial hole, little did we know that it would then take a further 60 minutes to clear the soil sufficiently from around the block to allow for its removal. It was not until four of us had finally managed to lever the concrete cube out of the hole and onto the path that we could fully appreciate why Andy had struggled. Measuring close to a yard across, the huge unearthed lump of concrete would have perhaps been more useful as one of the foundation stones for a nuclear reactor rather than just the footing for a washing-line pole. The one plus side of forming a huge crater in the middle of the lawn was that it provided the perfect place to dispose of the wheelbarrow loads of excess soil that Jon and I had spent most of the morning generating whilst digging the hedge-line trench.

With all four holes finally dug, the trench prepared and the trellis up, we stopped only briefly for an *al fresco* chicken stir-fry lunch, before I had to crack the whip again, as plenty more still had to be done before we lost the light. However, with most of the hard graft already completed, the second half of the work programme would be the fun part, as it was time to plant and prune.

Following the tried-and-tested methodology for hedgerow planting, the trench Jon and I had dug was back-filled with a mixture of compost and the soil we had already dug out. The whips, which we had also purchased from the local nursery in a job lot with the fruit trees, were then planted in two rows, half a yard apart and in staggered fashion, creating a zigzag pattern. As by far the most whips we had purchased consisted of the cheaper hawthorn, with a smaller mix of field maple, blackthorn, spindle and alder buckthorn, Graham had the excellent idea of planting the back row with pure hawthorn and then alternating the front row with the other pricier species.

It was inevitable during the morning's work that one or two of the primroses just pushing their heads above the surface would be in the wrong place, but, wherever possible, any plants in the way were carefully dug up and then relocated to a safer place elsewhere in the meadow. It was not just the primroses that were flowering; in addition to at least half a dozen varieties of daffodils randomly cropping up all over the garden, small golden rafts of another of my favourite early spring wildflowers were in full bloom too. Overlooked by many as nothing more than a small and inconsequential early-flowering buttercup, the lesser celandine is anything but, figuring heavily as it does in the writings of surely one of our most celebrated poets, William Wordsworth. Probably best known for his 'I Wandered Lonely as a Cloud' poem, where he waxes lyrical about daffodils, his favourite plant was actually the lesser celandine, which he honoured with an entire poem that begins thus:

> There is a flower, the lesser celandine
> That shrinks, like many more, from cold and rain
> And, the first moment that the sun may shine
> Bright as the sun himself, 'tis out again!

So adoring had Wordsworth been of this flower that it was decided after his death that the plant would be carved on his tombstone, but it seems the chap commissioned to carry out the work was no botanist and actually carved a greater celandine by mistake. To make matters worse, the greater celandine is not even related to its lesser namesake, but is a member of the poppy family instead – a grave mistake! In Wordsworth's poem he is of course spot-on when describing how the lesser celandine tends to be a bit of a fair-weather creature, only bothering to unfurl its petals properly when the sun comes out. And today was such an example, with the gorgeous weather having encouraged the flowers to emerge from the massed ranks of kidney-shaped leaves, to create the most wonderful golden splashes in amongst a field of green. But for me personally, he missed out the most interesting quirky feature of this plant, which is how all the flowers operate like miniature satellite dishes as they faithfully track the progress of the sun across the sky – this plant is in essence a botanical representation of me, a dedicated sun worshipper!

The planting of whips was of course kids' play, and involved no more than using a spade to create a slit trench into which the roots of the sapling were carefully placed before a boot was delicately applied to bed the plant properly in. So with Jon starting at one end and me at the other, in less than half an hour we successfully managed to plant ten yards of mixed-species hedge between the rear of the garage and the wooded bank – all we needed to do then was to water the whips and wait another decade for the hedge to mature and it would be job done!

Back over where Andy and Katy had been busy toiling away, the planned junction between formal garden and nature reserve had in the meantime been transformed into an orchard! Their last remaining job was to drive in the supporting stakes, at an angle of 45 degrees to avoid any damage to the root-balls, and also along a southwesterly orientation to give the trees the best possible support against the predominant prevailing wind direction.

The formation of a mini-orchard was something that Christina and I had both been keen on. Due to a combination of there nowadays being little room for small orchards in modern farming and the fact that supermarkets have been reluctant to sell home-grown apples, more than half of all our British orchards have disappeared since 1970. This is particularly shameful when you consider what hugely important wildlife habitats they have become, as orchards will often be the best places to find a wide range of wild-life, from the lesser-spotted woodpecker to rare beetles and mistle-toe. Probably as a result of the mild and wet climate found in the West Country there was also a strong tradition of growing apple trees in all the counties, spanning in an arc from Herefordshire and Worcestershire all the way to Somerset. This local long-standing regional association with the apple can also easily be verified by a visit to any public house within the area, as is this is probably the one region in the UK where cider drinkers outnumber ale-drink-ers! With all this in mind it would have been criminal not to do our bit both to halt the decline of the orchard and to continue support-ing a strong, local heritage. There would also hopefully be the small added benefit of a few apples for both us and the wildlife to share too!

Continuing our theme of buying local wherever possible, Christina and I had selected the three apple trees from three differ-ent varieties with both a regional heritage and a similar pollination group. With luck, the garden would be graced with 'Scrumptious', 'Cheddar Cross' and 'Discovery' apples for decades to come, start-ing with this autumn.

Last but not least, the technically adept pairing of Graham and Christina had done a marvellous job of erecting the trellis to hide huge sections of pebble-dashed garage wall. With something for the wisteria and clematis to be finally pegged back to, loppers and seca-teurs could at last be ruthlessly wielded to give them a radical short back and sides – with such unruly plants, you often have to be cruel to be kind!

With all the tools stowed away, Christina then brought ice-creams for the workers out of nowhere as we wandered around admiring our efforts. Thanks to the willing posse and the clement weather it had been our most productive day so far, and the trans-formation to the garden nature reserve was at last well on its way.

With Christina now back at work and my filming schedule of back-to-back trips still a month away, I was keen to capitalise on our good start by filling any spare time with garden chores, and the following Tuesday was one such opportunity to initiate phase two of the compost bin construction job. With my now trusty Workmate, Graham's borrowed saw and in the most beautiful weather, I soon made short work of sawing up the last of the recycled wood ready for the planks to be nailed together. Suddenly realising that a trip to the DIY store would be necessary to buy larger nails and screws than I had planned for, I decided temporarily to shelve the completion of the bins to provide some post-planting TLC to the apple and damson trees planted by Andy and Katy. Care for a tree should not stop the moment that it is placed in the ground, as the vulnerable bedding-in time is in many ways just as crucial to the tree's survival as to how it was planted in the first place. So with this in mind, all four trees were given a good soaking, and then in turn had their bases furnished with a mulch of bark chippings to suppress any weed growth, while they settled in. I was just down on my hands and knees finishing up the mulching when I suddenly caught a flash of sulphur-yellow out of the corner of my eye. Spinning round, I was ecstatic to see a male brimstone butterfly as it flew along the newly installed hedgerow which Jon and I had only planted a couple of days previously!

The first butterfly sighting of the year is always a red-letter day for me, testified by the fact that for the rest of the year I will always be able recall where I was and what I was doing when the butterfly made that appearance. I can remember bizarrely, for example, that in 2010 my first butterfly of that year was another brimstone seen flitting past a lay-by off the A1 in Hertfordshire; however, this year my first sighting would be doubly special, as for the record it was spotted in my own garden on 15 March at about 11.40am!

Being one of the few British species capable of overwintering as an adult, the long-lived brimstone is invariably the first butterfly of the calendar year to be recorded on the wing as the nomadic males emerge early from hibernation to begin fluttering around woodlands and along hedgerows in their annual search for virgin females to mate. The bright yellow-coloured brimstone was certainly well known amongst the earliest butterfly collectors, with some people still maintaining that the word 'butterfly' is nothing more than a shortening of the brimstone's old name of 'butter-coloured fly'. The paler-coloured and more scarcely seen females are also incredibly fastidious as to where they lay their eggs, only choosing either purging buckthorn or alder buckthorn. With this knowledge in mind, the sole reason why I had picked alder buckthorn as one of the constituents of our mixed-species hedgerow was to try and attract the butterfly into the garden – what I didn't expect was for it to take a mere 48 hours. This was more coincidence than design, I suspected!

Buoyed by my butterfly sighting and having collected the large nails I needed, I was soon straight back onto the bins assembly, which slowly but steadily began to take shape with the addition of each plank to the corner posts. Despite the near-constant noise interruption created by the sound of hammer on nail-head, I was surprised to still be able to count at least six different bird species singing from in or around the garden. Chaffinch, greenfinch, dunnock, blackbird, robin and wren could all be heard staking their claim for the chunk of real estate which also happened to be our garden – and they were most welcome to it! Putting the hammer aside for a break to properly enjoy this impromptu concert, I then suddenly picked up the call of a kingfisher as its shrill whistle cut through the other birdsong like a knife through butter – it was back again! Fully expecting it to have disappeared around the bend of the stream and out of sight by the time I stuck my head over the bank for a look, I was astonished to see it perching on one of the hazel branches arcing over the brook from our side of the bank.

Even without binoculars the red base to the lower mandible could be clearly seen and immediately identified the bird as a female. As far as I was concerned, the presence of an adult female in the middle of March meant that she was clearly the resident female and would be laying her first clutch within the month. How exciting was that? Not only did we have kingfishers whizzing past the bottom of our garden, but the presence of a female so close to the breeding season indicated that there would almost certainly be a resident male too, which in turn probably meant that the nest site would be close by. Our own resident kingfishers – it was too thrilling for words, and, for me, total vindication for having bought the house and garden in the first place. True, we knew that both needed a lot of work, but the garden particularly had the most enormous potential, and more importantly we were going to have the most fun this year unlocking it.

Christina was envious of the fact that I'd been able to spend some quality time in the garden midweek, and so, come the weekend, she was determined to make up for her GWS (Garden Withdrawal Syndrome) by spending a couple of full days capitalising on our good start. Despite the fact that it was now nearer April than March, there had been a ground frost over night, but once again the weather looked set fair. What an early spring we were enjoying!

The first part of the morning was spent in the front garden. While we had already agreed to prioritise the back garden, the front garden did represent the public face of our property – and what would our neighbours think if we hadn't made an effort? So while I carefully weeded, Christina's job was to heavily prune the buddleia just to the right of our bay window, which had obviously not been touched for years and was enacting out its plans for world domination.

Buddleia is perhaps much better known as the butterfly bush, and I have strong memories from my childhood in Stafford of a huge butterfly bush in our next-door neighbour's garden. Mr Hill also had the most amazing collection of pinned butterflies – a practice frowned on today now that digital photography has enabled collectors to create something every bit as good without harming a single insect. But what I remember even more clearly than his trays of butterflies was the thrilling sight of his huge butterfly bush alive with small tortoiseshells, peacocks and red admirals.

A native of China introduced here in the 1890s, the butterfly bush has proved a blessing and a curse in equal measure. While its long, honey-scented, purple flowering spikes are undoubtedly a big summer hit with all manner of moths and butterflies, its light winged seeds have also enabled its prolific spread across virtually the whole of Britain, with the exception of the far north. Certainly in Bristol you can't pass a piece of waste ground in the city without at least a few buddleia bushes exploiting the cracks in between the pavement or the tiniest of crevices in the surrounding walls. Certainly on the train journey between Bristol and Bath, the buddleia dominates the vegetation along the rail-side clinker to such an extent that the view out of the window often seems to be that of just one very long, sinuous butterfly bush. So in a nutshell, because of its excellent wildlife credentials, the bush would be able to stay in the front garden, but only in a much more diminutive and manageable form!

Taking a break from our work, we put the kettle on in preparation for the arrival of a VIP. We were both terribly excited as we were about to receive a visit from gardening royalty. One of my oldest and dearest friends, whom I first met at university, one of the few people I stayed in contact with during my five years of working in the tropics and also the person whose floor I slept on for 10 months when I moved down to Bristol in 1999, is Mark. Being a Senior Producer at the world-famous BBC Natural History Unit, Mark has worked on everything from *The Private Life of Plants* to *Human Planet*, but, more relevant to this book, he is also the most amazing gardener, and a man who also seems to have chlorophyll rather than blood running through his veins. Also, rather hilariously, his surname is, erm, Flowers!

Mark had kindly accepted our invitation to come and give the garden a once-over and to dispense some much-needed advice, but what we hadn't expected were the plants he also brought over, which were deemed surplus to requirements from his own garden. Arriving with the delightful surprise of his car boot chock-a-block with sedums, pulmonarias and phlox, Mark had also thoughtfully driven over in his gardening clothes, aware of the fact that he would have to sing for his supper!

Starting on the wooded bank, we were firstly keen for him to identify a few plants, which without flowers or foliage we were still unsure of. With the experience of having spent the best part of the last 40 years being obsessed with garden plants, this proved a straightforward exercise for Mark as he revealed with typical theatrical poise that we were also the proud owners of a magnolia, a viburnum and a winter-flowering honeysuckle. The magnolia was a particularly exciting find, but was really struggling for light and space and needed help.

Expertly handling the loppers, Mark began to prune the magnolia into a much more manageable size and a more aesthetically pleasing shape. Advising us that the surrounding shrubbery would also need pegging back, Christina, under Mark's direction, began brandishing her secateurs as she continued to make room for our surprise find. As the two clipped their way into the surrounding vegetation I then began to get alarmed at the amount that was being taken out, stating that while I, too, was keen to see the magnolia flourish, it shouldn't be at the expense of the native woodland species which had far higher wildlife potential. I also didn't want too much of the hazel and hawthorn removed before the breeding season, as this would deprive the birds of potential nesting locations. Christina, of course, sided with my old friend by stating that if progress were to be made, then some of the vegetation would simply have to go. With both actively ganging up on me, I was not only outnumbered, but left with little alternative other than to accede to their demands, and I was also delegated the job of tidying up the mess that they had been busy creating!

I was keen to give Mark something in return for all the plants he had kindly donated, and I noticed that his eye had been caught by some of the snowdrops from our front garden which had finally gone over after putting on a fine display over the previous six weeks. The best time to dig up and split snowdrops, Mark explained, was just after the flowers had faded. Removing some of the bulbs would not only give the opportunity to introduce snowdrops elsewhere into the garden but would ensure that the remaining bulbs would have more than enough room to put on an equally impressive show the following winter. Following Mark's lead, it really was child's play as we carefully dug up a few bunches with trowels, which were then split into smaller clumps of, say, half a dozen bulbs. Some of these small clumps were then either given to our horticultural consultant as a gift, or planted down in the woodland to repopulate our bank the cheap, easy and quick way, rather than having to wait the decades necessary for the snowdrops to spread under their own steam. This was also the first time that we had played 'botanical swapsies' – a game which hopefully we would continue to enjoy during the up and coming months.

After lunch, Mark and I headed off to Bristol, Mark to enjoy the rest of the weekend back in his own garden whilst I was away to feed one of my other addictions – watching football. Both watching and playing sport has often come a close second to my obsession with natural history, to the extent that Christina has long since given up fighting the constant drone of BBC Radio Five Live that I usually insist of having on in the background all weekend. Having chosen to support Bristol City since my move down to the West Country, it has to be said that, while skill levels are often seriously lacking, it is still a fun way to spend every alternate Saturday afternoon. Making me feel only slightly guilty that she was determined to carry on working whilst I was off enjoying myself, Christina wanted to begin digging up the weedy section of lawn running the length of the garage. Our aim was that this section would be turned into one of the real highlights of the more formal part of the garden – what better place to plant a huge herbaceous border?

I returned some three hours later, buoyed by an uncharacteristically adept performance and a 2–0 win by The Robins, and I couldn't believe how much Christina had achieved in such a short space of time. Having removed the turf, she had then created a lovely sweeping curve that would mark the front edge of the bed – the neck of which began at the defunct garage side-door, and widened out to a depth of three yards past the wisteria and newly erected trellis, before then swinging sharply back in to meet the corner of the garage wall underneath the hawthorn standard and by the water butt. This shape had the effect of a drawing the eye away from the garage and down the garden towards the apple trees. Not content to stop there, she had also turned over most of the soil, incorporating three or four pre-purchased bags of compost to create the perfect growing medium. In the space of three hours and out of nothing she had just created a herbaceous border in which to put all Mark's plants. This girlfriend was a keeper!

In fact, it would turn out to be a weekend of guests. I met Ed when we both worked on *Springwatch*; I was employed as Bill Oddie's researcher, and Ed and I have since become the firmest of birding buddies. Not content with regular birding excursions around the UK, we have also satisfied our unquenchable thirst for birdies with a whole array of trips to Europe, the Middle East and West Africa. A full decade and a bit younger than me, Ed is without doubt one of the finest birders of his age in this country, and in addition to having the largest private collection of feathers, skulls and wings I have ever seen, he has also found time to be one of Britain's top peregrine experts. Another addition to his mightily impressive CV was his recent qualification as a bird ringer, and it was in that capacity that I wanted to invite Ed round. Hopefully a siskin or reed bunting in the hand would on this occasion beat two in the bush!

Even penetrating above the buzz of my electric toothbrush and through the double glazing of the bathroom I could still hear the deep timbre of male wood pigeons serenading prospective partners with their endlessly repetitive 'I'm bor-ing I am, I'm bor-ing I am' call as I got ready for a morning's bird-ringing. The wood pigeon's call is possibly the sound that reminds me most of my childhood, as I have strong recollections of their call droning on in the background whilst I prised myself out of bed each morning for my paper round before school.

Befitting a man who's time-keeping is always nothing short of perfect, Ed pulled onto the drive exactly at our pre-arranged time of 7.30am, and without further ado we barrelled straight out into the back garden to work out the best locations to put up his mist nets. For those not familiar with mist nets in action, they are made of nylon mesh vertically suspended between two poles, giving a vague resemblance of an oversized volleyball net. When properly deployed, the nets are virtually invisible and, most importantly, are able to capture birds without causing any injury whatsoever. We decided to place a six-yard net alongside and parallel to the wooded bank and a 12-yard net running lengthwise along the garden just to the right of the feeders, so that any birds flying in to feed would hopefully become ensnared.

With a little cloud cover and no wind, weather conditions for trapping were initially perfect, but no sooner had we trotted back inside to leave the nets in peace, than the double whammy of both the sun coming out and a breeze picking up instantly made it trickier to catch large numbers of birds, for the simple reason that a billowing net is more easily spotted, giving the birds that vital extra millisecond to take avoidance measures. The protocol is that the nets should be checked at least every 15 minutes, so we were delighted on our first inspection to have caught both a blue tit and a great tit in the biggest net. Of course, extricating birds from mist nets is an art that takes years of practice, as birds can easily become heavily tangled in the net, are frightened and surprisingly susceptible to being damaged with inexperienced hands. So I confined myself to photographing the action whilst Ed carefully twisted, turned and rotated each bird with remarkable dexterity until both were free of the net and safely slotted into his ringing bags. My job then morphed from photographer to scribe as I noted down the measurements Ed took of their wing length, weight, age and sex before he placed a metal ring containing a unique code on each bird's leg which would identify it if it were re-trapped or found dead. The birds were then released back into the garden.

As someone who has watched great tits thousands of times through binoculars, I thought I knew this common garden visitor pretty well, so I was gobsmacked when Ed told me that the key to sexing great tits in the field is to look at the black breast-stripe, which is wider in the males than the females. I was slightly embarrassed that someone of my alleged repute hadn't even been aware of this basic fact. How come I had not read this somewhere or even realised it myself from all my years of birding? I suppose one of the most fascinating aspects about wildlife is that the more we learn about this huge subject, the more we realise how little in fact we really know. Even after a lifetime of studying birds, in many ways I was still only scratching the surface. One thing was clear from this revelation; I would have to start looking at my common birds through different eyes from now on!

As the morning went on, although a deluge of birds never materialised due to the weather conditions not working in our favour, we still managed to ring nine blue tits, four great tits, and one each of robin, chaffinch, dunnock, coal tit, wren, long-tailed tit and, best of all, a goldcrest – the latter being a bird I hadn't even recorded in the garden until we discovered one in the net! In between the net checks we'd also been royally entertained by a couple of jackdaws flying back to our uncovered chimney pots with twigs – it looked like the first nest of the breeding season wouldn't be constructed in one of the newly erected nest boxes but inside our chimney instead!

The lovely weather, while preventing the capture of any siskins or reed buntings, had managed to encourage a couple more male brimstone butterflies out of hibernation, but the best sighting of the morning was indisputably our first small tortoiseshell of the year. This butterfly was a particularly pleasing addition to our garden list, as this is a species which has seemed to have all but disappeared over the last couple of years, due to its larvae having been targeted by a parasitoid fly. Fingers crossed that this would be the year of the small tortoiseshell fight-back!

Having just spent the last couple of days in a sleep-deprived and ratty state hasn't been good. The nesting jackdaws I had been only too happy to observe with Ed a couple of days previously have been habitually at their most communicative at around 4.30 in the morning. And with the chimney breast actually passing en route through our bedroom between the fireplace and chimney pots, it has actually felt like the birds have chosen to nest at the foot of the bed instead. Enthusiastic though I was to do everything possible within my powers to encourage all nesting birds, I had just discovered that this welcoming attitude would not be at the expense of a good night's sleep. Nevertheless, I felt the painful irony in making the decision to unceremoniously evict the first pair of birds to have actually shown an interest in nesting. The best available option would be to remove the nest as quickly as possible before the female laid her clutch, meaning she would have time to re-build and raise a family elsewhere.

So a couple of days later I had to spend the morning watching, with mixed emotions, as Ben the local Chew Valley chimney sweep dislodged the most enormous jackdaw nest out of our chimney. Hopefully that would be the first and last time I would ever have to pay for a nest removal. I elected to spend the rest of the day cheering myself up in the garden, and I decided that I would get stuck into a couple of jobs that would allow me to show Christina on her return home from work how much progress I had made.

The first job would be to tidy up the mess that the lopping and pruning duo of Mark and Christina had created the previous weekend. While chatting to Marjory and Dennis as they put out their recycling the week before, my beady eye had also noticed a shredder hidden in their extensively stocked garage. Being the generous souls I now knew them to be, they instantly offered it out for loan on condition that I would also shred some vegetation they had recently generated from a spot of gardening of their own.

Once again I was blessed with the most beautiful weather as I powered up the shredder and set to work. By doing little more than feeding one branch after the next into the ever-voracious jaws of a shredder, there was something incredibly satisfying about seeing a huge, messy stack of brushwood converted into nothing more than a small pile of macerated twigs. In fact, in under an hour both piles of vegetation were polished off, leaving me more than enough time to finish off the composting bins in time for their inspection by my other half.

I was just in the process of moving my tools into the garden when I suddenly caught sight of a rather extraordinary insect buzzing around the primroses and lesser celandines in the meadow. Looking like a cross between a bee and a mosquito with a huge proboscis was surely one of our most spectacular early spring insects, the large bee-fly. With the wonderful Latin name of *Bombylius major*, the bee-fly is in fact a fly as it only has a single functional pair of wings in contrast to the two pairs owned by bees, and whilst its huge proboscis looked like a hornet's sting it is nothing more than an utterly harmless tube designed to tap into the deeply recessed nectaries of some flowers. This is a creature that has become an increasingly regular fixture in our towns and gardens over recent years, but for me it was a total surprise and a fabulous addition to my ever-increasing garden list.

Upon nailing the last planks in place, the compost bins were so heavy that I could scarcely move them into their allotted positions without either damaging them or my back. Finally, having managed to wrestle what must have been in excess of a 220lbs of timber into place I suddenly and belatedly realised that their uneven look was due to the fact that I hadn't taken enough care to level the ground that I had placed them on beforehand. Reminding myself that they were compost bins and not artworks, rather than risk a hernia I decided they were fine where they were, and, most importantly of all, at last they were ready to be used.

Dismissing their wonky nature out of hand, Christina was so pleased with all my hard work she immediately declared I should take the rest of the evening off. And proceeding to pour me a large glass of wine before cooking a terrific meal, she was true to her word. In fact, my only delegated job that evening was to dispose of the vegetable peelings – well, somebody had to christen the new bins!

APRIL

IF YOU DIG IT, THEY WILL COME

'Quick Mike, there's a badger in the garden!' 'What?' 'There's a badger in the garden!' With Christina up early ahead of a big day at work, while I would be working from home, it was one of those few mornings when she was up well before me. Dragging myself out of bed and half expecting it to be an April Fool's joke, I stumbled down to the landing-hall window where only a minute before Christina had apparently just glimpsed the first views of a badger from the light cast by the kitchen. 'I can't see anything!' I said, peering into the gloom of the garden and not sure, in view of the date, whether this was her version of an elaborate hoax. 'I tell you it was right there on the path!' she said, and as she seemed to be blissfully unaware of the date, it was obvious that she'd been telling the truth. The early bird had indeed got the worm – or in this case, the badger!

Whilst we already knew from the snuffling marks regularly encountered in the meadow that Britain's largest terrestrial carnivore was a frequent after-hours visitor to our garden, incontrovertible proof, in the form of a sighting, was still exciting news. Putting my disappointment to one side that I hadn't actually been there to share the moment, I was nevertheless thrilled for Christina, as my turn would surely come. I was tied to my office for the whole morning sorting out tedious paperwork, so it would not be until the afternoon that I was finally able properly to turn my attention to the garden, and, with the weekend just around the corner, what better time to set the ball in motion with two new fabulous projects? Of course, the initiation of any new project in our case inevitably involved the by now well-worn path to our local DIY store to purchase the necessary kit. But this time, buoyed by the unqualified success of the compost bins, I felt ready to tackle the biggest and most ambitious project yet: digging a wildlife pond!

From the moment our offer for the property had been accepted, we had decided that the addition of a pond was an essential pre-requisite for any self-respecting back-garden nature reserve. In a nutshell, ponds are teeming with life, and in my opinion adding one to your property portfolio is the single quickest way of instantly making your garden more attractive to a massive range of wildlife. Garden ponds have also over the last few decades become an increasingly important habitat, as their countryside cousins have either been filled in or become so polluted from agricultural run-off or other pollutants that the life they are able to support has become minimal.

Having a pond in my own back garden is something I have intensely desired for as long as I can remember. One of my most vivid early childhood memories is of a brush with aquatic wildlife at the age of four or five, when I recall being entranced by dragonflies dashing around a pond on Cannock Chase in Staffordshire, and it's fair comment to say I have been fascinated by them ever since. Of course, the presence of a pond will not only massively increase your chance of dragonflies making an appearance, but will also maximise the possibility of playing host to amphibians at some point during the year too. I can't tell you how happy it would make me to be the proud owner of a clump of frogspawn – does that make me sound strange?

Of course, with ponds it's not just about the charismatic mega-fauna of frogs and dragonflies, as any half-decent water feature should also provide a welcome home to pond skaters, water boat-men, pond snails, water beetles, water fleas, a whole array of differ-ent larvae and aquatic plants too. In fact the only group that most definitely would not be welcome in our pond-to-be would be fish. I'm afraid it's a cold, hard fact that garden ponds with fish are much less diverse and interesting – unless of course you are only interested in fish – but I wanted a wildlife pond not an ornamental pond. While I'm the first to admit that koi carp or goldfish are a lovely addition to water features of posh stately homes, it must be remembered that these fish are also voracious introduced predators in what is effectively a closed system. In a zoo, for example, no one would ever do anything as stupid as to open all the cages to see what would happen, as the obvious answer would be a few fat lions. Likewise, non-native fish would quickly clear out the eggs and larvae of all the species that I was far more interested in. So, the nearest any fish would get to my pond would be the ones swimming past in the brook at the bottom of the garden!

The other task that Christina and I would be tackling this month would be the building of a small raised vegetable bed. Although not as critical a feature of a wildlife garden as the pond, we knew that growing some produce would be desirable for a number of reasons. Firstly, there is something primeval and 'deep-rooted' in our souls about being able to support ourselves, even if only in a small way. Those who have tended and nurtured their own vegetables from seeds or seedlings to the final product will also vouch that they always taste better than anything bought in a supermarket. Finally, organically grown veg is undoubtedly more environmentally friendly than food that is mass-produced, as our planned patch, for example, would be pesticide-free and have a virtually nonexistent carbon footprint.

Importantly, it was only fair that as the garden was, let's not forget, equally owned by Christina, we should incorporate her wish to at least have some element of it as a smallholding. This wasn't for one minute an attempt to emulate the hilarious attempts at self-sufficiency by Tom and Barbara Good as seen in *The Good Life*, but the sacrifice of a small part of the garden to grow at least some of our own produce somehow also dove-tailed with the 'nature reserve' ethos that we were trying to create. With this in mind, the previous week we had hired a van to collect three old railway sleepers purchased from a huge reclamation yard in Wells. Our raised vegetable bed would be built with a rustic yet chunky design.

So in addition to buying a large piece of marine plywood to act as a simple lid for the compost bins, the shopping list at the DIY store also consisted of a bunch of canes and some spray paint to enable us to delineate exactly where the pond and the vegetable plot would go. Picking Christina up from work on the return journey, the longer spring evenings now meant that we would have at least a couple of hours in the garden to get some work done before bad light stopped play.

As Christina had by now finally relented to my request that the pond would indeed be located in the more formal section of the garden, close to the communal fence with Andy and Lorraine, we set about sticking canes into the lawn to experiment with different shapes and designs. The advantage of using canes meant that when we ran some twine around the outside of these markers, like a cat's cradle, it gave an immediate impression of how the finished pond would look. The pond's location had been chosen both because it was a sunny spot, with the resultant warmth helping to encourage an even greater diversity of wildlife, and also crucially because it was far enough away from any mature trees whose leaves would constantly clog the pond each autumn and block out all-important light. The hope was that we would then surround the pond along the shared fence line and around the rear with a sumptuous herbaceous border, full of places for dragonflies to perch, butterflies to sunbathe and amphibians to hide – or this was the idea.

While we wanted a pond of a reasonable size, we did have to bear in mind that the garden wasn't exactly huge, and so something the size of a small swimming pool would, frankly, have looked ridiculous. Moving the sticks in or out eventually resulted in a shape and size that we were both happy with and which vaguely seemed to resemble a 10- by 12-foot kidney bean. We marked out our agreed outline with yellow spray paint, and then removed the sticks to admire our work. True, at present it looked more like the crime scene where Mr Blobby had been killed in cold blood, but with time and skill levels permitting it would be transformed into the garden's star feature, to which the wildlife would come flocking!

Situated no more than a couple of large strides from the scene of the crime and butting up to the cherry-tree bird table sculpted by tree surgeon Rob, the water butt and the corner of the garage, would be the location of the raised vegetable bed. The overall plan was to funnel garden visitors down in between the pond and the raised bed, where they would then be confronted by the screen of apple trees, and through which they would pass to reach the meadow, the wooded bank and finally the brook. Measuring a standard railway sleeper length of 8 feet 6 inches, we planned for two of the pre-purchased sleepers to represent the longer sides, while the third one, which had already been cut in half, would complete the rectangle at either end. A total surface area of 40 square feet would hardly provide enough room to keep us in vegetables all winter, but with so many other features competing for space, we would have to cut our cap according to our cloth.

Sharp-eyed as ever, while I was busily marking out the raised bed with the canes, Christina had spotted a dunnock carrying what looked like moss back to one of the small ornamental *leylandii* cypresses which were within Andy and Lorraine's garden, but whose foliage spilled over the fence into our garden – making it just as much our nest as theirs! If we also factored in that the dunnocks seemed to spend most of their time in our garden, hoovering up any scraps dropped from the birds messily eating from the feeders above their heads, then I felt quite justifiably that we could count this as our first proper nest – apart from the jackdaw nest that we didn't talk about anymore!

To say that the dunnock is an unspectacular-looking bird would be an understatement, as plumage-wise the bird is utterly forgettable, but underneath that plain exterior is a bird with quite possibly the most complex sex life of any known in the UK. Put simply, in the world of the dunnock anything goes; whilst some pairings do persist with the typical male to female ratio of one to one, some males will have two females, with other females opting for two or more males. However, other individuals' relationships can be even more intriguing, and in some cases several males share several females. While the dunnock's sexual relations could in essence be described as being more akin to either a 1970s hippy commune or a more thoroughly modern swingers' party, it is always still the female who has the task of both building the nest and incubating the eggs, before either her one partner or the extended parental family chip in to help raise the brood.

With some light left before dusk drew a veil over the day and prevented further work, there was still the opportunity to get a few of the herbaceous perennials we had been steadily accumulating into the new garage border that Christina had so diligently and single-handedly created. So alongside the rejuvenated wisteria and clematis, in quick succession we were able to plant out all of Mark's recent donations plus a climbing rose and some bearded irises. Hopefully with the addition of a few more key plants, this bed would be a riot of colour in just a couple of months.

With Christina off to spend the Saturday morning catching up with family, this gave me the perfect opportunity to prepare the ground for the raised bed. Christina's brilliant idea at dinner the night before had been to get the sleepers in position before starting work on the pond. This meant the empty bed would be the perfect receptacle for absorbing most of the soil generated from digging the pond only a couple of yards away. It was so devastatingly simple, the only thing I wanted to know was why I hadn't thought of it.

I was acutely aware that I had slightly spoilt the final presentation of the compost bins by not having levelled the ground properly before positioning them, so this time I would be checking everything meticulously with a spirit level. Unlike the bins, tucked away out of sight behind the garage, the raised bed would be constantly on full show and therefore required a more exacting level of care and attention. Unfortunately the projected location of the raised bed would also be cutting across part of the concrete path which ran like a backbone down the centre of the garden, so before the sleepers were lifted into place this would have to be broken up. The concrete was initially laid down when the house had first been built, and it must have been at least a couple of inches thick. As my armoury didn't possess a pneumatic drill this meant I would have to do it the old-fashioned way, with a sledgehammer, a pick-axe borrowed from, you've guessed it, Marjory and Dennis, and brute force. For a job like this, a pair of eye goggles that I had just purchased would be essential, as doubtless small pieces would be flying all over the place. And with so much work to do, the last thing I wanted was to waste three hours down at Accident and Emergency having my eyes checked.

There is something incredibly satisfying about intense physical labour that makes you feel alive, and in no time, despite the cold, cloudy start to the day, I was soon peeling off layers. After trialling different methods, I soon found that the technique that worked the best involved initially swinging the sledgehammer with blunt blows to fracture the concrete, and then changing to the pick-axe to lever out the broken chunks. After an hour's solid graft, during which, quite frankly, I looked more like the missing link in a chain gang than a respected naturalist, I had completely cleared a two-yard section of the path and replaced it with a sunken mud pit. Ninety per cent of any hard landscaping job seems to involve making a mess and then having to tidy it up again, and having already ordered a skip to be delivered the following week, in a rare moment of forethought, the concrete could be piled up to one side in the full knowledge that the usual disposal issues wouldn't in this case be a problem.

With the weather suddenly beginning to clear and my first task completed ahead of schedule, it gave me a free hour to enjoy the garden before Christina came back to instigate a whole new raft of jobs. Taking a tour around the meadow, the primroses and lesser celandines were looking pristine and had just been joined by another top-notch plant which we had both been delighted to have discovered emerging in a couple of discrete clusters a fortnight ago. Surely there can be few flowers more charismatic or enigmatic in the whole of the British Isles than the snake's head fritillary. Largely confined in the wild to just a few winter-flooded hay meadows along the greater Thames Valley, of which the famous site is North Meadow at Cricklade in Wiltshire, the snake's head has now become an exceptionally rare plant. So while there was no doubting that the plants currently flowering in our meadow would have been introductions, their origin did little to detract from their beauty. And as I watched a queen bumblebee disappearing into the bell of one of the flowers in front of me, it was patently not only me who was enjoying them.

The snake's head fritillary's name is particularly interesting and is thought to emanate from both the pattern on the flowers, where the chequered design of purple and lilac seems to overlap like reptilian scales, and the long slender stem and nodding bell, which from certain angles bears more than a passing resemblance to the body and head of a snake rearing up to strike. While also a plant that can be quite easily purchased in cultivated form from many garden centres around Easter, when it tends to be at its blooming best, I have known a number of very technically proficient gardeners, including my esteemed friend Mr Flowers, who have attempted to plant them in their own garden but somehow failed to replicate their fastidious requirements, resulting in their time and money being wasted. Here, though, probably more by luck than judgement, they looked as much a natural component of the flora as all the dandelions, whose bright, brash flowers were beginning to crop up *en masse* in the main body of the meadow.

In addition to the bumblebee still systematically working the fritillaries, a couple more bee-flies had also been enticed out by the lovely weather and were doing their rounds of the primroses, and with the additional appearance of a number of hoverflies, they suddenly gave the garden an entomological gloss I hadn't up to that point seen. This was all hugely exciting as even the most basic student of ecology knows that most invertebrates are at the base of most biological food chains; in other words, if I was attracting six-legged creatures in healthy numbers then surely the four-legged and two-legged creatures would follow.

Christina arrived back, and she joined me in the garden. Almost instantly her presence brought out the star insect of the day, my first orange-tip butterfly of both the year and the garden too. I'm well aware that I keep going on about how I have favourite birds, plants, mammals and insects, but I think why I favour certain species more than others is because of what they represent, and in the case of a stunning male orange-tip, its arrival encapsulated, at the micro level, a lovely day (otherwise he wouldn't have been flying), and, at the macro-level, surely the most exciting time of year for wildlife.

Having spent close to the last nine months in chrysalis form, whereby, through the miracle that is metamorphosis, the caterpillar somehow manages to reconstitute its bodily ingredients into that of an adult butterfly, he then emerges into the world with just one mission, or his life will have been wasted. The male orange-tip's sole *raison d'être* is to pass on his genes by tracking down as many virgin females to mate with, before all his exertions catch up with him after a couple of weeks and he dies alone, a spent force. This explanation should hopefully go at least some way to explaining why I was jumping around for joy like a demented idiot – the orange-tips were back; the world was still turning.

Determined not to be left out of the action, the birds also belatedly began to find their voice. The chiffchaff is one of the earliest migrants back to the UK after a winter spent either in the Mediterranean or West Africa, and whose name is a perfect onomatopoeia of its repetitive and monosyllabic call. It is almost identical in looks to another closely related migrant, the willow warbler. When I was working as a warden at the RSPB's Minsmere Reserve after graduating from university, I remember eavesdropping on an elderly couple's conversation while taking a turn around one of the many footpaths. They had obviously taken up birdwatching as a retirement hobby, and while watching a bird singing away, I could clearly hear them debating long and hard as to whether the individual they were looking at was a chiffchaff or willow warbler, while the bird was actually busy trying to helping them out by handing out the biggest clue … 'Chiff-chaff, chiff-chaff'! So, like the orange-tip, the first chiffchaff of spring is always an exciting moment, but this enthusiasm soon wanes; the call quickly loses its novelty status because the bird never shuts up!

We were now approaching the peak period for migrants returning back from their wintering quarters, but 2 April was still probably a full week earlier than the average arrival date for the couple of house martins I spotted feeding in the airspace directly above the garden. This premature influx was almost certainly down to the glorious early spring we were currently enjoying; however, what was unusual was that this was the first year that I could ever recollect having registered a sighting of a house martin before a swallow. 'To hell with any more work' we thought. What's the point of having a garden if you don't take time out to enjoy it? So that's exactly what we did for the rest of the day.

Our planned 'big day' in the garden didn't get off to the finest of starts, with another argument about our different priorities. Christina thought the front garden looked a mess and wanted to spend part of the day tidying it up, but I had the bit well and truly between my teeth with the big jobs in the back garden and considered action in the front to be relatively low priority. This time, however, it was my turn to compromise, promising to help her out with some weeding and general tidying, but only after we had the veg bed up and running!

With the area now cleared of concrete and precisely measured using a combination of spade and spirit level to get the bed perfectly level, we were ready for the sleepers. Weighing the best part of 11 stone each, and with Christina only a mere slip of a girl, it wasn't

easy, but eventually both sides and then the shorter ends were eased into place. Resembling the most enormous open casket, I climbed in, testing it for size, whilst Christina took silly photos of me lying in state like Lenin in the place where our veg would soon be growing. It was at that point, lying prone with nothing to block my view of the sky, that I finally saw my first swallow. 'SWALLOW!' I shouted, pointing to the bird with long tail streamers gliding across our garden whilst trawling for insects. 'Click!' Christina had coincidentally snapped a picture of me at exactly the same time as I had spotted and pointed out the bird. Of course, unlike film cameras where the pictures have to be sent off to be developed, with digital photography the image is instantly displayed, enabling me to see immediately one of the most ridiculous photos I think I've ever been in. Looking like a cross between a prostrate Bee Gee from *Saturday Night Fever* and a horizontal member of the Hitler Youth, my 'swallow moment' had been captured for time immemorial!

The bed wouldn't be ready for any soil until we could put in some stobs to hold the sleepers in place, so we then had to re-jig our afternoon to involve a trip to Bath to buy some treated timber. Although irritating, this meant that at least we could pick up a few more plants to plug some of the larger holes in the garage border. The drive east to Bath is always enjoyable, passing the northern end of Chew Valley Lake before negotiating rolling woodland and open countryside, which shows off this part of the West Country to its best. On driving through a small piece of woodland just past the lake, I had to hastily apply the brakes to avoid hitting a male black-bird which had just shot out of the undergrowth before flashing across the road in front of me. I had barely had the chance to congratulate myself on my quick reactions in taking sufficient avoidance measures when ... 'thump'! Another male blackbird, which had been chasing the first one, had flown out, and been nailed.

Mortified, I instantly stopped the car and ran back, finding that the only blessing of the whole unfortunate incident was that the bird's death had been instantaneous. By hitting the second bird I had in all probability removed the incumbent territorial blackbird which had been too busy chasing an intruder out of his territory to concern himself with the Green Cross Code. The upshot of this meant that a prime piece of blackbird real estate, with a resident mate, had suddenly come on the market, and it didn't require a genius to work out who would be putting in a quick offer.

Having located the necessary timber in a still sombre mood, the only way Christina could cheer me up was by taking me on a huge plant crawl around the garden centre's herbaceous perennial section. April is of course a great time to go plant-buying, as at this stage of the year there is a bewildering variety to choose from. Not only will many of these plants soon be coming into flower, giving you that floral hit, but also as it was early in the growing season, they are still fairly small, so they shouldn't cost too much. This means that showing patience, from a gardening perspective, does have financial rewards. When choosing, Christina and I often liked to pick a plant each, so that we are both happy, and my selection on this occasion was a butterfly-friendly perennial wallflower in the genus *Erysimum*, whilst Christina plumped for a particularly striking and bee-friendly lavender.

Not for the first time I was struck by how fast we were becoming really knowledgeable plants-people, as both of us were now able instantly to identify at least the genus or common name of the vast majority of shrubs, annuals and perennials on offer. True, I did have a degree in botany, but it was native wild British plants that I was familiar with, and knowledge of cultivated plants was still very much a different discipline. Christina, however, was coming from an even more basic starting point than me, but such had been her speed of learning that I felt she would soon be giving a certain Mr Titchmarsh, Mr Don or Mrs Klein a horticultural run for their money!

One big change to the house during the course of the week, which would indirectly lead to an improvement in the quality and quantity of garden wildlife sightings, had been the much-needed installation of a new bathroom. While this work was being carried out, I'd had the bright idea of asking the fitter if he would arrange for the frosted bathroom window to be replaced with clear glass. Without any neighbours able to look directly into our bathroom, the normal need for discretion wouldn't be necessary, so the installation of a window we could actually look out of would enable valuable data to be garnered without the wildlife being disturbed.

Work commitments over the following few days conspired to keep me out of the garden most of the time, but during the brief periods spent at home, the bathroom window immediately began to pay dividends, with my first garden views of a male bullfinch surreptitiously coming to the caged feeder before dashing back to the safety of the wooded bank with its booty. Another bathroom visit later that day also fortuitously gave me my first sightings of holly blue butterflies, probably the only representative of all the blue butterflies that I would record in my garden, as all the other blues are primarily stay-at-home grassland specialists. The holly blue, as its name suggests, prefers shrubs to grass, and also has much more wanderlust than its cousins, which would explain why it is only the blue butterfly commonly recorded in southern British gardens.

Friday finally brought the first opportunity that week for anything more than just the occasional sneaky peek into the back garden, as a day free of work or tedious life administration enabled the opportunity to start the most ambitious project in the garden yet – digging the pond. Once again the weather was simply stunning, leaving me not only struggling to remember the last time it had actually rained, but equally remarkably reaching for the sunblock – a burnt pate so early in the season would not have been good form!

I removed the turf first with the spade, and I quickly began to make serious inroads into the dark topsoil just below the surface, which was then placed into the wheelbarrow before being wheeled the two-yard distance over to the raised bed, sieved through a garden riddle into the bed and finally mixed up with a peat-substitute compost.

Of course, with ponds it's not all about size, as the profile is, if anything, even more important. As a simple equation: the wider the variety of different depths, the higher the diversity of wildlife. Some plants, for example, need to sit with their feet in the shallows, while pond lilies will not flower unless they are in much deeper water where the temperature fluctuates less. The shallower and warmer areas also tend to best suit the amphibians, as opposed to large numbers of insect larvae preferring to plough a furrow through the mud right at the bottom. With this in mind, I had planned the deepest section to be about three feet deep with the rest of the pond effectively consisting of a couple of increasingly large concentric rings radiating out from the deepest point, each at a different level and incorporating a shelf so that baskets with aquatic plants could be placed without fear of them sliding into the murky depths. The end closest to the communal fence with Andy and Lorraine would also feature a large shallow area, giving any amphibians an easy entry and exit point. This area would also, I hoped, be the place where I would ultimately find frogspawn the following year.

As I dug deeper, the topsoil soon began to give way to subsoil, which was lighter in colour due to being of a lower organic content, but rather than putting this into the raised bed, it was placed to one side for later use. I have already admitted to not being the most practical of people, but a technique I've learnt along the way to compensate for this weakness is to read extensively around the subject before launching into a new project, and in this case the related topics that fell under my gaze were 'pond construction' and 'pond ecology'. This should mean that the decisions I made would at least be based on sound ecological principles. One of the wildlife gardening books I'd read had suggested that after the pond liner had been put in, the excavated subsoil could then be re-used as both a planting medium and habitat, instead of wasting money on expensive pond compost. This is because the subsoil's low nutrient levels help ensure against the build-up of too much algae, and this in turn would prevent the water from firstly turning the colour of pea soup and then becoming short on oxygen. This was the theory – I would soon find out whether it would actually work.

With the attitude that 'Rome wasn't built in a day', I was keen to take my time digging out the pond, mostly because going at it like a nineteenth-century railway navvy would only have resulted in me putting my back out, so by lunch I'd downed tools, taking the executive decision that I'd put my body through enough exertions for one day. As I stood back and looked on, from a stranger's perspective it looked like the sum total of my efforts had been to have half-dug one hole whilst half-filling another one in, but I knew I'd done much more than that; this had been wildlife gardening multi-tasking at its best.

I took a rare weekend away from Chew Stoke and the garden to spend a couple of days with Christina up in Manchester, and it felt good for both of us to draw breath and take a complete physical and mental break from a project that had quickly taken over our lives. Having secured a couple of tickets to the Theatre of Dreams to watch Manchester United play, there would be no talk of best composting techniques, no discussion of the various merits of different bird food and certainly no debates on coppicing strategy. We were good to our word – apart from that one weak moment … well, the garden centre we briefly stopped at for a cup of tea on the way home *did* have a lovely range of plants!

The following Monday brought a day of contrasts for both Christina and me. While Christina was up and out early to earn an honest day's crust, I was due to spend the whole day in the garden. Such were the joys of being a freelancer – I wouldn't be earning any money today, but at least I could enjoy it, free of guilt! Getting my early-morning fix of the garden from my usual landing-hall window watch-point, I was able to see the squirrels taking advantage of that small window of opportunity between dawn breaking and when my presence would result in their exclusion for the rest of the day. While the two bespoke anti-squirrel feeders were proving excellent acquisitions, and had so far deterred all attempts to ransack their contents, the caged ground feeder's defences were being regularly breached by at least one particularly lithe squirrel. A wooden peanut holder, in the form of a small house with a slate roof, that I had hung from the quince just behind where the pond would soon be, was taking a pasting too.

It was not until closer inspection that I realised the brutal levels of vandalism to which the peanut feeder had been subjected. By gnawing away the wood of the housing in an attempt to circumvent the mesh holding in the peanuts, the little vandals had rendered the feeder virtually useless. I was appalled at the damage, but also in quiet admiration of their astonishing tenacity. One thing was sure: the squirrels' guerrilla tactics were working!

With the hired skip now in place on the drive to enable the disposal of excess spoil, I was finally in a position to break the back of excavating the pond – hopefully before my own back gave out. Upon filling the first wheelbarrow load of the day, the first problem arose when I realised I wouldn't be able to tip the spoil straight into the skip, as its lip was too high. I needed some ingenuity. I scoured the contents of the garage, and I had the idea of using a couple of the old pergola stanchions as the sides of a ramp, then nailing to these a spare piece of the marine plywood left over from the compost bin lid. By additionally nailing a small wooden batten across the underside of the stanchions at the elevated skip end, to form a letter 'T', this would then catch onto the lip of the skip to ensure the ramp wouldn't slip and fall flat while I and the full wheel-barrow were wheeling up it.

I tested this with an empty wheelbarrow and it seemed to work perfectly, and more by accident than design the stanchions poking out beyond the plywood at the skip end of the ramp also proved the perfect mechanism for emptying the contents without the fear of dropping the barrow into the skip, as the wheel struts would catch on the stanchions enabling the barrow to be easily and safely pivoted through 90 degrees. Put simply, it was quite possibly the best thing I had ever built, so brilliant that had I not got a pond to dig I would have been straight down to the Patents Office with my design – 'The Dilge Ramp'. It would have been the ramp of choice for years to come.

As I dug deeper with the removal of each wheelbarrow load of spoil, at last it began to resemble less of a hole and more of a pond, and I was just beginning to think that pond digging was a piece of cake when I suddenly felt that jarring clang from the spade, which seemed to indicate I had hit something very solid indeed. I brushed the soil away from the obstruction, and it was obvious that work had suddenly become a whole lot tougher as I uncovered what seemed to be a huge concrete lintel, lurking like an iceberg about a foot below the surface. Two options were available: either the concrete would have to come out, or another location for the pond would have to be found, and, realising it would have to be the former, the spade was laid to one side as the job now necessitated a recall for the goggles, sledgehammer and pick-axe.

Slowly but surely, I started to drag hard-won lumps of concrete out of the hole, each piece removed taking a one-way ticket to the skip. However, unlike the path, which had been comparatively easy to break up, working in the confines of a hole with limited space made swinging the tools much more demanding. After a cold start, the weather was once again turning the day into one bathed in glorious sunshine, and, not realising how engrossed I'd become in the work, it wasn't until a mid-morning break for liquid refreshment and the re-application of sunblock, that I gave myself a moment to stop and appreciate the garden.

As I took a few minutes out to watch and listen, rather than dig and swing, in addition to the usual cast of characters singing away, I suddenly caught just a snatch of another bird which up to that point I hadn't recorded in the garden. A male blackcap, freshly arrived back during the night from Spain, Portugal or even West Africa, was pressing his claim for a territory from the ivy and bramble-infused scrub at the very bottom of the garden around the base of the oak tree. The RSPB *Handbook of British Birds* describes the blackcap as living in 'deciduous or mixed woodlands, copses, thickets and other bushy places, including mature gardens and parks', and it was indeed a thrill that a blackcap, having flown such a long way, had decided that our lil' ole' garden was of sufficient merit to look no further.

For me, the song of the blackcap is the quintessential sound of that point in the year when we're never quite sure if it is still spring or whether summer has started, so with summer still officially some way off, this bird was probably very much at the vanguard of blackcap arrivals. The song always sounds like an interesting jumble of sweet and sour, as it contains pure, melodic notes interspersed with harsh, churring tones, but always ending in a bit of a flourish.

The blackcap was not the only species to have made a sudden appearance in the garden; a cursory glance in the meadow revealed that little clusters of powder-blue field forget-me-nots had just burst into flower and were joined along the bottom of the beech hedge by an instantly recognisable plant – one with probably more local names than any species in the British floral kingdom. Variously called lords-and-ladies, cuckoo-pint, parson in the pulpit and willy lily, while arguing over the name, everyone seems to be of accord that this common plant of woods and hedgerows has an incredibly bizarre look. With its shiny arrow-shaped leaves and pale green sheath, which hoods the yellowy-purple spadex, perhaps the most evocative name, and the one I use, is cuckoo-pint. This name emanates from both the fact that it generally flowers around the same time as the arrival back of the first cuckoos, and that 'pint' (to rhyme with mint) is thought to be an abbreviation of 'pintle', which rather hilariously seems to be slang for penis. So rich in colloquial names, this is also a plant that totally changes its appearance during the year; looking weird and wonderful in spring, it then produces an autumnal splash of colour later in the year with an amazing spike of orange-red berries.

My enjoyment of both blackcap and the 'penis plant' was cut short by a couple trying to catch my attention from the garden gate. I immediately recognised the lady as Jane, the daughter of the previous owner Mr Gregory, and soon discovered that the gentleman was her husband, Peter. They had dropped by to pay a visit to Marjory and Dennis, but they were also desperately angling for a nose around the garden to see what Christina and I had been up to since we had moved in. I was keen to prove to them that Jane's childhood home was now in good hands, but I also had a couple of questions of my own in mind, so I took them up on their none-too-subtle hint and invited them in for an impromptu tour of the garden. Almost immediately Jane noticed that the middle rowan had been taken down and, strangely feeling like I was under pressure to justify its removal, I garbled a response that it had not been enjoying the best of health and was also deemed a little too close to the others. The tour then quickly developed into a game of spot the changes, as the removal of the fence and the pergola both necessitated comment. But by now up to speed as to how the game worked, I was prepared with answers to which Jane seemed more than satisfied.

When they encountered the huge hole in the lawn, I explained that I had been in the middle of excavating a pond when I had hit a problem, and was keen to find out if they knew why huge shelves of concrete were buried in the garden. 'Well, you've just hit the foundations of dad's old greenhouse' was Jane's response, in a manner which suggested the answer should have been evident. Choosing not to retort with the obvious retaliatory question as to why they hadn't bothered to dig out the concrete when the greenhouse had been removed, rather than bury it under a bit of soil and turf, I decided to change tack and enquire after her father.

Apparently, he was as well as could be expected given his advanced years, but one bizarre side-effect of the dementia was that, having seen his Military Service out in Germany after the Second World War, during which time he had apparently learnt a good deal of German, some 60 years later it seemed this was the only language in which the great man felt the need to communicate. It made me want to meet him even more, but only after I'd removed his greenhouse foundations and polished up on my incredibly rusty German!

Jane and Peter weren't the only visitors to drop by that day, as Christina's father had planned to turn up and help finish sanding the floorboards of the third bedroom, which was in the process of being converted to Christina's painting studio. I was aware that Graham had an impressive arsenal of tools which were potentially at our disposal, and I had asked him to bring his angle-grinder so that we could dig out and then cut down the last of the washing-line poles into a number of skip-sized pieces. After a charming lunch out in the sun, Graham started on the sanding while I began the onerous task of digging out the concrete base. Just as Andy had discovered when planting one of the apple trees, it must have taken the best part of an hour to dig a hole large enough to finally be able to lever the pole's foundations out of the ground. Graham then ground the pole down to size, but it still took two full-grown men the best part of another 20 minutes to drag it down the path and up the 'Dilge Ramp' before seeing it drop with a satisfying 'clang' into the skip. Another legacy of the old garden had been removed, but I was now a spent force, so the remaining concrete still in the pond hole would have to wait for another day.

Seeing how hard I had been working on the pond, and being equally impressed with the 'Dilge Ramp', Christina was keen to make up for having spent so little time in the garden (due to work commitments) with a big push over the weekend. So while I was off feeding my football habit, she made a start turning the lawn surrounding the pond into a border similar in size and ambition to the one we had just dug and planted up along the side of the garage. Arriving back after a disappointing 1–0 defeat, I was even more disappointed to find that Christina, having grown tired of the bed construction, had decided to take a bowsaw down to the wood and had sawn down a couple of small trees! While I had to admit that the wood looked better without the 6-foot stump and twisted holly she had cut down, I also felt compelled to point out that it was only fair that each should be consulted before any major operations were carried out. The main issue I had with work being carried out in the wood at this time of year was that it might disturb any potential birds prospecting for nesting locations in any of our boxes – I wanted nests!

One positive impact of Christina's unilateral actions had been to uncover the most sublime patch of lily-of-the-valley at the edge of the woodland, which, like the snake's head fritillaries, would have been purposefully planted in the garden, rather than growing naturally wild on the bank, but which still smelt wonderful. The same could not be said of the ramsons, which had suddenly begun to emerge in a huge green and white carpet across the floor of our bank, belatedly matching the show put on by the same plant on the south-facing warmer bank on the opposite side of the brook. Otherwise known as wild garlic, for good reason, when the plant does emerge in profusion the smell is so overpowering that it can make your eyes water and catch in your throat. But, the pong aside, it was a display to make any botanist jump with delight, as ramsons is also one of those plants that is considered an ancient woodland indicator. The plant's very presence hinted at a little bit of the history of the bank, and in this case revealed that it may well have been covered by woodland for hundreds of years. This meant we owned the tiniest strip of ancient woodland – now that was something to write home about!

With a filming trip planned to East Anglia for later the following day, it was vital that after breakfast we hit the ground – or should I say concrete – running. With Christina helping, we finally managed to remove the last of the concrete that impeded further progress in the hole, allowing Christina to continue her good work digging out the soon-to-be pond's herbaceous border, whilst I was left with tidying up detail, i.e. shredding all the vegetation she had sneakily cut down the day before. I found it easiest to carry out the shredding on the drive, where it was close to the power supply and easier to sweep up any mess, and I was happily feeding in branches when Christina ran across from the garden to grab my attention above the constant whining and crunching sound of vegetation meeting its maker. 'HAVEN!' she shouted, to which above the noise I responded 'haven?' To which she loudly responded 'NO! RA-VEN!'

A new bird for the garden was becoming a rarity, and thus worthy of immediate action in the form of a sprint around to the front garden, where I arrived just in time to catch the diagnostic wedge-shaped tail and stonking bill so distinctive of this King of the Crows before it sailed out of sight in the direction of the Mendips. To make the moment even more precious, Christina had actually identified it by call. All my constantly boring her with the subtle differences in call between different species over the years had at last begun to pay dividends – a call for celebration, in the form of a visit to the garden centre, would be in order. Time to reward our hard work and undoubted birding skills by selecting the vegetables for our raised bed – we knew how to party!

Good Friday is an important date in the Christian calendar, but for us it meant the first of three whole days in the garden. With high pressure forecast all weekend, the finest spring in living memory would hopefully 'spring' a few surprises on the wildlife front too. Even in the space of just a few days, the warmer temperatures and lengthening daylight had caused the garden to change immeasurably. Even from a cursory glance at the trees, the rowan could be seen to be in both leaf and flower, the birch too was in leaf, and with their buds bursting left, right and centre, the oak and beech were not far behind. In fact, the only one of our mature trees yet to have joined the party was the ash on the bank, although this was not unusual as it is invariably the last of our native trees to come into leaf anyway.

The meadow had also changed substantially since the first days of spring. The lesser celandines, fritillaries, daffodils and primroses were now all but over, but with the next wave of plants in the form of meadow buttercups and ox-eye daisies still not quite at their best, the meadow had a 'twixt cup and lip' feel.

Having gone to great lengths in the construction of the compost bins, herbaceous borders and the pond, in many ways the meadow had been the easiest habitat creation of all. By merely demarking the area where we had wanted the meadow to be, in other words the whole area between the apple trees and the wooded bank, the basic technique to establish the habitat had been to do nothing – no lawnmower, no fertiliser, no weeding – just nothing. When attempting to create verdant lawns or voluptuous herbaceous borders, for example, some of the most important jobs are fertilising and mulching, as cultivated lawns, and fastidious flowers and shrubs, are always constantly hungry for supplements, but with meadow plants it is exactly the opposite. The second worst thing you can do to a beautiful flower meadow (the worst is to build a housing estate on top of it) is to stick fertiliser all over it, as the meadow flowers that you are so keen to see flourish will be beaten up by the ugly, gas-guzzling invasive species like rye grass and nettles which thrive in environments where nutrients are abundant. So the whole idea in the meadow was to drive nutrient levels down, but before I could attempt to do just that later in the year, the most important first job was to record what plants were where, and this in turn would give me clues – like the ramsons did – as to how big a job I had on my hands.

Meanwhile, back over at the pond Christina had noted a problem. A small hole which had developed in the wall of the newly dug pond had suddenly been converted into what appeared to be a bees' nest, with individuals pouring in and out. Now, having worked all across the tropics of South America, East Africa and Southeast Asia, there is very little wildlife that I'm afraid of – apart from bees. This is because every sting I've received over the last 20 years has caused an allergic reaction resulting in the most hideous swelling, and so swarms will always be something I give the widest possible berth. Not only were these bees, but they were also bees in the wrong place, and as the next step in the pond construction would be to line the hole prior to the addition of water, this meant that, as with the jackdaws, the only course of action would unfortunately have to be a drastic one – a prospect I did not relish.

As I looked more closely through my binoculars from a distance of a few yards, rather than risk getting stung, it was obvious, much to my relief, that these were not honey bees after all, but in fact just one representative of the 250 species of solitary bees that can be found in the UK, as our hole had become an impromptu home to some harmless red mason bees. Even though they were swarming around the hole and giving the impression of being in a colony, it was obviously just a communal entrance, off which each female would be busily excavating her own individual brood chamber, before laying a batch of eggs, with each bee larva being provisioned in turn with its own mini-larder of pollen and nectar. The 'mason' element of this insect's name comes from the fact that in addition to collecting mud to use as a building material to form nest structures, they will also often resort to using pre-existing holes in soft mortar to raise their brood, which explains why people often report seeing bees seemingly emerging from solid brick walls during the spring and summer. They are also important pollinators of commercial crops like fruit trees, and some orchard owners will even buy pre-populated tubes of red mason bees to make sure there are sufficient numbers to carry out this crucial service.

Knowing the background to this fascinating insect made me feel even worse about the fact that I would be evicting them barely three yards away from the apple trees that had so carefully been planted and which were currently in blossom. So it was with great regret that I carefully collapsed the part of the wall they had been actively excavating, trying not to squash any bees in the process. By nipping it in the bud, I hoped my actions would still give them enough of a chance to nest elsewhere during the season, but it didn't stop me feeling like a ruthless landlord.

Elsewhere in the garden, the rising temperature was attracting yet more new butterflies to the garden, as in quick succession I managed to spot my first speckled wood, large white and green-veined white butterflies of the year, making a grand total of nine species recorded in the garden so far. The dunnock we had spotted making a nest in the cypress right at the beginning of the month must have recently hatched her eggs, as we watched a whole series of different partners flying in to feed the ever-hungry chicks – she was obviously one of those birds with slightly looser morals! In addition to the dunnock, Andy and Lorraine's garden was clearly ahead on 'nesting' house points, as we could clearly see a pair of wood pigeons making the beginnings of a nest in their huge *leylandii* hedge. Having already admitted to detesting these ornamental cypresses, which are invariably only planted because they will grow to a huge size in any type of soil and without any effort, often taking over gardens in the process, I had also reluctantly to admit that they were good for nesting birds. So while love was patently in the air, it most definitely didn't seem to be in any of our nest boxes, which were disappointingly all still void of residents. It had to be said that all was not yet lost, as there was still time for occupancy, but the *lastminute.com* fraternity would have to get their act together quickly otherwise they would miss the boat and we would draw a blank … Which got me wondering whether garden centres did 'sale or return' on nest boxes?

With the herbaceous border along the fence shared with Andy and Lorraine now ready for planting up, Christina set to making a dent in the collection of plants that we had been accumulating on the patio, which had begun to resemble a miniature garden centre in its own right. We were keen to establish some kind of living border to hide the ugly old fence, so we had purchased a couple of yew and a pyracantha, which in the future would hopefully take on the dual purpose of providing both a dense structure for nesting and winter food. With Christina happily planting away, this freed me up to do what I generally do best in the garden – and certainly most of – tidying up. The skip was due to be collected the following day, so it made sense to use it to give the garden a 'spring-clean', and I spent the rest of the afternoon clearing up any spare turfs, woodcuts and excess soil, in addition to enjoying my last few trips up the 'Dilge Ramp' before it would be consigned to the garage for eternity – patent pending, of course.

For the trip to the DIY store the following morning we had a big shopping list. Going for one of the flat-bed trolleys that stated we 'meant business', we swept up and down the aisles collecting:

Six bags of stone-free sand to line the pond
A lawnmower, as it was embarrassing that we were still
    borrowing Marjory and Dennis's
Six bags of vegetable compost to finish off the raised bed
A few obligatory extra plants in the form of hollyhocks and
    cornflowers which had caught Christina's eye.

When we reached the till, it was obvious not only that we had spent a lot of money, but also that we were potentially about to cause irreparable damage to the suspension of my car. Creating ponds and setting up vegetable plots was proving an expensive and heavy business. After dispensing with an eye-watering amount of cash that I would quite happily have lived off for an entire term as a student, we eventually managed to get all our purchases back home without any major incidents.

We immediately mixed the newly acquired vegetable compost with the excavated topsoil, hoping that we had now created the perfect growing medium, and the fun of planting out all of the seedlings we had bought earlier in the month into neat little rows could begin. As the red onions, carrots, parsnips, shallots, leeks, Savoy cabbages, beetroot, courgettes and runner beans were all planted out, it soon became obvious that we had bought far too much for the growing space on offer. This resulted in the seedlings being planted far closer together than had been recommended on the labels, but we declared this to be of little concern as our adapted plan would be to thin out the weedier specimens later in the season, so giving the rest the room to flourish – it would be a Darwinian 'Survival of the Fittest' in our veg patch. Cleverly using some hazel poles extracted from the wooded bank, rather than having to use pricy bamboo canes, Christina was then able to fashion an A-frame for the runner beans to climb up at one end, which meant the only work remaining, apart from a spot of watering and weeding, would be to reap the dividends later in the summer.

Leaving Christina to tidy up, I went in to grab a shower as I was due a night out with the lads! My birding buddies, Ed the ringer,

Ant and Simon were all coming round, hoping for a quick tour of the garden before we went out for a meal, beers and no doubt a whole evening of hardcore bird chat. As opposed to my old flat where I positively discouraged people from spending too much time in the garden, there was something special about seeing people's reaction on walking around the side of our bog-standard house and being confronted with what was turning into a gem of a garden. As I took the fellows on my standard five-minute tour, taking in the hole in the ground, the meadow, the herbaceous borders, the newly planted raised bed and finally the bank and brook, they made suitably impressive noises as to how much we'd already achieved and of course what other birds I'd expect to record in the garden.

'Have you recorded swifts yet?' asked Ant, and on hearing my reply of 'not yet', said 'well you have now!' It must be said that I've been birding quite a few times with these boys and Ant seems to have the most incredible bionic eye that would eclipse even Steve Austin from *The Six Million Dollar Man*. Of course, sure enough, following the direction of Ant's gesture some 200 or more feet above the garden we could just make out a single mini-anchor scything through the air. The immediately diagnostic silhouette indeed revealed it to be a swift, the undoubted aerial master of the universe, and a species which, upon fledging, will *not* touch the ground for at least two years. Of course, whenever birders meet up there is always healthy competition amongst each other to be either the first to spot a bird or recognise a song, and it can often become a bit of a game, so I couldn't begrudge Ant his audacity in picking out a new bird on my own manor.

Swifts are usually one of the last migrants to arrive back in the UK after a winter spent eating tropical African insects, so 23 April was indeed an early date for the first swift of the year and Ant's observation made a fine end to the day, an excellent addition to the garden's burgeoning bird list and a good start to an evening about to be filled with four blokes talking about how much they loved birds – of the feathered variety, of course …

Having a hangover is never conducive to doing something as technically demanding as putting together a lawnmower, and it didn't help that, after struggling away for two hours or so, peppered with a large number of profanities, I realised much to my irritation that I'd put the handle on the wrong way round. On the bright side, however, at least Christina had found my alcohol-induced ineptitude funny … but suffice to say, she had been the only one.

Deciding that some fresh air would do me good, the rest of the morning was spent spreading sand in an even layer all around the inside of the pond-hole. With the addition of some old carpet donated from the floor of Christina's new studio, the idea behind the introduction of these layers was to ensure that when the water-retaining butyl pond-liner was inserted into the hole nothing would puncture this lining from below, causing the water to drain away just like when a bath-plug is pulled out. With the carpet inserted and cut round the edges to provide a snug fit, it wasn't just a hole any more, it was now a carpeted hole ready for the liner! As if to give my work the ring of endorsement, a comma butterfly – the tenth species of butterfly we had so far recorded in the garden – promptly flew into the hole for a spot of sunbathing and in the process added a touch of glamour to a piece of carpet that had long since seen better days. With the lawnmower now properly constructed, I took my leave of the pond and cranked it up for its first test-run whilst Christina pricked out the seedlings of red hot pokers and verbenas that she had carefully been tending from seeds.

With the garden tidied, the beds at least partly planted, the raised bed up and running and the lawn mown, the back garden was starting to look like something we could be proud of. Our efforts were being rewarded and hopefully the message was spreading around the wildlife community that this garden was definitely the place to be seen.

29 April 2011 will be the date forever associated in the nation's psyche as the day on which Prince William married Kate Middleton. But for me I'm afraid the date won't be bringing back memories of that kiss on the balcony, Princess Beatrice's ridiculous hat, or the couple driving off in the Prince of Wales' Aston Martin, but of an exceptional occurrence in our garden instead.

Being a little bit of a Republican (even though I admire Prince Charles's environmental stance), I wasn't too keen to waste my precious time off watching the wedding on television, so I decided the day would be better spent playing golf with a couple of pals, followed by a tea party of our own at home with Christina and her parents. I returned victorious from the golf, having completed the round in 94 (which, for the record, was 22 over par – and a good score for a decidedly average player), and arrived back mid-afternoon just as Christina and her mum were setting out tea and home-made cakes outside. Despite the weather having been a bit hit-and-miss for street parties elsewhere in the UK, in the south-west it was once again unseasonably balmy, so before pouring the tea we decided to move the table and chairs to the centre of the lawn to enjoy the sun on our faces and the best the garden had to offer.

There is something about taking tea outside in lovely weather that somehow elevates the level of conversation to a more interesting, eloquent and certainly more aspirational level than can be often attained elsewhere, and such was the case that afternoon, as the topics meandered from royal weddings to roses and from Westminster Abbey to wisteria. All of a sudden our chat was interrupted by the tinny whistle of a kingfisher down at the brook, but this time it was much more than just a 'look out, I'm coming' call, and as we turned to the brook, two little bullets emerged from the natural hole in the undergrowth created by our steps down to the water and raced towards the centre of the lawn! As they tore past

only marginally slower than the speed of light, we watched in open-mouthed disbelief as both kingfishers flew right over the table, and no more than a few feet over our heads, as they looped over the garden, round the garage, and down Marjory and Dennis's garden before joining the brook again. I had hardly got the syllable 'king …!' out of my mouth before they did the entire party trick again!

Travelling at such a speed they'd had to bank severely in order to make the turn around the garage, so on both occasions I'd only seen their orange bellies, while Christina's mum Laura, sitting on the other side of the table, had only seen their electric blue backs! It looked like two birds were having the most incredible territorial ding-dong and we had been treated to a ring-side seat. It was only then that Laura admitted that this was the first time she'd ever seen a kingfisher, and all I could muster, by way of a reply, was … 'Hell of a first view!'

MAY

MORE WILDLIFE THAN YOU CAN SHAKE A STICK AT

For me, the month of May equates to hawthorn blossom, deafening dawn choruses, emerging mayflies, fox cubs appearing above ground and more spectacles than you can shake a stick at. If cloning were a subject not just confined to the realm of sci-fi books, but a matter of reality, sometimes I think I'd like to create a carbon copy of myself for just this very month, to enable me to catch up with all the wild-life events in this most wonderful, yet ephemeral, time of year without fear of missing anything. So rather than seizing the opportunity to rush out into the garden to see what natural history delights were waiting for me to discover at the beginning of this fabulous month, what did I do? Well, I went off to buy bark chippings and rubber – that's what!

Starting the month off with a visit to the DIY store, where I swear they now rub their hands in glee on seeing us walk through the entrance, we began the morning's purchases off with half a dozen bags of bark chippings to help suppress weed growth in the flower borders we had just planted up. With Christina simply unable to help herself, as we passed the plant section we quickly added a rock-rose, two different salvias and a scabious to the trolley before I could finally drag her away from the plants to the tills. I joked to the cashier that I was now living with a 'plantaholic', but I wasn't laughing as she responded to my flippant remark with a straight-faced 'that'll be £74.35 please.' With the next planned purchase being a pond liner, it was going to be an expensive day.

Of all the different types of pond liners available on the market, from my extensive prior research on the subject the only one that doesn't need a remortgaging of the house, yet is able to stand up to the reasonable rigours of time, is that composed of butyl rubber. Having at last made the decision that this would indeed be our liner of choice, the next thing for me to fret about had been the size of liner we'd need. As ponds are of course three-dimensional shapes, simply measuring the length and width of the hole would be insufficient, as the depth would also have to be taken into account too. Obviously any miscalculation could result in the purchase of a liner too small, which would be nothing short of disastrous – it's not as though you can just glue a bit on the end with this material if you find yourself caught short. But at the other end of the scale, if I ordered a liner far too large, this would mean having to cut swathes off when fitting it, which would of course be a waste of both time and money.

A specialist pond book I had ordered over the internet had attempted to tackle the tricky question of calculating pond size with a natty formula:

Length of liner = 2 x depth + 1.2 x length
Width of liner = 2 x depth + 1.2 x width

Apparently this calculation would give you the size needed with an extra 10 per cent, which could be used to anchor the liner down. Now bearing in mind that maths was never my strong point, I decided that erring on the side of caution with the dimensions I put into the equation would be the wisest move, and so after rounding up both the length, width and the final result, just to slightly increase that safety margin, it seemed that a 20 x 16-foot sheet of liner would suffice.

Being a specialist product, the purchase of the liner necessitated a visit to a proper aquatic centre dedicated to all things watery.

Once again the retail assistant assigned to help smooth our purchasing experience did anything but, by firstly asking about what gauge of butyl liner we required. Unaware that there were even different thicknesses of liner, as this hadn't been mentioned anywhere in my research, we both stood there looking like the pond-liner novices we were, as he went through the pros and cons of the 0.75mm butyl as opposed to the 1mm. 'B…b…but what does everyone else use for garden ponds?' I stuttered, and, on hearing the response 'well, the 0.75mm is the one recommended for what you need', felt my temper flare as I wanted to reply with 'well why bloody bother with all that unnecessary bullshit then?' However, I checked myself at the last second, and what came out of my mouth instead was 'in that case we'll have the 0.75mm please'.

Having already got my back up, the assistant then went on to demand confirmation from us at least twice that we had the right dimensions, before proceeding to take the scissors to a huge roll of the stuff, and stating with relish that once it was cut there would be no turning back. Knocking off a 10 per cent discount because Christina smiled sweetly at the much more pleasant cashier, I was still flabbergasted at the £192.80 price tag. By way of an apology at relieving us of such a large amount of money for what was nothing more than a big sheet of rubber, the cashier did remind us that the liner had a guarantee of 10 years, before waiting just a beat to add the caveat 'if it's fitted properly, that is'.

The liner was composed of material similar to that of the inner tube for a bicycle, and I had been all too aware that if we did accidentally puncture the liner, either during the fitting or when adding the soil substrate or planting baskets, then it wouldn't be quite as straightforward as just getting out the puncture repair kit. In other words, buying another liner might in the long term have been the easier option. Still, if we got the statutory 10 years out of the liner, then I wouldn't for a second begrudge paying a mere £19.28 a year for the joy of watching frogs, dragonflies and pond skaters take up residence in the garden – cheap at twice the price!

We realised that we would need a full day to fit the liner properly, and that other garden chores could wait, so we decided to accept my friend Mark's offer of an extended tour around his garden in Bristol. Having moved into their house only a year before we had made the plunge, Mark and his partner had since set about single-mindedly creating one of the most astonishing floral gardens I've seen in a long time.

Like us, Mark had bought a somewhat ramshackle house that needed a lot of work, and also like us, he had decided to start the overhaul outside rather than inside, putting every ounce of his energy and creativity into turning round the garden. What he had achieved in a relatively short space of time was simply astonishing. Their vast, sweeping herbaceous borders with drifts of plants so beautifully colour-coordinated and layered were something that Christina and I could only look at in open-mouthed admiration. Despite Mark freely admitting that all his plants were primarily chosen for their aesthetic appeal, in contrast to our garden where decisions were mostly based on their benefit to wildlife, the abundant numbers of birds, bees and butterflies patently attracted to his garden were testament to the fact that they were equally at home here as well. Mark's garden was just one example amongst many that blew away the misconception that gardens have to be messy and full of teasels, brambles and nettles to be wildlife-friendly – and wildlife obviously doesn't mind prissy manicured cultivars either!

Once again Mark had kindly sorted out some more plants for us to take away that either he hadn't found room for or didn't fit in with his colour schemes, in the form of some white foxgloves, pink phloxes and raspberry canes. Feeling guilty at this generosity, we agreed that these plants could only be taken on the condition that they would be part of another 'plant swap' with Christina's verbena and kniphofia seedlings when they were large enough to be planted out.

Our aim the following day was simple: by the end of play we would be settling for nothing less than a pond filled with water – talk about ambitious! Having devoured all the pond-related literature, the one technical aspect that most of the books seemed to have slightly fudged was how to dispose efficiently and effectively of the liner edge in a way that wouldn't leave the liner either exposed to the elements or improperly anchored. The best possible options seemed to involve either burying it under soil or weighing it down with large stones, but we'd cross that bridge when we got there, for now our primary concern would be to get the liner in position – without puncturing it.

We cleaned the carpet in the hole with a hand-held vacuum cleaner to ensure nothing would cause a puncture and invalidate our guarantee, then we slowly unfurled the liner, and with Christina minus shoes climbing in to ensure that it was properly fitting the contours of the hole, it was gently lowered and shaped into place. The liner was, of course, huge, and could have easily lined a pond half as big again, an oversight that was undoubtedly due to both a combination of my generous measuring of the pond's dimensions and paranoid rounding up of figures, rather than any inaccuracy in the formula. But being way too big was definitely the lesser of the two evils. Carefully cutting off most of the excess, with probably more than enough rubber left over to kit out a fetish party, we then weighed the margin down all the way round with bricks before inserting the hose.

With the generally considered belief that it's fine to fill a pond with tap water, providing it can be left to stand for a week to allow the chlorine to evaporate and minerals to disperse, we slowly began to add water, the pressure of which forced the liner to mould to the shape of the hole. With the pond around half-full we belatedly realised that as the hole had in fact been dug out on a very slight incline, while the lower end towards the centre of the garden looked almost full to the brim, the other more elevated end of the pond unfortunately still had a large slice of liner visible above the water line. In an attempt, at least in part, to correct this, we used a combination of techniques for disposing of the liner edge. By burying it at the higher end below the turf, but anchoring the liner edge at the lower end with bricks on the surface, this height differential was reduced somewhat. This was more of a bodge than a permanent solution to the problem, but for the time being at least it would do the trick.

Despite all the problems encountered when digging the hole and the obvious stress of fitting the liner, watching the hole being transformed simply by the addition of water somehow seemed to have made it all worthwhile, and as we stood back watching our handiwork being topped up, one of those coincidences happened which retrospectively you couldn't even make up. Suddenly flitting around the pond, seemingly inspecting the work, we spotted a damselfly – our first of the year and for our garden too. 'Large red!' I shouted, almost involuntarily, immediately deducing from the time of year and the type of habitat which species it was.

Although marginally bigger than its other closely related species, the unimaginatively named small red damselfly, the large red damsel, confusingly, isn't particularly large either. It is, however, most definitely red, well, at least the males are, and we were definitely looking at a male as the darker females tend to emerge later and keep a much lower profile. The large red is also almost always the earliest of all our 13 resident damselflies on the wing, and, with a wide distribution around the UK, is one of the most commonly seen species in gardens with a pond. For naturalists to confirm any identification, it is always good to eliminate any potentially confusable species, which in this case was its aforementioned diminutive cousin. The small red damselfly, however, is much rarer, as it is mostly confined to acid bogs in southern England and west Wales and also is never on the wing before June. Large red it was, then!

Most species of damsels and dragons will always be on the lookout for opportunities to colonise new sites, but it would have been stretching credibility somewhat to believe that this damselfly had tracked down our pond only minutes after it had been filled. A far more likely scenario was that this damselfly had emerged from Andy and Lorraine's pond and was probably in the process of establishing his territory for the oncoming breeding season when it coincidentally stumbled across our pond. What could not be disputed was the symbolism of its timing, and if this was a taste of things to come around the pond during the summer, then I would be a very happy wildlife gardener.

And then it began to rain. Now this would not ordinarily have been something worthy of comment were it not for the fact that in this extraordinary spring it simply hadn't rained for weeks. In fact, one regular chore over the last couple of weeks, and more associated with high summer, had been to keep the garden well watered, particularly as so many tender young perennials had only recently been planted in the herbaceous borders. Normally I detest wet weather as it puts a 'dampener' on everything, but on this occasion, with the feeling that it was 'good for the garden', we both retired inside for a cuppa to watch the garden get its first proper soaking that spring. The rain would not only save us the bother of having to water all the plants but would finish the extra job of topping up the pond too!

With the shower short and sharp we were soon back outside again. There is something lovely about being outside immediately after a downpour. The air smells fresh, the plants have a shiny, vibrant look, and the wildlife, having hunkered down out of the rain, suddenly emerges as one to make up for lost time. Taking a turn around the garden, it also gave us the first proper opportunity during the month to observe some of the newest developments at this time of profound, yet constant, change. Centre stage in the horticultural glamour stakes were the hawthorns in the wood and the standard hawthorn next to the garage. Otherwise known as the May tree, in honour of the month when its blossom first opens, the hawthorn really is a world-class wildlife plant. For starters it is cheap to buy and incredibly easy to grow, irrespective of whether your preference is for it to be in the form of a sculpted hedge or a small garden tree. In addition to the astonishingly beautiful blossom, which makes the plant look like it's been suddenly caught out in an unseasonal snow shower, its leaves and thorns double up to make it both the best cover for birds and insects and a fabulous wind-break. The vibrant green foliage, which unfurls marginally before the blossom (unlike blackthorn, with which it can occasionally be confused, but whose flowers appear before the leaves), also turns a vivid red in the autumn, by which time the red berries, or haws, will have swelled sufficiently to sustain our blackbirds, redwing and fieldfares throughout the winter months.

As a result of our changing climate, the plant seems to have responded by moving its flowering period ever earlier, meaning 'April Tree' might ultimately end up becoming a more accurate alternative name. But with a flowering date in our garden of 2 May, at least for the time being, nothing would need to change. Judging by the amount of blossom, particularly on the standard tree next to the garage, a bumper crop of berries would be due later in the year – the thrushes would be thrilled. Additionally, in contrast to the other two hawthorns in the wood, the middle plant didn't possess the usual white blossom, but instead had a lovely spray of pink flowers, making it probably one of the cultivated varieties that would have been purposefully planted a few years before.

Other supporting cast members that had chosen early May as their time to shine included the irises in the garage border, an old spindle shrub incorporated into the new hedge-line we had planted up to cover the fence, and last but definitely not least, the wisteria. This once-neglected climber had responded magnificently to being pruned back and re-trained by rewarding us with a line of pendant flowers the colour of Parma Violet sweets right across the top of the garage – a marvellous vindication of our decision to give it a second chance.

Also waiting in the wings for the sun to put in an appearance were the insects, with both orange tips and large whites appearing in quick succession with the accompanying rise in temperature, the latter somewhat unsurprisingly sniffing around the raised bed, no doubt having already spied our young Savoy cabbages. Also known as the cabbage white because of its caterpillars' voracious appetite for all forms of cultivated brassica, I knew I would soon be facing yet another of those classic club versus country dilemmas I was becoming familiar with. Unlike the earlier issues with the jackdaws and mason bees, however, if the large whites had indeed set their mind on selecting our cabbages as egg-laying material, then this might just have to be one of those occasions where we took the losses on the chin.

Then blow me, the garden seemingly not content with giving us lovely views of the large red damselfly earlier in the morning, topped off the afternoon with the gift of our second damsel of the day. With their flying technique more reminiscent of a butterfly flitting elegantly around the vegetation rather than a damselfly, the demoiselles are easy to identify even amongst spotters with very little experience of this wonderful group of insects. With only two species of demoiselle to get to grips with, the way to tell the difference between the showy males is to look at their wings; one species has a dark band across its wings, while the wings of the other are almost entirely pigmented. The aptly named banded demoiselle, and its close cousin the beautiful demoiselle, also frequent subtly different habitats. The banded, for example, favours slow and sluggish streams, rivers and canals with open bank-sides and adjacent meadows, whilst the beautiful demoiselle is more at home in fast-flowing, clean-bottomed brooks often running through woodland.

Along the majority of Strode Brook's length, it took the form of a fast, gravel-bottomed watercourse, surrounded by woodland, making the beautiful demoiselle the more likely candidate, and this was indeed borne out by a quick verification of the presence of dark wings. Unlike the large red damselfly, which we fervently hoped would be encouraged back to mate and lay eggs in our new pond when it was finally ready, the beautiful demoiselle would never be anything more than a passing visitor, but a very welcome one at that!

Having just arrived back home from a couple of days filming terrapins living in a London boating lake, which had been released as unwanted pets originally kept during the Teenage Mutant Ninja Turtle craze in the 80s, my immediate thoughts were to quickly check the pond hadn't sprung a leak and was still actually full of water. I popped straight out to the back garden, and not only was I flabbergasted to find the water still in there but some aquatic wildlife had moved in too.

Immediately recognisable as the predatory bug which spends its time whizzing around on the surface of the water, what is less known about the pond skater is the ability of some of them, having overwintered, to then take to the air in search of new freshwater locations. It is believed that whilst dispersing in spring these bugs are able to colonise new ponds by honing in on the reflections created by water. Having found a suitable pond (like ours), the dense hair pads on the ends and undersides of their second and third pair of legs trap air, enabling the insects to propel themselves over the water without breaking the surface film. The middle pairs of legs essentially function like a pair of oars – used in a rowing action with the rear pair for steering. If disturbed, one escape mechanism involves moving away quickly in a series of rapid hops.

Pond skaters normally feed on dying insects which have fallen into the water but are unable to break away from the surface tension. Attracted by the disturbance, the pond skaters will quickly 'row' over to the prey, then grasp and hold it with their short, sturdy front pair of legs before using their needle-like proboscis to pierce the body and suck out the poor victim's juices. This ability to move between water bodies and their method of catching dinner ultimately goes to explain why pond skaters are very much pioneer species to new habitats – all they need is still water and a continuous supply of prey and they will be able to make a handsome living. If pond skaters were to find the pond sufficiently attractive after just

72 hours of the water being added, then heaven only knew what I would be seeing with a full range of plants and a soil substrate in place.

After a few days of wet weather, which limited the time we were able to spend outside, the weather looked set fair for a very important day in our household – Christina's birthday. 10 May should have been a work day, but Christina had taken the day off so she would be able to spend it doing her favourite thing; hanging out in the garden with me! After taking breakfast outside, it then seemed to make sense to follow up with an amble around to check up on the progress of various projects, a habit which, with the garden changing so quickly, often ended up proving as enjoyable as it was informative.

The raised vegetable plot had already proved a bit of a mixed bag, which was the least that could have been expected from novice vegetable growers. With everything packed a little too closely together, some serious thinning out would have to be carried out, otherwise little would have room to mature properly. On first inspection the red onions, carrots, beetroot and Savoy cabbage were showing potential, whilst the runner beans, shallots, leeks and French beans seemed to be struggling. Just behind, the herbaceous border running alongside the garage was beginning to take on the appearance of a proper flowerbed, and in addition to the irises which had been flowering for a few days, the phlox and aquilegias were coming into their own too.

But for me the undoubted star performer was the meadow. Simply by letting the plants grow without threat of a lawnmower chopping them off at the ankles, a whole raft of lovely grasses and wildflowers was beginning to make its presence felt. The definition of a 'weed' according to my dictionary is that of 'a wild plant that grows where it is not wanted, especially among cultivated plants', and plants like dandelions, herb Robert, cleavers and petty spurge would all be on most gardeners' hit-lists of their Top 10 Most Annoying Weeds. Here in the meadow, however, instead of being vilified these plants were being actively encouraged to flower and set seed, even though I was well aware that ultimately I would be creating a rod for my own back as and when the seeds blew into the cultivated part of the garden. As far as I was concerned, the extra weeding we would have to carry out as the meadow flowers suddenly transmogrified into weeds elsewhere in the garden would be a small price to pay.

Wild grass species are also often underrated components of meadows, and very rarely seen in gardens where most British lawns tend to be a limited, but robust, mix of ryegrass, bents and meadow grasses, but just by leaving the meadow to grow I could see lovely species like sweet-vernal grass and Yorkshire fog taking a hold. Both of these species were additionally interesting, as an understanding of their ecological preferences can also give clues to help reveal a greater awareness of the garden itself. Sweet vernal, for example, as well as being the grass renowned for giving hay that lovely smell, is also a species that favours a low pH. Yorkshire fog, on the other hand is very susceptible to trampling, which is why it struggles to survive in well-used lawns, but it also tends to grow best in moist, disturbed soils. So purely from the presence of a couple of grasses, I was now wise to the fact that the meadow soil was poor, wet, acidic and had been recently disturbed – probably not the best combination of attributes for fastidious, cultivated flowers, but not bad for my equally cherished meadow flowers and grasses.

Following the smallholding theme we had initiated last month with the construction of our organic raised bed, Christina had also been trying to persuade me that the addition of chickens might be a good idea. Initially I wasn't keen, as I was only too aware that not only would they involve extra time and effort, but also they would have to go somewhere, which would inevitably mean losing some of my beloved meadow. Christina pointed out that very little grew in the shady spot behind the garage, and suggested that for her birthday treat she would like to go and see some of the different chicken breeds on offer, supremely aware that I would firstly never deny her birthday wish, and secondly that my stance would probably weaken upon finding what engaging animals they were. Pressing home her advantage, she additionally pointed out the undeniable fact that the constant presence of chickens would give me more opportunity to indulge in a spot of birdwatching whenever I wanted!

So with a mixture of trepidation, foreboding and more than a little curiosity too, I took Christina for a fact-finding tour. Ellie Smith's Poultry Farm was a combination of a one-stop shop selling everything the part-time chicken owner would ever hope to need, alongside a huge electrified field with the most unbelievable number of different type of chickens, primed and ready to go to good homes. Ellie could immediately see we were beginners, and therefore might just conceivably be in the 'starter package/big spend' category, so she agreed to take us for a tour to show us the chickens.

Running around the field in the most enormous feral flock must have been at least 300 chickens of what looked like eight or nine obvious breeds. Ellie explained that all the various coloured chickens we could see were not actually 'breeds' but 'hybrids', which were created by crossing different pure-bred parents. The hybrids could not be elevated to the level of 'breeds' themselves, though, as they wouldn't breed true if placed together. This means that if you wanted more of a certain type of hybrid, then you have to go back to the pure-bred parents again. The advantage of owning hybrids, as opposed to their pure-bred parents, was down to a genetic process called 'hybrid vigour', whereby the cross-bred offspring tend to acquire many of the best attributes of both their parents, but relatively few of their worst, so they are often much fitter, healthier and hardier as a result. Additionally, Ellie only selected those hybrid crosses which were prolific egg layers, with some capable of producing up to 300 eggs a year!

All the chickens sold at 'point of lay', which was at around 16 weeks after hatching, and Ellie went on to explain that all her hybrids were also vaccinated against various poultry diseases, and, being low maintenance, were ideal for beginners. It was utterly fascinating and I really enjoyed soaking up all the information about the one bird that I had both seen and eaten on thousands of occasions, but admittedly didn't really know the first thing about. Also, being the kind of nerd whose appreciation of any animal immediately doubles once I know what it actually is, I then got Ellie to point out all the names of the different types of hybrids in the flock and list their various attributes. The Gold Lines were apparently the friendliest hybrid, the Cou Cou Marans were the classic speckled hens with darker eggs, and the White Leghorns were quite noisy and timid but produced beautiful pure white eggs. I also managed to spot, with Ellie's help, Silver Sussexes, Blue Bells, Syston Black Tips and a number more.

Ellie hadn't even needed to give us the big sell, as both she and Christina could see I was hooked. It would be fine after all to lose a small, shaded part of the meadow, and with Christina promising to look after the chickens whilst I was away, and with the birds available for sale the following week, the only decisions we had to make were how many and which types we wanted. By way of celebrating our decision to become part-time chicken farmers in addition to both gardeners and nature-reserve wardens, it would have been remiss of us not to pop into a garden centre on the way home, as there were some lovely plants I'd noted down at Mark's which I was keen to add to our garden too!

When we arrived home, I went inside to send some emails whilst Christina wanted to spend an hour enjoying the garden before getting ready for her birthday meal. I'd barely read my messages before Christina rushed in with something so urgent that it had to be wildlife-related. 'We have a nest in the garden!' she announced breathlessly. 'Where and what?' I replied, grabbing my binocs and hurtling for the back garden, fervently hoping it would be a tit in one of our nest boxes. Raising my binoculars it was immediately obvious that I'd received one of my two wishes, as I watched a blue tit with food disappear through a hole, not in one of our nest boxes, but in a tiny little barrel that had obviously been wedged in the middle of one of the hazels for years. Not even sure what it was but believing it to be an eyesore, I'd tried taking it down the previous week, and had given up when I found I couldn't reach it – what a good job I wasn't taller! Turning their noses up at the brand, spanking-new penthouse suites we'd recently installed, there was more than a hint of irony that they had opted instead for a ramshackle, filthy, old one-bedroom apartment, but as any estate agent worth their salt will tell you when moving into a new property, it's all about location, location, location – and at least they'd got that spot-on. Now all I needed was one of the house martins currently feeding above my meadow to decide that the pebble-dash render on the side of my house would look far better with a bit of wet mud and saliva stuck to it – or maybe I was getting just a touch greedy?

With Christina's birthday now over for another year, she was straight back to work, giving me one more opportunity to try to sort out the pond edge before I too became tied up with work. Having decided that the only permanent way to try to level the pond would be to create a concrete collar at the lower end, I had called in a favour from a good pal who was decidedly more practical than me. Big Ben was Bristolian born and bred, and I had met him when he briefly harboured aspirations to work as a wildlife cameraman back during the early days of *Springwatch*, when I was working on the programme as a researcher. Ben had eventually decided that his technical skills might be put to better use running his own handy-man business instead.

I explained beforehand what I hoped to achieve, and Ben thought it a big enough job to warrant a cement mixer, so jumping in his van in Bristol we swung past various stores, picking up the mixer, chippings-to-dust aggregate, sand and cement ready for an afternoon of concreting. With the liner already obviously containing water, the task of building up the rim, whilst not collapsing the sides or puncturing the liner, was hardly straightforward, but with Ben mixing and laying the concrete while I lifted the liner to ensure it wouldn't be damaged, rapid progress was made. By forming a half collar, like a doughnut ring around the back and the lower side, the liner would then be able to be anchored on the surface by heavy stones, with the rim finally at the same level all around the pond. This in turn meant the pond could now be filled to the brim with a minimal amount of liner showing. At last it was ready to be planted up!

With Ben away back to Bristol and me still filthy from a combination of sand, cement dust and sweat, I decided to take a quick bath to freshen up before Christina arrived home for the pond inspection. While the bath filled, I looked down on the garden through the bathroom window, which now gave the finest overview. Dreamily staring out, I was pleased with how much we had achieved in such a short space of time: the compost bins were composting, the herbaceous borders were bordering on beautiful, the pond was virtually done and the meadow ... HAD A FOX! It took me a moment to register it; bold as brass, and in broad daylight, I couldn't believe I was watching a fox strolling through the meadow! It was one of those moments when I understood exactly why Archimedes ran naked down the street shouting 'Eureka!' after discovering that his body displaced water from a bath and thus he could calculate the volume of objects. Mammal-wise, our nature reserve didn't just have squirrels and the occasional badger, it also played host to a fox as well. Hardly worth getting arrested in the street for, but reason to celebrate nonetheless!

By the look of its 'pencil' tail and bare patches on its haunches it was obviously not a particularly healthy animal, as many foxes across Britain have seen their numbers plummet due to mange – a horrible, debilitating infection caused by the same mite that gives us scabies. Bristol, for example, was thought totally free of mange until

1994, but since the first recorded case the disease became so rampant that in just a twenty-month period it was thought to have wiped out an astonishing 95 per cent of all the city's urban foxes. Due to this highly infectious disease being transmitted between different animals, mange was considered to be less of a concern in surrounding countryside (like Chew Stoke), as rural foxes are present at a much lower density in the countryside. Thrilled as I was to see the fox, I was hoping this poor individual would be very much the exception rather than the norm.

Christina, of course, was both thrilled to see the pond progress and hear about my fox moment on her return, and with it being such a lovely evening we thought we'd take a bottle of wine and a couple of glasses down to the bank by the oak tree to see what wildlife would be about in the lovely 'golden' hour before dusk descends. We sat incredibly quietly, tucked up with our backs against one of the hazels. It's amazing how much you can see if you only take the time to stop, look and listen. To our right along the bank, the blue tit parents were busy collecting caterpillars for the barrel brood, the ramsons were still both looking and smelling stupendous and the blackbirds were making their usual chattering alarm call as a precursor to settling down for the evening. With the light levels having dropped a couple of notches, we then spotted a couple of bats, possibly pipistrelles, trawling above the water for any emerging insects like mayflies at exactly the same time as one of the kingfishers whizzed straight past – which was certainly the first time I'd ever seen both bats and a kingfisher in the same view! As light faded still further, we were at the point of retiring inside when we both noticed a female blackbird acting very suspiciously just below us at the bottom of the bank with what looked to be food in her bill, as it disappeared in amongst the vegetation barely five or six yards away. Straining to see anything through the gloom, what we did clearly pick up was the unmistakable cry of hungry baby chicks begging for food. We'd only gone and located another flipping nest!

One of the questions I'm asked on a surprisingly regular basis is which is my favourite month for spotting wildlife. While all the months hold their own particular delights for me, this is always an easy question to respond to, as my answer is the same every time – the last two weeks of May and the first two weeks of June. The only problems with this four-week period of frenetic wildlife activity are that firstly it always seems to pass way too quickly, and secondly it tends to coincide with my busiest filming period, giving me little time to stop and enjoy it. So this year I was determined to ensure any spare time would be properly prioritised – or in other words, spent in the garden.

The morning of 16 May was an early start, as I was due at Television Centre in London for my first experience of filming for *Blue Peter*. As a guest contributor I was due to appear on a strand they were running called 'Freaks of Nature'. I arrived on time and I was surprised at how many cameras would be used to film the item and how small the *Blue Peter* Garden really was. With all television, the majority of time is spent standing around waiting, with the actual filming process itself often rattled off in quick measure. But with the three presenters, Andy, Helen and Barney, being so charming and good at their jobs I was able to quickly impart my knowledge about leafy sea-dragons, and so was away, with my *Blue Peter* badge safely stowed, before lunchtime. A prompt getaway on this occasion was a bonus, as it would now free up the extra time needed to get back home to prepare a meal for a special guest we had invited over.

Gary is one of my best mates in the business; a sound recordist, whose job it is to record all the sound on any film shoot, whether it be my voice or the somewhat more attractive sound of a nightingale's song. I have forgotten the number of days I have been lucky enough to spend in this fine gentleman's company, as we've filmed everything from nightjars flying around our heads to dolphins leaping out of the water right in front of us. I suppose Gary would be best described as a big vegetarian with a rapacious wit, who, like me, is passionate about birdsong. I was also delighted he'd been able to accept my invitation to come over to make a recording of the garden's dawn chorus, which we'd planned for the following morning. With the birdsong commencing at around 4am, I suggested that it might be easier if we cooked him dinner and he stayed over in the guest bedroom, meaning all he would need to do was to roll out of bed and start recording!

Gary had brought a bottle of red with him, and this was soon polished off while the mushroom lasagne was in the oven. When it was ready, dinner was washed down with another bottle of our own, as Gary and I no doubt bored Christina with stories she'd probably heard before, of the various hilarious events that had occurred over the last decade spent filming together. As time always seems to fly when good company and booze are mixed together, it wasn't until close to midnight that we realised the time, and hastily bid each other goodnight with an arrangement to meet downstairs in the kitchen in just over four hours' time.

In my inebriated state I accidentally set my alarm for 4pm, and so the first I was aware that it was time to get up was when I heard a gentle tapping on our bedroom door. Having waited downstairs for 15 minutes, Gary realised I had overslept and so had come back up to rouse me. Stumbling around with a hangover in the darkness as I tried in vain to get dressed whilst not waking Christina, I eventually met Gary downstairs some 10 minutes later, full of apologies. Then, laced with coffee, we quietly slipped outside.

Immediately we could hear the dawn chorus was already under way, which was not a good start as I would like to have recorded it from the moment the very first bird had piped up. There is quite often an order about when birds join the chorus, with some species patently earlier risers than others. Of course which bird sings first tends to depend on the habitat, and in gardens, for example, it is often a toss-up between the robin and the blackbird as to who kicks off first, but because I had overslept we were none the wiser as to which species had begun this particular morning as both birds were already up to full speed by the time Gary was ready to start recording.

His audio equipment was state-of-the-art, and consisted of a parabolic reflector, which looked exactly like a TV satellite dish, with a microphone attached to the centre. Connected via a cable, this then plugged into a mixer which controlled the level at which the recording was made, before in turn being placed on to a hard drive that stored each recording in separate computer files. The clever idea behind the shape of the reflector is that when pointed at a sing-ing bird, for example, the song is funnelled by the dish to the sensi-tive microphone, and so even when you can't see the bird, because it's still too dark or obscured by vegetation, it can often be pinpointed quite accurately by gently swivelling the reflector until the song is at its loudest and purest in the headphones. When you hit that 'sweet spot' all you have to do is hold the reflector as steadily as possible and then press 'record'!

Despite the morning being a touch windier than Gary and I would have liked, in no time we rattled off recordings of both the blackbird and the robin before easing down to the middle of the garden to record the wren and the song thrush that had just added their voices to the chorus. The wren's song is remarkably strident for such a small bird, and even though Gary couldn't actually see it, a thumbs-up from him meant that he was pleased with the quality of the recording. Many birdsong beginners often struggle to learn a wren's song, but the secret is to listen for the two trills within the body of the song, the first one drilled out at rapid speed in the middle, followed by the second delivered at a much slower pace as a finale – it's a five-second work of art. The song thrush was next to come under Gary's forensic examination and listening to it made me wonder whether it was indeed the very same male that had been belting out its welcoming song on the very first day we moved in – I certainly hoped this was the case, as I wouldn't ever forget my special moment with that bird.

Slowly but surely some later arrivals entered the fray. The next bird to get the treatment was the dunnock perched directly on top of the ornamental *leylandii* and above the nest, which in the dunnocks' case had also doubled as a den of iniquity. Their song is a short, fast and quite scratchy warble which barely seems to deviate up or down the scale. Next for recording were the uncharismatic songs of the endlessly repetitive onomatopoeic chiffchaff and the 'teacher-teacher' call of the great tit, which is superficially similar to the chiffchaff but always places the emphasis on the first syllable, or the 'teach' part, of its call.

As we moved down to the wooded bank we were delighted to find a singing blackcap, which had plumped for a territory on the opposite side of the brook in amongst a patch of brambles. Sitting quietly down on the bank we listened enraptured to its much-underrated song. Slowly, as the tiredness from the combination of our late finish the night before and our incredibly early start began to wash over me, I decided the more relaxing position from which to enjoy the concert would be horizontally in amongst the ramsons, with Gary's spare set of headphones clamped to my ears. I often find that when listening to birdsong your hearing becomes more attuned by shutting off the sense of sight, so on closing my eyes I firstly heard the reflector pick up the plaintive but insistent song of the male blue tit, reminding us of his nest just above our heads, and then a greenfinch wheezing away from further off. By now all the birds had joined in, with the chorus emulating a symphony reaching its crescendo; while revelling ever deeper in the wondrous performance, at some point I must have slowly dozed off.

I was suddenly brought to my senses by a squeeze on my arm. In my befuddled state I wasn't initially sure what was causing the pressure until I realised Gary was still seated right next to my prostrate figure on the bank. I half opened my eyes and looked down, and I could indeed see it was Gary's hand that was responsible, and for an awful moment thought that Gary had chosen this impossibly romantic moment to declare suddenly that he was gay and that he'd always been attracted to me. As my mind spun like the reels of a one-arm bandit, as I tried to gain my senses, I realised that this was a ridiculous notion … he had a baby son and a partner … maybe he just wanted to attract my attention instead without making any noise … maybe he had spotted something. Sitting bolt upright without making a sound I caught Gary's eye, whose expression seemed to be like a cross between someone who'd just won the lottery and someone who'd also just had an unfortunate accident in his trousers, and followed the direction of his finger which was pointing in an ET-like manner over my shoulder and upstream. Immediately I picked up the movement in the water that had caught Gary's attention, and in one of those euphoric moments, the likes of which happens on just a few occasions throughout one's lifetime, I realised not only that my garden played host to a wonderful dawn chorus but that it was also being visited by an otter.

The otter was swimming downstream towards us, and it immediately became obvious that it had no idea we were there. As it drew level with the two open-mouthed idiots, no more than three yards away on the bank, I saw its broad, flat head, whiskers and powerful tail as it half swam and half paddled past us. I also had the accompanying thought that were a bus to run me over later that day, I swear I would have died with a smile on my face. Like all the most memorable natural history moments I've ever had, there was a dream-like quality to the encounter, and although in reality we probably watched the animal for a good 10 or 15 seconds, it felt somehow that the sighting was over in a blink of the eye, as the otter, still oblivious to our presence, disappeared out of sight around the meander.

We forgot that Gary's hard drive was still running, and I don't mind telling you that a few expletives and whoops of sheer joy were sprinkled in amongst the dawn chorus that was still being recorded as we realised the enormity of the moment – an otter on the garden

list had been so far off the radar that I hadn't even considered it! The likelihood was that this had been an otter covering a much larger area, which would have included all of Strode Brook, the adjoining and larger River Chew and probably Chew Valley Lake as well. With adults being territorial and largely solitary, we had obviously just been sitting quietly at exactly the moment that it was moving through this section of its territory – an unbelievable stroke of luck. This wasn't the first time I'd seen an otter, having been lucky enough to see and film them on a number of occasions up in Newcastle and Shetland, across on the Somerset Levels, in Pembrokeshire and down in Dorset, but believe me, it's a thousand times more exciting seeing one swimming past your own back garden!

Christina, who was now in the process of kindly cooking us breakfast, had to tell us to slow down and speak clearly as we relayed the unbelievable events of the morning in a barely intelligible gabble. Upon deciphering the exciting news, she was as thrilled for us as we were with ourselves. True, otters had made a remarkable recovery since swimming back from the brink of extinction in England during the 1970s, and they had also very recently been recorded as being back in every single English county with the final addition of a couple of sightings in Kent, but this was still a moment to cherish.

Buoyed by the dawn chorus and the otter sighting, and after recharging our batteries with a full-on veggie breakfast and coffee, Gary and I decided that a little further exploration of the river would be in order, and so, donning our wellington boots, we tramped back down the garden and into the brook. We waded upstream first, and it took us no time to pinpoint the blackbird's nest that Christina and I had located only a couple of days earlier. The nest itself was embedded in the bank, with a piece of plastic litter interwoven in amongst the grass and twig cup at a height of no more than six inches above the level of the water. Inside we could see three chicks, which already had their eyes open with their first flight feathers emerging from the down, making them around a week old and just another week away from fledging.

Blackbirds will generally have a clutch of between three and five eggs, which meant this brood size was at the lower end of the range, but it was not until we looked closer that the chicks, thinking we were the parents returning with food, reached skyward with their mouths open in full-begging mode, revealing at the bottom of the nest a fourth egg which hadn't hatched and may have been sterile. The chicks suddenly realised that there was no food forthcoming and that something was alarmingly different, so they shrank back down into the nest, covering up the egg in the process – no wonder so many blackbird nests were predated if the chicks were that unwary. This would in all probability have been the parents' second brood of the season; as one of our earliest birds to commence nesting, first broods can occasionally fledge as early as March in mild years.

We retreated upstream to leave the chicks in peace, and we had gone barely 50 yards when I showed Gary the bank where Christina and I had thought, back in February, that the kingfishers might have been tempted to nest, and, sure enough, partially hidden behind some trailing bramble tendrils was a newly excavated hole positioned towards the top of the bank, a full five feet above the water. The tell-tale sign that the hole was currently occupied was the most enormous white stain of guano emanating from the lip of the hole and running for the best part of two feet like a white waterfall down the face of the bank. Obviously not keen to soil their own nest, the chicks were not fussed about sullying their own doorstep! It was turning into the most amazing day of revelations; not only did our garden play host to a passing otter, but we also had a kingfisher breeding just 50 yards from the garden!

I thanked Gary profusely for coming over and for waking me up to see the otter, which I would otherwise have missed, and I bade him goodbye and snatched an hour's catch-up sleep before I was back out in the garden, this time with Christina, to tackle the edge of the pond liner. Having decided after much debate that stones would indeed be the best way to both anchor down and cover the liner, Christina had come up with the inspired idea of using a few of the stones from the river bed to give the pond surround a rockery feel. Feeling slightly guilty that I would be removing an excellent habitat from the brook for all manner of aquatic life, my partner in crime was quick to point out that there would still be an awful lot of stones left, so a few wouldn't be missed too much, providing we washed off the aquatic life back into the river beforehand.

I waded back into the brook for the second time that day, and my job was to lift the stones out of the water as Christina gave a Caligula-style thumbs up or thumbs down as to whether, in her opinion, they were aesthetically pleasing enough to be on permanent view around the pond. On each stone being lifted (which were not light either, I can tell you), all the minuscule freshwater shrimps immediately started wriggling their way back towards the water and safety, no doubt thoroughly peeved that their world had, quite literally, just been turned upside down. Most rocks also had a few clusters of empty larval caddis-fly cases attached, each one shaped like a tiny cigar and composed of sand and fine gravel. Assiduously glued together into tube shapes by underwater larvae, they are an amazing feat of engineering, and are designed thus to protect their soft bodies as they grow and mature in preparation for the climax of their lives as winged adults.

Eventually about a dozen carefully selected stones, having been assiduously washed free of life, were then placed on the bank before being hauled up to the pond, where they did indeed give a lovely, rustic feel to the pond, which was itself, at least in part, surrounded by the herbaceous border. We decided that we would properly set the stones in a bed of sand and gravel the following day, and that we would quit for the day while we were ahead. I was just about to hop into the shower when Christina called me quickly to the landing-hall window, 'Bullfinch!' she said, and as my binoculars were now permanently stowed ready for action by the window, I was able to get a great view of a male looking resplendent with his rose-pink breast sitting in one of our newly planted apple trees. Now I hate to go on about my 'favourite species' topic again, but if I had to pick my all-time favourite British bird then without doubt it would have to be the bullfinch. I could go on and on about how much I adore this bird, but in essence it's because it looks stunning (or at least the males do), it's shy, it's usually an indicator of a lovely habitat and, just like the jay, is one of those birds which, when it flies off, leaves you feeling slightly crestfallen.

When out for a walk in the countryside, the most common view of a bullfinch is usually of the bird's white rump as it zips out of view along a mature farmland hedgerow having been disturbed, so to see one sitting out in broad daylight oblivious of us watching was a real treat. Suddenly the bullfinch did something quite unexpected. Launching off the apple tree branch, it flew a couple of feet into the meadow, where we watched it hover like a turbo-charged humming-bird whilst extracting one of the parachute-bearing seeds from a dandelion clock. Having successfully plucked out a seed by the feathered end, it then flew straight back to the apple tree and proceeded to manipulate the seed and parachute around in its bill with the most astonishing dexterity, until the parachute was jetti-soned with a quick snip, leaving the seed to be cracked open like a tiny walnut.

It might be stating the obvious, but this was something that neither I nor Christina had ever seen before. I'm sure that someone at some point must have watched a bullfinch doing exactly this, but watching such an utterly fascinating facet of this bullfinch's life made me realise how little even so-called experts like myself really know about our birds at all. I meet many birders when I'm out and about these days, who are seemingly only interested in rare or unusual birds, often not bothering to give common birds a second glance. I too have been firmly in this category of birdwatching on numerous occasions, wishing, for example, that just one of the indi-viduals in the small flock of goldcrests I was watching would instead end up being the far rarer and therefore far more interesting firec-rest. Maybe the antidote to getting off the merry-go-round of endlessly chasing rarities is instead to stop, look and enjoy what the more common birds are *actually* doing, rather than dismissing them as second-class citizens. I'll go even further by saying it had

taken this one defining moment to realise that ownership of a garden had been the key to falling back in love with garden birds all over again.

My voiceover work was done and dusted by lunchtime the next day, so this freed up the rest of the afternoon to finally get to grips with the border around the pond. Stopping off at the DIY store on the way home gave me the opportunity to purchase some limestone chippings, sand and treated timber, hopefully all the necessary ingredients to finish the job. Cutting up the timber to 3 foot x 6 inches first, and this was then slotted in to create a very small retaining wall to demarcate the boundary between the back of the pond and the surrounding herbaceous border. This was kept firmly in place with embedded wooden stobs, and the stones from the brook were then placed to one side whilst I covered the area between the liner and the retaining wall with off-cuts of the butyl liner, to prevent any weeds coming through. This area was then covered in a layer of sand, and all the stones could now be repositioned, but this time on much firmer footings. The finishing touch involved placing limestone chippings to fill in the gaps between and behind the stones up to the level of the retaining wall. The hope here was that this would create a tidy and functional surround, the edge of which would be softened with plants spilling over to hide the retaining wall.

Christina arrived back from work just as the last chippings were being sprinkled into place, and she couldn't believe what a thoroughly competent job I'd done. While still true that I shouldn't consider giving up my TV career for one in landscape gardening any time soon, I had somehow managed to transform myself, as a result of all the back-garden projects, into someone for whom the phrase 'practically inept' might at long last now be considered wholly inappropriate.

Seeing my diligent work, Christina too was keen to be seen not to be slacking, and having spent the previous weekend visiting the

Malvern Flower Show, from which she had returned with quite literally her own body weight in plants, the rest of her evening, with my help, was spent plugging gaps in the garage herbaceous border, as heucheras, cultivated achilleas and irises were added to the mix. By the time we had finished it was so dark we could barely see the bed in front of us, and so we would have to wait until the following day to see the riot of colour. Fingers crossed, a whole panoply of insects would enjoy it too.

Work in London the following day meant an early train and an even earlier rise to ensure I would be able to catch it. Leaving for the train station at 6am, I almost immediately came across a dead badger at the top of the road that had obviously been struck by a car in the night. Having still not seen badgers in the garden, despite the fact that digging marks and a small latrine indicated that they were probably passing through on most nights, it was disappointing to think that this might have been one of the badgers from our closest sett down by the brook. I jumped out of the car to move the badger off the road and into the hedgerow, where it would cease to be a distraction to drivers and be safely disposed of by a variety of scavengers, and I then realised that the badger had been a lactating female. With badger cubs born underground between mid-January and mid-March, but not weaned until around 12 weeks, this meant that unless her cubs had been born particularly early in the year, they would by now be very hungry indeed.

I had barely driven another half-mile along the road when I was astounded to encounter yet another badger on the outskirts of the village that had also been hit and killed during a night of heedless badger slaughter. Having been chastened by the blackbird"s death I had caused some weeks earlier, I made a mental note that I for one would from now on attempt to drive at night with more care and consideration for my wild neighbours than some of my human neighbours patently had.

In my opinion London is always best appreciated during a flying visit. So with my meetings safely negotiated, and my appearance on *The One Show* sofa done and dusted, I was straight off to Paddington to head back west for the rural idyll I had grown to adore. Christina, who had been out on the tiles with friends in Bristol, had kindly arranged to meet me at the station to give me a lift and enable us to catch up with each other's day on the way home. The journey home takes us through south Bristol, before driving up and over Dundry Hill which usually gives an amazing view of the Chew Valley as we drop over the ridge on the home straight. It was pitch black by then, and we couldn't see anything away from where the beam cast by the headlights had caught the road in front of us and the hedgerow either side. Suddenly an ethereal flash of white was caught in the headlights, before ghosting over the road. 'Barn owl!' we both sung out in unison as we watched the floating apparition disappear into the inky night. This was certainly the closest to the city that I'd ever seen a barn owl, and to catch up with one, albeit briefly, barely a couple of miles from our house made it even finer.

The barn owl is just one of a sorry list of birds that has been on a long-term decline in the UK over the last 30 or 40 years, with recent population estimates thought to be as low as just over 2,000 pairs. The main reasons for their disappearance from swathes of our countryside seem to be down to a combination of a loss of vole-rich hay meadows and rough grasslands, the over-use of pesticides and the lack of suitable nest sites as suitable barns become converted to homes with no allowances made for the sitting tenants. To add injury to insult, the staggering rise in the number of cars on our roads has also exacted a heavy toll on a bird that often hunts along linear features like the hedgerows which border many a country road. It was a good job I'd taken heed from the badgers to slow down earlier in the day; if I'd been upset at killing a blackbird I'd have been inconsolable at hitting a barn owl.

I pulled on to the drive, still thrilled at our brush with the barn owl, and I was just preparing to turn off the engine and lights when out of the corner of my eye I spotted a small creature shuffling along the side of the house bound for the garden. If you think a barn owl is easy to identify then surely a hedgehog is right up there as being Britain's most instantly identifiable animal. Is there a person over the age of two who doesn't know what a hedgehog looks like? Somehow I doubt it. As the hedgehog disappeared under the garden gate, I ran around instead to the car boot, fumbling for the torch in order for us to get a closer look at what represented another fabulous mammal tick for the garden.

Upon seeing the torch pointed at it, the hedgehog did what hedgehogs have been doing for thousands of years in response to any perceived danger, and battened down the hatches; turning itself from the lovable Mrs Tiggy-Winkle into a ball of around 5,000 spines. Like the barn owl, the hedgehog is a creature that has been on the downward spiral for a number of decades in the UK now, and it cannot be overestimated how important gardens have become to its survival. Not only do they provide a refuge from the constant menace of traffic, as rolling up into a ball is a fat lot of use when confronted with about a ton and a half of motorcar zooming towards you at 50mph, but the mosaic of habitats offered by gardens is the perfect place to hunt down the beetles, slugs and earthworms that make up a hedgehog's diet.

The hedgehog provides such an excellent pest-removal service that gardeners should be positively encouraging their presence in the borders, rather than seeking the quick and easy, but environmentally naïve, option of using slug pellets or insecticides. Blasting the flowerbeds with these chemicals may keep your hostas and roses looking immaculate all summer, but it can ultimately result in the garden becoming soulless and sterile, as the hedgehogs, which may eat the poisoned slugs, will become poisoned themselves through the process of bio-accumulation. If you want a garden with about as much wildlife value as green tarmac then spray away; however, if you don't object to a few holes in your hostas or aphids on your roses then you will be singing from the same songsheet as me – and good on you!

While cars and chemicals could definitely be described as unnatural predators, the only animal that a hedgehog will go positively out
of its way to avoid is the badger. Using their powerful limbs and
kitchen-knife claws, badgers are quite capable of rolling open
hedgehogs like a tin of sardines to get to their soft underbelly, and
would definitely be in their 'mortal enemy' category. In certain areas
of high badger density, predation pressure can be so intense that it
may even be enough to exclude hedgehogs entirely, which is why I
was so surprised to see a hedgehog in an area so heavily frequently
by badgers. Maybe it felt emboldened after having passed the two
dead badgers earlier in the evening! Leaving the slightly startled
hedgehog to go about his business, we retired for the night. What a
mammal-centric month May was turning out to be!

We wanted 21 May to be a seminal day – the day when Mike and
Christina would become a family, for, before sundown, if everything
went to plan, we would be responsible for three chickens. As it was
also my last day off for quite a while and there was a lot to be sorted,
the organisation needed to be meticulous, so with the coop already
in place behind the garage, I sorted out a large cardboard box to
bring the chickens back in, while Christina, who was barely able to
contain her excitement, checked the opening time on Ellie's
website.

Ready and raring to go, I popped back inside to see what was
holding Christina up, only to come across her staring at the
computer screen in my office with a look on her face which I can
only describe as that of devastation. 'They've hardly got any chickens left,' she said, reading out a hastily posted sign on the home
page, which seemed to indicate that the flock of 300 we had seen
just a couple of weeks ago had now dwindled to just a handful of
birds. To make matters worse, the notice had also added a list of all
the hybrids which had sold out, which, as sure as eggs are eggs,
included two of the three types we had decided we liked the most:

Cou Cou Marans and Light Sussexes. 'Well, that's that,' I said, 'she'll have some more in a couple of months and we'll be first in the queue then.' This response didn't stop the tears rolling down Christina's cheeks, though, as for all the world she looked like a child who had suddenly been told that Christmas had been postponed indefinitely. 'Sod it!' I said, as I always hated seeing Christina so upset, 'let's go up anyway and see what they do have.'

Seeking out Ellie on our arrival, she put us more at ease with the news that despite some of the hybrids having indeed sold out, there were still more than enough lovely chickens from which to choose. On our previous visit the adjacent field had looked like the chicken equivalent of wildebeest grazing in the Tanzanian Serengeti, but this time there was not a chicken to be seen. 'They're all in the sheds,' Ellie said, on seeing our quizzical looks, going on to explain that they were impossible to catch when the flock became smaller, so with all the birds captive it would make it easier to view and select from the full range still available.

Half-opening the door, so we could all look in but the chickens couldn't get out, we were confronted by about 40 looking nervously across at us of at least half a dozen varieties. My first mistake was to ask Ellie if she could help us spot which were the healthiest birds, to which she responded tartly that all her chickens were in tip-top condition. We quickly decided that we should select three chickens that looked totally different from each other so that we could easily identify them in the future, and furthermore that we would each pick one, with the third being jointly chosen. We were keen to start with a friendly one, and the first chicken to come under the spotlight was our joint choice, as we plumped for a very inquisitive Syston Black Tip just by the door, which was a light chestnut brown with a black tail. Entering the shed and then closing the door behind her, Ellie then emerged into the light some 30 seconds later, with what we presumed to be the same bird, which was then gently but expertly placed into the box we had brought along. Reopening the door, Christina then took only an instant to point to a very pretty Blue Bell which was blue-grey with a darker head and chestnut-fringed feathers on her upper breast. With two now in the box, I decided my pick would be the chicken which gave me the best eye contact, and as I scanned the shed the one that looked most interested in me also happened to be the one who seemed head and shoulders above the others, a big Silver Sussex, which was misleadingly mostly velvet-black, with silver fringes to her breast feathers. Once more, as Ellie emerged with the bird, it produced the most enormous squawk whilst simultaneously making the most enormous impromptu toilet visit right down Ellie's fleece, jeans and trainers as I opened the box for it to join the other two.

Ellie was quite literally covered in shit, and I for one couldn't stop laughing. We tramped back to the shop with our chickens and I suspect it was Ellie who had the last laugh, as we then went on an unparalleled shopping spree purchasing the rest of the chicken-related paraphernalia. Apparently back-garden chicks don't just need a garden but also require a drinker, a feeder, some hay as bedding, layers' pellets, food containers, treats and a starter kit including vitamins, mite powder and grit. With a grand total of £249, minus £48 which my mum had kindly offered to pay for the chickens as a belated housewarming present, this meant that, if we ate half a dozen eggs a week, our initial investment would take around two and a half years to pay off. 'They'd better be worth it,' I muttered under my breath as Ellie, having now changed into clean clothing, confirmed that she did indeed accept MasterCard.

When we got home, with the chooks sitting quietly in their box, blissfully unaware of the brave new world they were about to enter, I began sorting out a place in the garage to store all their food and bedding whilst Christina prepared the chicken coop for its new tenants. Essentially the coop was the shape of a triangular prism, about two yards long with a covered and uncovered outdoor run, linked by a small ladder to the nesting and roosting space accessed through a sliding door.

'I've been thinking about names for them,' said Christina. 'Go on,' I said, slightly fearful that we would be in for an argument if she had set her heart on Nigel, Colin and Derek. 'How about April, May and June?' she said, immediately trying to gauge a reaction from my facial expression. She shouldn't have worried, they were inspired choices; April, May and June it was, and they would be named in the order they had been selected. First to be carefully lifted out of the box was April, the Syston Black Tip, closely followed by May, the Blue Bell, then June, the Silver Sussex. To our utter delight and relief they could not have settled in more easily, and they immediately began eating, drinking and exploring the rest of the coop. As we watched from the sidelines, we also saw the first hint of a pecking order being established as May began to throw her weight around with June, despite the size difference, whilst April seemed to ignore both of them. This hierarchical system in chickens has been noted ever since humankind first started domesticating fowl. By determining who is the 'top chicken', the 'bottom chicken' and where all the rest fit in between, a pecking order is essential for reducing the incidence of conflicts that can cause the unnecessary expenditure of energy, and for preventing the risk of injury.

Having canvassed the opinions of a few of my chicken-owning friends beforehand, they all independently testified that a real inner peace comes from watching chickens going about their daily business. And as we stood there for the next hour, utterly fascinated by our three girls, I sincerely can't ever remember having felt that happy or complete. I was not only a naturalist, TV presenter and wildlife gardener, but I was now also a part-time chicken farmer too!

STOP PRESS: 'Egg-cellent' news ... two eggs have been found in the coop just 24 hours after the birds' arrival!

JUNE

WHO SAYS MOTHS ARE BORING?

Having just spent marginally over £295 plus VAT on a moth trap, Christina was not best pleased with me. To be fair, she had been at pains to point out that, working as hard as I did to earn my money, I was indeed entitled to spend it exactly how I saw fit. But what she had found irritating was that I preferred to use my disposable income on expensive equipment to trap 'bloody moths' when the house was crying out for a new front door and our bedroom was desperately short of a wardrobe. She had a fair point, because all modernisation of the house had come to a standstill since the installation of the new bathroom back in early April, and all my time, money and energy went into improving the garden and recording the wildlife that appeared in it. Taking on board her constructive criticism, I thought it might then be only prudent to wait a while before mentioning the additional purchase of a bat detector in the same order, which had elevated the final bill to marginally over £500 – my expensive acquisitions would have to be on a 'need-to-know' basis.

We had barely been at home for a couple of weeks because of work commitments, and the first weekend in June was our first opportunity that month to spend most of the day in the garden, so it was important that as little time as possible should be wasted with an argument. We agreed that the moth trap would be the last large expenditure of natural history equipment in the garden for a while, and I also promised to try my best to address some of the more pressing issues relating to the house. But just not quite yet, as today would be the day when the water-filled hole in our garden at last began to resemble a pond – it was time to get some plants in!

Before we shipped off to the aquatic centre on another of our plant-buying sprees, I was keen to see how the garden had changed in the last couple of weeks. With spring having slowly but inexorably given way to summer, our main flower border running the length of the garage was beginning to look sensational. The yellows of the lysimachia and achillia, possibly more by luck than judgement, perfectly complemented the purples of the allium, erysimum, geraniums and lavenders. Not content with letting the purples and yellows have it all their own way, the bed was also dotted throughout with the vivid blood-red splatters of poppies and astilbe too. The so-called 'June Gap' which gardeners talk about, in reference to the supposed dearth of nectar for bees during this month, patently wasn't showing any sign of occurring in this garden!

In contrast to the garage border, the pond border was at a more embryonic stage, with plenty of gaps available for plants, and it was the area Christina was keenest to devote her time to, to ensure it wasn't going to let the side down. Likewise the pond still needed some serious attention. With the sand-subsoil mix that would ultimately form the pond's substrate having been carefully placed onto the shelves in the pond a week ago, it had finally settled out of suspension, re-clearing the water in the process and giving the green light for planting. Unfortunately the pond had also been green-lit for algae, which was now beginning to create large blooms in the water. The sooner we would be able to put oxygenating plants down in the green murk, the better.

Alongside the pond, the vegetable patch had developed into a huge shock of green produce. With the carrots already harvested and consumed and the leeks ditched, which for some reason had been nothing short of a dead loss, this had created space for a green carpet of salad leaves which had sprung up in double-quick time and would soon also be ready for the dinner table. Barely a yard away, the blossom on the apple trees had served its purpose and long since withered away, and was now replaced by a small number of steadily swelling apples which were already beginning to weigh down some of the more slender branches to an uncomfortable degree. The meadow's cast of floral characters had subtly changed too, and was currently being dominated by a lovely white-and-gold patch of ox-eye daisies – one of the first meadow flowers to recolonise grasslands devoid of chemicals, and a good sign that this habitat was moving in the right direction. This is one of the flowers that has recently benefited as a result of the Highways Agency having belatedly realised the huge potential of many roadside verges as linear meadows. The ox-eye daisy is also, to my mind, the classic midsummer meadow plant, and almost seems to glow in the evenings when the golden sunlight catches its simple but timelessly stylish flowers.

To the right of the meadow and behind the compost bins, the chickens were proving the real surprise package. Not only were they little or no trouble to look after, and endlessly entertaining to watch, but at a current rate of around two eggs a day (meaning each bird must be laying on alternate days), we had not needed to purchase a single egg since the girls had come to share both our lives and our garden.

Near the wood, with the hazels, hawthorns and in fact all the trees in full leaf, the whole bank gave the impression of a huge green curtain, so it was not until we passed through, via the steps, that we were fully able to appreciate that the ramsons had finally passed their sell-by date. The drifts of white flowers had now been replaced by massed ranks of the caper-like seed heads and the once-luscious green and deliciously pungent leaves had largely lost their smell, wilted and turned a jaundiced, sickly yellow. With woodland flora having evolved to be at its peak before the trees above have unfurled their leaves to block out the light, their moment in the sun had definitely passed for another year. What a good job that the pond flora was just about to come into its prime!

With Chew Stoke equidistant between Bristol, Bath and Wells, a game of scissors, paper, stones, which Christina won, meant that it would be the garden centre in Bath where we purchased the pond plants. With different species of aquatic plant happiest at specific depths, we wanted not only to select a variety to sit in baskets on the different shelf depths I had created within the pond, but also a number of submerged oxygenating plants and floating plants. Fortunately, for once we wouldn't have to spend a king's ransom, as Lorraine next door had kindly offered some of the plants from her pond, which frankly needed a major clear-out anyway, as had Christina's parents' pond, too. As our hole was big and our need great, all offers would be gratefully received!

While Christina was looking at evergreen shrubs to ensure the garden wouldn't look a wasteland when all our perennials finally died back in winter, I began filling my basket with aquatic specialities. I decided, wherever possible, to go for native British species such as yellow flag iris, water plantain, tubular water dropwort, lesser spearwort, lesser reedmace and hard rush. A couple of oxygenating plants and a pond lily were soon added to my trolley, as well as a range of planting baskets, a small bag of aquatic compost, and pea gravel for planting out those specimens donated by family and neighbours. We had arranged to meet at the tills, and Christina had been unusually restrained, having only bought a hidcote lavender and a rosemary, and it also helped assuage our financial guilt by convincing ourselves that every plant purchased was also an investment in the property. Still, not for the first time in the last couple of weeks, I had to let the plastic take the financial strain, in the knowledge that the garden was currently being constructed on credit!

I was keen to keep the aquatic plants out of water for as little time as possible, so upon our return home the first job was to get them into the pond. By placing the taller flags and reedmace at the back to act as a green screen, the rest of the plants were then dotted around the pond according to their depth preferences. It's amazing how a trolley-full of plants at the garden centre suddenly looks terribly inadequate in a large pond, but hopefully they would soon grow and spread out to fill the void. We were also still awaiting the plants from our aquatic benefactors, after which the pond would hopefully begin to look like the real McCoy.

With our planting duties duly completed, it felt the perfect opportunity for another break and phase two of the day's enjoyment of the garden, as we retreated to the patio to see what was fraternising the bird feeders. Many regular feeders of garden birds consider that the only time it is really necessary to put out food is when they're struggling in winter. But the general consensus amongst various bird charities in the know, such as the RSPB and British Trust for Ornithology (BTO), now seems to be that by feeding the birds all year round you'll give them a better chance of surviving the periods of natural food shortage, whenever these may occur.

I also think that feeding the birds in early summer presents an opportunity to give supplementary food to those that may have recently fledged, and so may still be relatively inexperienced at finding sufficient natural food. As we sat watching the birds, it became immediately apparent that this indeed seemed to be the case, as scarcely an adult blue or great tit was noted coming into the garden for food, with the feeders dominated instead by both species' juveniles. The young of both blue and great tits were immediately recognisable as yellowy washed-out versions of their parents, and would stand out as birds with 'L-plates' on their backs for a while yet to come, not even beginning to resemble their parents until they had undergone a partial moult, commencing in late summer.

It was nice to think that a number of the blue tits we were watching filling their yellow faces would have belonged to the barrel brood, which had fledged while I'd been away. Of course, being unable to open the barrel without risking either damage to the nest or desertion by the parents, neither I nor Christina had any idea how many eggs had initially been laid or how successful the fledging had been. Generally the average clutch size for blue tits is between eight and ten, but it's thought that for those blue tits nesting in gardens, broods tend to be smaller due to the more limited availability of their natural food, such as caterpillars. But with mature trees close at hand and a whole woodland corridor beside the brook along which the adults could have scoured for food, it was hoped that a high proportion would at least have been well fed. Judging also by the sheer number of young birds piling in, it looked to have been a very healthy breeding season. This was particularly good news for blue tits, as in the vast majority of cases they only ever have a single brood in Britain – talk about putting all your eggs in one basket!

Of course, it wasn't just juvenile blue and great tits that we managed to spot, as a couple of recently fledged blackbirds also graced the garden with an appearance. Hopping around in the meadow, these brown-speckled and scruffy-looking birds were probably the very same fledged chicks that Gary and I had seen in mid-May from the nest down by the bank.

I had recently taught Christina the call, and it was her keen hearing that first picked up the soft, plaintive 'peeuu, peeuu', the sure-fire sign that both we and the garden were about to receive a VIB – a Very Important Bird. Entering the garden by the woodland, the rose-pink breast of the male bullfinch was immediately obvious as it then flew to the birch, followed in quick succession by three more individuals – a bullfinch family! With mother and the two juveniles watching from the sidelines, the male then flew down to the sunflower-heart bell feeder in the rowan tree, before grabbing a beak-full of food and flying back up to the two juveniles who were fluttering their wings like crazy as they both competed to be the recipient of the food. Though initially one seemed disappointed to miss out, it didn't have to wait long as its father flew back with more food and its begging had the desired effect.

Racking my brains, I was really struggling to remember the last time I had been lucky enough to see juvenile bullfinch, before eventually coming to the conclusion that if nothing immediately sprung to mind then this could indeed have been my first ever time. The juveniles were much browner than the female, and without the black cap that is so distinctive of both the adult birds, and while I'd like to have given you a far more complete description, I'm afraid that was all I managed to note down, before they melted away back into the woodland and out of our lives again. To reiterate, that sums up why the bullfinch is my favourite bird – it is a species that both surprises and delights you, before ultimately disappointing you.

Due out at a ridiculously early hour the following morning to film (of all things) kingfishers in east Bristol meant that I didn't have the time to check the contents of my new moth trap, which I'd set up in the aftermath of our 'bullfinch moment' the previous afternoon. Filming the kingfishers had entailed sitting quietly on a bank in camouflage gear for around five hours in the relentless, pouring rain while waiting for a kingfisher to land on a stick in front of me. The kingfisher did eventually turn up, but only after a very long, damp wait.

Moth-trapping or 'moth-ing' is an activity from which I've derived the most enormous amount of pleasure since first coming across it in the early 1990s. I had moved to North Wales for a three-month contract as a reserve warden on Anglesey, and I fell in love with the fascinating and endlessly varied landscapes and amazing wildlife and ended up staying there for the best part of five years. I look back upon my stint in *Gogledd Cymru* (North Wales) as the time when I made the change from being just a keen birder to a hard-core naturalist, and this conversion was in no small part down to an amazing naturalist and lecturer at Bangor University called Nigel Brown. Everybody who has studied an environmental discipline at Bangor University over the last 25 years will surely have come across Nigel at some point, and having met a number of his ex-graduates over the years, to a tee they all talk in the most glowing terms of his gentle but inspiring nature. In a nutshell he is simply both the most charming person and the best naturalist I've ever met.

After my wardening contract finished I decided I fancied a crack at a second degree, in the form of a Masters degree in Ecology. At the university, it was Nigel's job to take the students out on various field trips across the region. He was keen to educate his disciples on both the finer points of identification and the precise ecological requirements of everything from ferns to fungi and birds to bumble-bees, and he soon garnered a huge following amongst wannabe ecologists like me. Nigel lived at the university's Botanic Gardens in Treborth, and it was his job to operate a couple of moth traps within the grounds throughout the year. As I lived only a mile away from the Gardens, in the small town of Menai Bridge, I soon manoeuvred myself into the position of chief scribe, whose responsibility it was to write down the names of all the moths collected in the traps after identification by Nigel. I cycled to the Botanic Gardens before breakfast, and I was basically given a one-on-one tutorial with the great man each morning, as we sat supping tea whilst identifying hundreds of species of different moths, an activity I carried out with the enthusiasm of a religious zealot for the best part of two years. It was the most wonderful ritual, and also a time of which I have the fondest of memories.

Of course during this period of religiously identifying the moths day in, day out, my knowledge of many of the species became white-hot, but on leaving North Wales, and without a trap of my own to use or a place to safely trap in, my moth-ing career began to stall somewhat over the following years. However, with a garden to my name at last, I was determined that my moth-ing would be resurrected, if not every night, than at least whenever possible.

For those who have never seen moth traps in operation, they are really simple but very cleverly designed bits of kit, which are based on the fact that the vast majority of moths are attracted to light. Using a special Mercury-Vapour light bulb, which emits a high proportion of its light in the ultraviolet range (making it especially attractive), on a summer's night the moths can often be seen to almost pour in. Exactly why the light is so attractive to moths has baffled scientists for generations, but the hypothesis that seems closest to the mark is based on the premise that moths use the moon for navigation by a technique called transverse orientation. By maintaining a constant angular relationship to the moon, they can then fly in a straight line, and as celestial objects are so far away, even after travelling great distances, the change in angle between the moth and the light source is negligible. Furthermore, the moon is always in the upper part of the visual field and above the horizon. However, if a moth accidentally uses a much closer artificial light for navigation, the angle will change substantially after only a short distance, causing the moth to simultaneously plummet down and spiral towards the light source in ever decreasing circles – which moth catchers will testify is a commonly seen incoming flight path amongst many of the moths attracted to the light.

A funnel positioned directly below the bulb collects the moths when they collide with a series of projecting baffles, then the trap operates in the same manner as a lobster pot – with a large opening but small exit, meaning that once the moths have dropped down into the bucket part of the trap, their chances of escape are minuscule, until released by the moth catcher.

Amongst the ignorant and uninitiated, moths often have a bad press as nasty, fluttery things that fly through our open windows at night and eat our clothes. Even with the less hysterical commentators dismissing them as the dull, boring and drab cousins to butterflies, I'm the first to admit that they do have something of a PR problem. Of course, moths will occasionally be drawn to house lights, and out of the 2,400 or so species recorded in the UK there are admittedly a couple of species that can cause damage to our clothes, but as anyone who has ever seen an elephant hawk-moth, garden tiger or merveille-du-jour will tell you, dull, boring and drab they are not! While British butterflies total around 60 species, even if we just count the macro-moths alone (which consist of the mostly larger species and are usually identified by wing-shape and pattern), these number around 800, making them an incredibly diverse and interesting group.

To maintain the ability to recognise wildlife to species level, as with many other hobbies or specialised areas of interest, the phrase 'use it or lose it' is incredibly applicable. From a natural history perspective this means if you don't practise your identification skills on a regular basis, they quickly become rusty. Of course, when I was identifying moths up in North Wales on a daily basis, sometimes weeks would pass without the need to consult my moth book to confirm any identifications, but as I was now out of practice, I suspected that I would probably need at least a couple of hours to even come up with a species list. But with the rest of the afternoon clear, I did indeed have the time and inclination, and so, lifting off the moth-trap lid, I dived in.

To ensure that the captured moths don't damage themselves inside the trap, the general protocol is to fill the bucket with empty egg boxes, meaning that rather than bashing themselves on the sides the moths will usually crawl into any one of numerous nooks and crannies. Another of the great joys of moth-ing is that you never know what you will find, and so each and every egg box lifted out in turn has the potential to hold something unusual or surprising.

It's not just moths that are attracted to light, and the first egg box extracted from the trap revealed one of the most immediately distinguishable of all our large beetles – the unfortunately named cockchafer. Also known as the May bug, as this is the month when it's first regularly recorded on the wing, this beetle has a black head and thorax, with brown sculptured wing cases and the most magnificent stalked antennae, which look like a pair of hairy eyebrows. The short-lived adults are occasionally seen noisily buzzing about their business on an early warm summer evening, so it is easy to forget that this beetle was once so abundant that it was considered a pest. With the adults feeding on the leaves of trees such as oak, and the 'C'-shaped grubs feeding on the roots of crops and other grasses, this species was nearly eradicated due to the extensive use of pesticides in the middle of the twentieth century, only making a comeback as a result of an improvement in the regulation of pest control in the 1980s.

The next egg box out brought my first moth and one that I instantly knew. The heart and dart moth is virtually a ubiquitous and abundant presence in most traps the length and breadth of Britain between mid-May and July, and having made the sweeping statement that moths aren't dull and boring; this one is well … fairly dull and boring. The forewings can vary in colour, but are usually a shade of brown and bear both a distinctive little dark dot (the heart) and a line (the dart) adjacent to each other. I would have been incredibly surprised if there were not more heart and darts tucked away in the trap, and would go as far to say that I'd bet my house (and garden) that this would be easily the most abundant species in the trap.

As the egg boxes were removed one by one the number of heart and darts grew, but the species tally also began to increase as well. Moths with wonderful names like the setaceous Hebrew character, beautiful golden Y, flame shoulder and willow beauty were soon identified and then promptly added to the list without too many identification issues. In fact I was pleased with how much I remembered, taking at least a dozen moths before an individual I either couldn't quite remember or hadn't seen before necessitated a quick look in 'Skinner' – *The Colour Identification Guide to the Moths of the British Isles* by Bernard Skinner, to the uninitiated, or the Bible, for all old-school moth-ers like me!

At least being familiar with the taxonomic family to which the moth belonged meant that I was in a position to quickly narrow it down, and in no time Skinner was able to confirm that I was indeed looking at my first lobster moth. Described as being found in the southern half of the UK, its distribution obviously didn't stretch quite as far as North Wales, so I'd never seen it before. It is quite a large, hairy moth with cream and brown rounded wings. Admittedly, it is not the most stunning moth, as the wings are designed to blend in perfectly with a tree trunk when it is at rest. Its caterpillar is, however, an entirely different story, and would surely take first prize in 'The Most Extraordinary-looking Larva Competition' as it resembles a miniature cooked lobster! As a naturalist, there are few more satisfying feelings than seeing something that you have never seen before, and in that moment the £350 I had spent on the trap felt like money well spent.

As I steadily worked my way to the bottom of the trap, in amongst the heart and darts I was also able to record several buff ermines, a clouded silver and a couple of large yellow underwings, amongst others. The final egg box provided one more surprise in the form of another moth, which I instantly recognised due to its fame in the world of genetics: the peppered moth. This moth is well known to any student of genetics or evolutionary biology as it is used as the classic textbook example of natural selection and evolution in process. Its use has not been without controversy, however, as Creationists have tried to argue that the evolutionary explanation behind the moth's genetics is fundamentally flawed.

The peppered moth exists in two genetically controlled forms (or morphs), a peppered (or black-and-white speckled) form and a melanic (or dark) form. Historically, the vast majority of the peppered moths encountered were of the peppered form, which meant they were camouflaged effectively when settled against the lichen-covered trees whilst resting during the day. However, due to the widespread pollution from the Industrial Revolution in England, many of the lichens died out, and the trees on which the moths settled became blackened with soot. This caused the peppered forms to die off due to the high levels of predation by birds as they stood out, while the melanic forms flourished due to their ability to melt into the background of the darkened trees. Since that time, and with improved environmental standards, the peppered form has again become more common.

This is not the place to wade into the pros and cons of whether or not this does indeed represent a convincing example of natural selection and evolution in action (and, for the record, I personally think it does). But the fact that my moth in the trap was indeed of the peppered form and the abundance of lichens, particularly on the ash and oak tree, told me all I needed to know about the high quality of the air around Chew Stoke. With all the moths identified, the final total represented 115 moths, of which 79 were heart and darts (meaning my house and garden would be safe!), consisting of 20 species, already close to twice the number of butterflies I'd identified since we moved in, and not bad for a night's work.

I came back from filming a couple of days later to find some botanical gifts in the back garden. True to her word, Lorraine had cleared out some of the plants from her own overcrowded pond and kindly placed them in polythene bags over the garden fence to help green up our pond too. Her very generous selection had included marsh marigold, water dock and a couple of oxygenating plants in the form of hornwort and crisped pondweed. In addition to the water forget-me-not and watercress gleaned from Christina's parents' pond, we now had a collection of plants fit to grace any wildlife pond.

Picking up Christina from work, who had managed to slope off early, we dashed home and cracked on with a big planting session, with my allocated job being to slot in the aquatic plants while Christina tackled the bed surrounding the pond. Having decided that the bed would look more impressive if marginally increased in size, Christina first stripped back a small section of turf, before mixing up the soil with a couple of bags of peat-free compost. In the extra space created, delphiniums, hostas and salvias were planted after their positions had been agreed by committee. The aquatic plants needed a slightly more exacting technique, in that they first needed to be placed in planting baskets lined with hessian, which was then packed with special aquatic compost (with especially low nutrient levels, designed to keep down algal blooms), before being covered with pea gravel and submerged to the correct depth. Doubtless also in amongst the mud attached to Lorraine's plants would have been all manner of aquatic creepy-crawlies which were now transported to our pond, too. In fact one the best ways quickly to populate a new pond with aquatic invertebrates is simply to take a bucket of muddy water from an established pond – you'd be amazed what's in there!

While we toiled away around the pond, we were also conscious that our every move was being monitored by the beady eyes of April, May and June. Having settled in incredibly well, our chickens had well and truly got used to their daily routine of being let out into the run within the coop first thing in the morning, as we cleaned out their roosting quarters and collected the egg booty, before being locked up last thing at night after they had put themselves to bed at dusk. This seemed to work well as a first measure, but it was clearly unsustainable in the long term as the run, where they spent all day pecking and scratching around, was quickly stripped to a rectangular patch of bare mud. This then necessitated the coop's near-constant movement to ensure the run below didn't end up becoming a quagmire. Ultimately we were keen to give them more room by cordoning off a larger area surrounding their coop with an electric fence, which would ensure that unwelcome intruders like 'Pencil Tail' wouldn't get any bright ideas.

As an interim measure we thought that maybe letting the girls roam free-range around the garden, as long as we were present to keep an eye on them, would both give the grass in the run brief respite and provide the chickens with a change of scenery, while crucially ensuring they didn't come to any mischief. So with more than a touch of trepidation we removed the side of the coop, and stood back to watch them emerge into our garden. After taking a full 15 minutes to realise they were actually free to leave the coop, first April, then May and finally June jumped up on to the rim and out. During the short space of time they'd been in our possession, their pecking order had just about established itself with April mostly ruling the roost and with poor old June bringing up the rear. With April being the smallest, it also seemed there must have been a strong element of brain beating brawn, as despite June being the largest she was also quite comfortably the daftest. Despite this clearly defined order of dominance, most of the time they seemed the best of friends, and as they wandered around the meadow demolishing the dandelion leaves and kicking leaves out of the way to reveal juicy grubs, they were never more than a couple of feet apart from one another.

Watching them behaving perfectly naturally, if I were of an anthropomorphic bent I would say they were blissfully happy, but irrespective of whether it is right and proper that professional naturalists like me should be attributing human emotions to animals, all I can tell you definitively is that Christina and I *were* blissfully happy. The decision to take on the monumental task of creating a wildlife garden to be proud of was, for the time being at least, paying off.

I was committed to working for most of Saturday filming the story behind the remarkable re-introduction of the large blue butterfly back into Britain, and so it wasn't until mid-afternoon that I arrived home. As I dropped off my bags indoors I could see Christina out in the garden and down on her haunches in front of the pond, staring so intently at something that she wasn't even aware I'd returned. On hearing the squeaky gate open as I came round to join her, she spun round on her heels beckoning for me to join her quickly. 'Are they egg-laying?' Christina said, pointing to a couple of large red damselflies perched on one of the leaves of the newly donated marsh marigold. 'They most certainly are,' I said, delighted to see the darker female curling the tip of her abdomen just under the surface of the water as she carefully attached her eggs to the submerged vegetation.

In common with many of the damselflies, egg-laying is rarely an act the female large red will carry out alone, as the male usually stays attached in tandem to ensure no other males will be given the opportunity sneakily to introduce their own sperm into the mix. The male was positioned in the typical guarding pose for this species, with his claspers (situated at the end of his abdomen) keeping her held firmly and securely just behind the head. Grasping her in this seemingly brutal way positioned him virtually bolt upright and in the best possible position to repel all borders should any interloper attempt to dilute his genetic destiny. This whole egg-laying procedure was thrilling for both of us to see in such a young pond, and with large red damselfly larvae usually taking two years before finally emerging as adults, this would definitely be something to look out for the spring after next.

Now that the chickens had tasted freedom, and as life beyond the coop was so much more exciting, they seemed desperate to be let loose on the garden again, so Christina let them out for a roam as we put our backs into a few necessary chores. We looked up periodically to check on them, and they seemed more than happy investigating every little corner of the garden as a tight-knit gang of three. My job was to suppress any weeds in the herbaceous border around the pond by putting bark chippings down, and looking up to check on them quickly after a period with my head down in the flowers, I realised I could only see April, who was next to the beech hedge by the playing field. The other two were nowhere to be seen.

Alerting Christina, I felt the rising panic as we immediately downed tools to investigate. 'They're never far apart, what's happened?' I wailed, as it became apparent that a mini-crisis was unfolding. Before properly looking for the other two, we first caught a now solitary April in a pincer movement up against the fence before placing her back in the coop. Forming an impromptu search party, we then split up to maximise coverage, but after what must have been a couple of minutes of rummaging around it seemed they had simply vanished. Checking the wood, I suddenly became fearful that a fox might have come in unseen and just snaffled them right under our noses, but surely we would have heard the commotion? As I searched down by the water, I then heard Christina issuing a muffled 'I can see May!' from back above me in the garden, and running back up the steps I was confronted with Christina's bottom sticking out of the beech hedgerow. I can only guess that her head was poking into the playing field …

No wonder April was down by the beech hedge; she'd obviously not seen the other two pop through the small hole at the bottom of the fence, through which we supposed the badgers and foxes entered our garden most nights. I climbed up and over the fence, and jumped down into the playing field, almost landing on a surprised June who had been wading through beech leaf litter with her massive feet, utterly oblivious to the consternation she'd caused, and a quick glance around spotted May some 50 yards away contemplating a turn on the swings and slide. It was only then that I finally realised that finding them wouldn't be even half the battle, for how in the devil's name would I actually succeed in capturing them? My mind spun back to the *Rocky II* boxing movie, where Rocky Balboa, played by Sylvester Stallone, has to try and catch a chicken as part of his training, and after initially failing famously calls himself 'a Kentucky Fried Idiot'! That was me. How could I have let this happen?

The most important task was first to get the chickens back into the garden. On my request, Christina threw over a long-handled brush and a hoe, as I decided to work on the premise that if I could just corral them to the beech hedge then perhaps I could gently cajole them back through the same hole they'd previously come through, leaving Christina to block it up. Like most animals, the chickens sensed something wasn't quite right and picked up on my anxious vibes, meaning they wouldn't let me anywhere near them. Even though my two props might have made me look just a touch like Edward Scissorhands, they worked surprisingly effectively as I ushered them both back to the hedge and, eventually, after a bit of a cat and mouse game, back through the hole. Climbing back over the fence, by now both chickens were obviously scared witless, maybe suspecting that they were for the pot, and they had both hidden under the euonymus shrub behind the pond.

Not wanting to freak them out, a brilliant idea suddenly came to me – an occasion that unfortunately happens all too infrequently for my liking – as I suggested to Christina that we retrieve from the garage the huge role of chicken-wire fencing that had originally been used to demarcate the garden from the wooded bank when we had first moved in. By using this fencing to create a large 'V', with the coop situated inside the base of that 'V' and the open ends either side of their hiding place, and based on the principles of a Heligoland trap, we were then able to shove the two chickens out from underneath their hiding place below the shrub and force them down the ever more narrow sides of fence line until they had two options – to try and charge past Christina and me, or to hop into the sanctuary of the coop – fortunately they chose the latter!

Having already formed an emotional bond with the chickens in such a short space of time, we would have been gutted and also slightly embarrassed to have to return to Ellie's Chicken Emporium after just a couple of weeks for replacements. To wilfully misquote none other than Oscar Wilde: 'to lose one chicken may be regarded as misfortune, to lose both looks like carelessness'. To avoid a ridiculous fracas like that again, we would need to buy and install that electric fence – and soon!

With more than enough emotional and physical energy expended for one day, we decided instead to put the kettle on and our feet up, as we were determined to spend the last couple of hours of daylight left enjoying the garden. The bird feeders as usual were still busily entertaining all manner of juvenile birds, but for once attention-wise they were eclipsed by the pond, which in a short space of time was really beginning to reward us.

Having already seen large red damselflies egg-laying, we were then treated to the second species of the day, which had obviously made up its mind that our pond was also of sufficient merit to be the repository of its eggs. With the fat, flattened shape to its abdomen, the broad-bodied chaser is an instantly identifiable dragonfly. It is usually the males, with their powder-blue abdomens, that are the more common sight around shallow, sunny garden ponds in early summer, where they will often take up a territory, and are also well-known for colonising new sites. But in this case there was no male to be seen, as just the brown-bodied female was present. Her way of egg-laying was also completely different to that of the large red damsels, and involved hovering just an inch or so above the water, periodically tapping the end of her abdomen onto the surface, which caused the eggs to be washed out. These eggs are surrounded by a mini-capsule of jelly that immediately absorbs water on contact, causing each one to swell and become sticky, before floating off and sticking to the surrounding plants.

In addition to the egg-laying chaser, we also spotted the omnipresent pond skaters, a number of aquatic beetles, which also must have recently flown in, and hundreds of tiny *Chironomid* midge larvae, which would double-up as food for the many aquatic predators waiting further up the food chain. From a 'geological' standpoint the pond was not even five minutes old, but from an ecological perspective it was already close to being a fully functioning ecosystem. By simply digging a hole in the ground and filling it with water we were actually attracting a whole range of wildlife that otherwise wouldn't have thought our garden worthy of even a second glance. Maybe the new mantra for every gardener who loves aquatic wildlife should be: 'dig it and they will come!'

We had planned Sunday to be a big day in the garden, but we were beaten by the wet weather. Having had the most glorious spring, the summer was already turning into a damp squib; and with the rain coming down like stair-rods we opted to stay in and watch the garden from the dry instead. Although the squirrels had been largely thwarted in their attempts to pilfer from the two main bird feeders, they were still an active presence, and given the weather we didn't have the heart to chase away the squirrel that had managed to get through the anti-squirrel bars on the ground feeder.

The day was broken up by a visit for lunch from my good pal Ed the ringer. He dashed out in the rain for a quick garden inspection, and he couldn't believe how much had changed since he'd last been ringing birds here in March. Barely able to see the feeders, let alone any birds feeding on them, we decided that an easier way to get our natural history fix might be to retire instead to the garage and empty the moth trap I had set the night before.

One of the other fascinating elements to moth-trapping is that throughout the year there is a constantly changing cast of characters as most species have a defined flight period during which they will be attracted to the light, and when this passes it means that the adult moths (or imagos) will not then be seen again until their allotted slot the following year. This is why, for example, the March moth is most commonly seen in March, the September thorn in September and the December moth in, you've guessed it, December. Even in the space of the few days since I had first put the trap out, the species composition caught had already changed subtly. For example, one of the very first moths out was a moth called an ingrailed clay, which looked a really fresh specimen, and according to Skinner was only on the wing from late June through to August.

Because the weather had been foul during the previous evening, the total moth catch, in terms of both numbers of individuals and number of species, was much lower than before, with the number of heart and darts barely reaching double figures. It was, however, still capable of throwing up a few surprises, the main one being my first hawk-moth for the garden. To the uninitiated, the hawk-moths are the Jumbo Jet, Ferrari and Gucci of the moth-world, all rolled into one. For starters, they are almost all an impressive size, and with beautifully aerodynamic swept-back wings they are also patently sleek flying machines too. Finally, the livery on their wings and body often contains a glamorous variety of psychedelic colours and patterns that would eclipse any airline carrier I know. Having seen the elephant, poplar, and eyed hawk-moth in abundance up in North Wales, I knew immediately it was not one of those, and a quick glance in Skinner revealed it to be a lime hawk-moth. It was a species of only middling size and beauty for the group but with a far more localised distribution in the southern half of England. It might still have been raining outside, but for me the day had just got a whole lot brighter – it had been a long time since I'd seen a new hawk-moth!

With work frenetic, it wasn't until the following Saturday that I had my next opportunity to enjoy the garden. Usually I like to try and get up as early as possible to immerse myself in what I consider to be the best part of the day, but as it had been a tough week, on this occasion I immediately took Christina up on her kind offer to feed and water the chickens, which gave me an extra 20 minutes in bed. Comfortable and warm, I must have dozed straight off again, only coming round on hearing Christina's voice talking to me with what sounded, in my befuddled state of mind, to be a sense of high urgency. 'There's been a murder,' she said, seemingly half-shocked and a touch thrilled too. 'Not the chickens!' I said, and, by now fully awake, I must admit that I was ever so slightly relieved when I heard that the innocent victim was not in fact April, May or June but a poor hedgehog instead. I then felt guilty for having instinctively put, in my own mind, a stronger emotional attachment to the lives of my chickens as opposed to that of a declining UK mammal which I had only seen in the garden once before. Maybe in that instant I had become more of a smallholder than I ever thought possible.

I got dressed quickly and went down to inspect the crime scene and I have to say it was fairly gruesome. Right in the middle of the meadow was a dead adult hedgehog that had patently been attacked and then uncurled before being killed, going on to suffer the indignity of having its back end partly eaten. Now I'm not an expert on the timings as to when rigor mortis sets in on dead hedgehogs, but the fact that it was still limp would have suggested the murder had taken place in the last few hours. The list of suspects was also somewhat short – in fact, it only had one name on it. Dogs were never in my garden, and neither a cat nor a fox was able to inflict this kind of damage. The only weapons capable of ripping through a hedgehog's prickly defences belonged to a badger. I suddenly understood Christina's emotions; it *was* both shocking and slightly thrilling to think that this titanic battle to the death had been played out in our own back garden whilst we were innocently sleeping just yards away.

To rationalise the phrase 'slightly thrilled' I have just carefully used in relation to my feelings surrounding the hedgehog's death, I do so only because for a hedgehog to be killed by its *natural* predator the badger is, ecologically speaking, perfectly natural. Badgers have been predating on hedgehogs for thousands of years, just as a hedgehog in turn will eat hundreds, if not thousands, of slugs in its lifetime. This also explains why I would also be 'more than slightly thrilled' if I were to see a sparrowhawk ploughing through my garden and successfully catching a blue tit – as that's what sparrowhawks do for a living. In fact, the precise reason why blue tits have such large broods is to counter the fact that a high proportion will be taken by predators like the sparrowhawk. Imagine, for a minute, if all sparrowhawks were to be instantly terminated tomorrow, we could conceivably have a plague of blue tits on our hands in just a couple of breeding seasons! These examples illustrate Tennyson's famous comment 'nature, red in tooth and claw'. This very phrase was then used much later by the celebrated evolutionary biologist Richard Dawkins in his book *The Selfish Gene* to summarise the behaviour of all living things in relation to Charles Darwin's theory concerning the survival of the fittest.

What does make me angry are the acts of deliberate cruelty to these animals, such as death by badger baiting or indeed the idiotic student in Birmingham who thought it would be funny to microwave a hedgehog. All the animals killed in these ways are creatures that have died *unnatural* deaths, and they contrast sharply with the hedgehog's death in my back garden, which, whilst undeniably untimely for the hedgehog itself, in no way could ever be said to have been unnatural.

With the final weekend of the month upon us and the nights once again drawing in with the passing of midsummer's day, there was still much we were keen to achieve for our half-term report. The first important job was to get the electric fence we had just purchased up and running. It had arrived, courtesy of the internet, a couple of days previously, and I had found the instructions so bamboozling that I suspected the only person technically competent enough to install it would have been an engineer or an electrician. Fortunately Christina's brother, Jon, was a physics graduate who was now working in research and development for a rather well-known vacuum cleaning company, and as such certainly knew the difference between AC and DC. Having been tempted to come around the night before with the offer of a curry, beers and a bed in which to sleep both off, Jon was also aware of the maxim 'there is no such thing as a free curry'. So after a delicious breakfast of smoked salmon and scrambled eggs, the latter produced by April, May and June, Jon got to work earning his board and lodging.

As befits a man whose brain seems to be wired differently to mine, Jon understood the instructions perfectly, and had the fence up and electrified in less than an hour. The fence formed a rectangle, and it ran from the corner of the garage close to the water butt and down the garden for around seven yards, before turning at a right angle to link up with the communal fence dividing our garden from Marjory and Dennis's. The 35 square yards that would now be the chickens' extended quarters and entire universe had also enclosed the compost bins and roughly two-thirds of the mixed-species hedgerow that Jon and I had planted back in mid-March, which was now greening up nicely.

Christina came to join us for the Grand Opening Ceremony, and we decided that fanfares, speeches and champagne were probably slightly over the top, and so without further ado I hopped over the fence, carefully ensuring not to electrocute my undercarriage in the process, before removing the side panel and joining the others back over on the other side to watch the proceedings. Almost immediately alpha chicken April was out of the coop, realising she could make good her exit via the ladder which led to the loft. Both the other two were desperate to follow their glorious leader into the enclosure, but instead of stopping to think for a second, they preferred to run around the coop panicking that they were missing out, like the two daft brushes that they were. Eventually, more by luck than design, May stumbled upon the entrance and was out in a flash, followed by June who, whilst certainly not the smartest, having copied May exactly, had at least elevated herself above the status of 'congenital idiot'. Once they were all out they looked as pleased as punch with themselves as they wandered around exploring their new area, and accepting the fence as the boundary. Doubtless they too would reduce this section of the meadow into bare mud over time, but for now they were in seventh heaven!

We thanked Jon for his sterling work, and we let him get back to enjoying the rest of his weekend while we took an al fresco lunch with some of the carrots, beetroot and salad leaves from our own raised bed. In my opinion food does indeed taste so much better outdoors, and if I could add to this sentiment, it's even tastier if it is from produce you have lovingly grown yourself! To our relief the weather seemed to have at last perked up after a couple of pretty wet weeks and the sun on our backs certainly felt fine as we tucked in.

Our dining table was positioned close to the pond, and it was amazing how quickly the birds coming to the feeders became both accustomed to and accepting of our presence, so I barely had any need to hold my binoculars in one hand while the fork was in the other. With juvenile birds still dominating the feeders it was noticeable that large numbers of immature greenfinch had joined the food-fest. Given that the numbers of greenfinch have been dropping nationally as a result of trichomonosis, the large number of young birds I was seeing meant that, at least locally, it had been a good year. I was also surprised that it was only now that I had begun to see large greenfinch numbers in the garden when I had been observing juvenile tits for at least three or four weeks. Whether this was down to greenfinch laying their clutches later than the tits, or because of the possible extended care greenfinch parents offered their fledglings, was hard to say. One thing was for sure; watching my garden birds so intimately was certainly leaving me with more questions than answers.

With my focus on the feeders, Christina's gaze must have been elsewhere as I felt a fork tap me on the arm, snapping me immediately out of my quandary just in time to hear her say, 'Isn't that a newt?' Looking down to the pond, I just caught sight of what seemed to be a newt swimming down and out of view, which needed immediate investigation! Barely a second later and I was down on all fours with my nose virtually touching the water ... this could potentially be our very first amphibian in the garden! For somebody who is generally terribly impatient by nature, the one area where I seem to have developed the patience of Job is when I'm *actually* waiting for nature. I'm basically one of those irritating people who starts to tut and sigh when I have to wait in a queue for anything more than a couple of minutes, but if I'm in a hide waiting for a bird to turn up then I can adopt the attitude of a Zen Buddhist. Of course, newts, being amphibians, breathe air and so have to surface at some point for a gulp before heading back down below, but sure enough, as I lay there on my belly waiting, I noticed what looked like a female smooth newt swimming up to the surface to take a lungful of air, before disappearing below the duckweed. Our pond had newts!

On reflection, given that Andy and Lorraine's pond, situated less than ten yards away, already had newts; and being an animal that is not just mobile but spends most of the year either feeding or hibernating away from the water, it would have been disappointing if the summer had passed without any newts having stumbled across our pond at some point. But this still didn't detract one iota from how exciting a find it was, and it re-confirmed for me how right I had been to insist on a 'no fish' policy in the pond in the first place. As I continued watching from my pond skater's eye view of the water, I saw a second newt coming to the surface, which, being a male, confirmed my initial identification that they were indeed smooth,

rather than the closely related palmate newts. The females and juveniles of our two common newt species look very similar, and it is the males that can easily be differentiated. Despite being close to the end of the breeding season, I could still clearly see the male's wavy crest running the length of his body and tail, which in conjunction with the spotted flanks are so diagnostic of 'smoothies'.

It was from this low profile that I also realised that we would now be able to add another species of damselfly to our list, as buzzing around with a few large reds were a couple of common blue damselflies. This is generally a species that is at its peak in mid-July, so late June was still quite early in the season for this species, and it was no surprise that one of the individuals low down on a shrub to the side of the pond was still at the teneral stage. Dragons and damsels are often labelled as 'tenerals' immediately after emergence; at this stage they are still sexually immature and easily identified by the drab colouration of their bodies and shiny appearance of their wings. With the maturation process taking a week or more before completion, during this time they often assume a low profile away from the pond itself as this tends to be the arena for the aggressive, sexually active males and no place for a young 'un not ready for gladiatorial combat!

There are a number of 'blue damselflies' that look virtually identical to the inexperienced odonatist, and the key to the successful identification amongst this sometimes-difficult group is to look at the second abdominal segment. Damselflies, like all insects, are composed of a head, thorax (or body) and abdomen (often inaccurately called the tail). The long, thin abdomen in damselflies is made up of nine or ten segments, each of which can be numbered, with the first being closest to the thorax and the ninth or tenth situated at the end of the abdomen. In the case of the common blue, the second abdominal segment is characterised by a club-shaped mark 'Ω', as opposed to the 'U' shape on the equally abundant and closely related azure damselfl. It's easy when you know how!

Without a cloud in the sky the Sunday promised to be glorious, and with uninterrupted sunshine looking more than likely, it also threatened to be the hottest day of the year so far. With such a promising day ahead I was loathe to spend too much time in bed and so was up and out at 6am to carry out my daily task of cleaning out and feeding the chickens. As I opened the back door, my presence immediately flushed a whole raft of wild vandals out of the garden, which up until my arrival had been doing exactly as they pleased. Quickly noted before they flew off were a magpie standing in the hanging water bath to reach the fat balls, squirrels both in and around the ground feeder and a flock of around a dozen jackdaws guzzling the food in the open chicken pen.

After sorting out the girls, I got on with mowing the lawns as Christina chopped back and attempted to re-shape the euonymus behind the pond. With the lawn looking suitably smart and the grass clippings placed into the compost bin, I then went to help Christina in her valiant attempt to eradicate the heinous bindweed which had crept in under the fence from Andy and Lorraine's and had slowly begun to envelop this corner of the garden. Topping a 2009 *Gardeners' World* poll as 'England's Worst Weed', this really is one plant that you don't want to get in your borders, as it not only invades, occupies and overtakes but is also devilishly difficult to eradicate. Even if just a few remnants of its thick, white roots are left in the soil, the plant will use these as a starting point from which to recommence its plan for garden domination – so despite my aforementioned fondness for weeds this was indeed one that would have to go.

Down on our hands and knees raking and sieving the soil to remove the infernal roots was hard work in the full sun, so regular refreshment breaks were the order of the day. Because it was so warm, the garden was positively humming with hoverflies and butterflies, and in addition to the large whites fraternising a whole variety of flowers I was really pleased to be able to add meadow brown butterfly to my garden list, which I saw actually in the meadow itself! Like most of the 'brown' butterflies, female meadow browns lay their eggs on a variety of grasses, and as the lawnmower had been kept well away from the meadow, allowing everything to grow unfettered, the grasses had returned the compliment by attracting an insect into the garden which we just wouldn't have recorded otherwise. Once again I was over the moon with how simple changes in the way we were managing the garden were having a positive impact on the wildlife.

Using the stones surrounding the pond as stepping-stones to get back round to where we were carrying out the bindweed eradication work, a sixth sense suddenly told me to stop stock-still in my tracks and look down – and what a good job. Just one more step and my size-nine steel-toe-capped work boots would have squashed a small common frog as it hopped out of the flower border on the way to the pond! In the space of the weekend we had recorded our first two amphibian species for the garden, which by any definition was a result. Crouching down for a better look, it patently had some way to go before reaching the same dimensions adult common frogs are capable of achieving, and as such was still some way off reaching sexual maturity. But just by having got this far, the frog was already in the incredibly lucky top one per cent of tadpoles that had avoided predation to reach metamorphosis – and it didn't have bad taste in garden ponds either!

By now there was so much going on in the garden that I could barely get any work done due to being constantly distracted by the wild delights the garden had to offer. The pond in particular was endlessly fascinating and a constant hive of activity, with hundreds of dark-coloured flies constantly landing momentarily on the surface before taking off again. What they were, or what they were doing, I simply had no idea. Another female broad-bodied chaser was egg-laying again with her patented 'dipping abdomen' technique, and with a number of large red and common blue damsels either egg-laying or holding territory above the pond it was difficult to know where to look. And then it suddenly became easy – as out of the corner of my eye I spotted what was for me quite comfortably the insect of the year.

During certain summers a rash of reports will suddenly come in of people recording hummingbirds in their gardens. I'm afraid to say these are all erroneous, as hummingbirds are a specialised group of (admittedly lovely) birds that are confined to the Americas some 3,200 miles away on the other side of the Atlantic, and to my knowledge not a single hummingbird has ever arrived in the UK under its own steam. To be fair, the hummingbird hawk-moth's habit of hovering in front of flowers as it sips the nectar, does confusingly lend it much more than just a passing resemblance to the hummingbirds themselves: in fact the moth's feeding technique is so similar that this is how it got its name. So this was not just any old moth, it was one of the small clique of moths that prefers the daytime and additionally is a species that is only ever seen out on sunny days. It is also a member of the fabulously charismatic hawk-moth family and in all likelihood may well have flown to our garden all the way from southern Europe or even Africa.

Christina and I watched transfixed as it unfurled the most enormous proboscis, which was then deployed to extract the nectar from the delphiniums and salvias we had only very recently planted at the back of the pond border, all the while hovering on the spot like a little hummingbird. Who says moths are dull, boring and brown?

JULY

BIRDS, BATS AND BUGS BY THE BUCKET-LOAD

The wildlife was getting to be a bit of a problem. Or maybe I should clarify and say it was mainly the magpies and jackdaws that were the issue. Getting up for my early morning appointment to clean out, feed and water the chickens, I once again found myself flushing a couple of magpies and around a dozen jackdaws out of the chicken coop, which prior to my rude interruption had patently been guzzling down beak-fulls of the chicken's food. With the electric fence installed we were able to leave the coop's side panel off all the time, which enabled April, May and June to move between the coop and the enclosure whenever they wanted. However, with the system patently being abused by interlopers, procedural changes would have to occur.

I was keen, wherever possible, not to practise a form of 'wildlife chauvinism' in the garden, whereby, for example, blue tits were more welcome than magpies, but just standing back and giving the crow family free rein in the garden would also have tipped the balance the other way in their favour and to the detriment of the other wildlife. Additionally, operating this 'open house' policy in the long term simply wouldn't be financially viable, as I wanted to attract the wildlife to my garden, but not at the expense of being eaten out of house and home!

Early morning was a lovely time to be outside, once the chickens were sorted and while waiting for Christina to come and join me, and I didn't need any encouragement to spend a quiet 15 minutes watching the garden gear up for another day. In the space of five months since our move to the country, I had changed from someone who used to quickly shuffle through our old garden, embarrassed at the state it was in, to somebody who couldn't have been happier at the knowledge that a full day in the garden lay ahead. Staring dreamily ahead, my senses suddenly came sharply back to the present as a bird that somehow looked just a little bit different flew from the wooded bank to the birch tree and landed on the trunk some ten yards from my where I was seated. I was aware that very few bird species in Britain made a full-time living by gleaning the trunks of trees for their insect prey, so my list of possible candidates quickly began to narrow. The clincher then came a split-second later when it began moving up the tree in jerky fashion, spiralling around the trunk, as it disappeared around the back only to reappear from around the other side slightly higher up.

In Britain there are only really two bird species that scour tree trunks for a living, and even if we totally disregard for a minute what they look like, they can easily be distinguished by their respective idiosyncratic feeding habits. The nuthatch is the only British bird capable of descending a tree trunk head first and often seems to spend more time upside down than the right way up. This technique contrasts with that of the treecreeper, which prefers a head-up strategy, with the direction of travel only ever being upwards. So pronounced is this behaviour with treecreepers that on running out of trunk they will then usually fly off to the base of a neighbouring tree, to repeat the same 'bottom up' strategy all over again. As I watched the bird, it was just like it had read the 'Treecreeper Manual', as the moment it reached the top of the birch it flew straight back to the sanctuary of the wooded bank undoubtedly to find another tree to ascend. To have attracted a *bonafide* specialist woodland bird into the garden was really thrilling, and maybe it was time to stop calling the bottom of the garden 'the wooded bank' and time to start calling it 'the wood', as that's what the treecreeper obviously thought it was!

Christina and I had decided the morning's priority would be to tackle the beech hedge that ran alongside our border with the playing field. Although we loosely termed it a 'hedge', it was really no more than a long, neglected line of saplings that hadn't been touched for years and so, rather than filling out to provide an effective screen of the playing field, which had obviously been the original plan, the young trees had instead shot skywards like lanky, unkempt teenagers. Despite hundreds of miles of hedgerows having been ruthlessly grubbed up over the last thirty years, and many more in terrible condition due to being slowly flailed to death (the botanical equivalent of death by a thousand cuts), I have still yet to visit a country anywhere in the world with more statuesque hedges than can be seen in Britain. Of all the different types of hedges, in my opinion, there are none finer than that of a beautiful mature beech hedge. At their best they are works of art; resembling vibrant green walls in the summer, before being transformed into shields of shimmering copper from the autumn onwards. Acting as living walls, these hedges not only lend gardens an element of structure throughout the year, but offer privacy from prying eyes too, which is precisely the reason why they're so attractive to nesting and roosting birds and able to offer the perfect tucked-away location for a hedgehog to pass the winter unmolested. If our hedge were ultimately able to achieve these lofty ambitions, however, it would need a lot of help.

Like the wisteria along the garage, which Christina and her father had successfully managed to turn around, the only proper course of action had to be equally brutal surgery. So armed with loppers, we set about cutting all the saplings back to a height of around six feet, trusting that by removing the apical meristems or growing points this would force the production of side shoots, theoretically leading to thicker growth. Like all these types of jobs, the hedge appeared far worse initially, and after over an hour's work it looked like all we had achieved was a large mess and a bizarre array of stunted and disfigured saplings. It would not be until the end of the year, when we checked for lateral buds, that we would know whether it had been worth the effort.

Rather than helping with the unglamorous task of reducing the brash to a decent, disposable size, Christina promptly decided that a far more pressing concern was to spend some money down at the garden centre on plants we barely had room for, leaving muggins, as per usual, to do the tidying up. Having said this, there's something I quite like about the unglamorous, grunt-type jobs; and so on this occasion didn't feel like I was getting the short straw.

Taking a break for some liquid refreshment and a quick stock-take of the pond, the newts were once again showing well, but it was noticeable over the last few days that a large algal bloom had built up in the pond, almost certainly as a result of nutrients leaching out of the potted plants that I had recently placed in. Removing the worst of the algae by hand wasn't particularly difficult, and I was able quickly to clear at least a couple of sections of the pond, but I was also aware that this was hardly a long-term solution. Ultimately what I was aiming for was the creation of a much more natural equilibrium, with my hopes being pinned on algae-grazing snails and oxygenating plants to be key elements in redressing the balance. However, it was far from doom and gloom with the pond, and if someone had said to me that I would already have recorded common frog and smooth newt, and seen egg-laying from three species of dragonfly and damselfly barely a month after adding the water, then I simply wouldn't have believed them.

I was just about to turn my attentions back to the diminishing pile of brash when I noticed that one of the large, flat river stones surrounding the pond was covered in small fragments of snail shell. I could clearly see that they were the remnants of the shells of both the common garden and brown-lipped snail. The former species can often be the curse of many a gardener attempting to grow fruit, vegetables or tender bedding plants. It is also the one snail encountered during garden tidy-ups due to its habit of sheltering in various nooks and crannies, such as behind flowerpots, during dry weather or through the winter. Here, though, rather than causing havoc amongst Christina's carefully assembled plants, these particular snails had come to a sticky end at the hands, or should I say beak, of our resident song thrush, with the rock doubling up as a thrush's anvil.

It was a totally unexpected but superb discovery. Seeing a song thrush deftly dismantle a snail's armour should be labelled as one of the great wildlife garden spectacles and something I have only been lucky enough to see on one previous occasion. Each song thrush often has its own favourite stone where it likes to conduct business, and by grasping the shell's lip, the thrush then smashes it against the surface of the stone until the shell succumbs under the constant barrage of blows and the bird is able to winkle out its reward. Like the hedgehog, whose murder we had pieced together from the evidence, this was just another example indicating that Christina and I were probably observing only a tiny percentage of the daily action occurring in our garden. Life and death struggles were obviously commonplace – it was a jungle out there!

Aware of the limited space now available in all of the beds, Christina had shown a laudable restraint at the garden centre, having confined her purchases to just a couple of beautiful white echinaceas. Then I did something that, in retrospect, I wasn't terribly proud of. By using her impulsive purchases in a Machiavellian and, if I'm honest, not entirely honourable manner, I seized upon this as the perfect time to come clean that I had also bought a bat detector when I'd acquired the moth trap. It was a tactical masterstroke on my behalf, as Christina was hardly in a position to criticise my extravagant purchase, having just made a couple of her own. Feeling guilty at my underhand tactics, and by way of an indirect apology, I suggested that if I cooked the evening meal then maybe she'd like to join me dining outside whilst we trialled the new bat detector for the first time. What can I say? I have a very forgiving girlfriend!

Although I'm certainly no Jamie Oliver, I suppose my cooking could be described as being 'half-decent', and so while I prepared my signature dish of chilli con carne, Christina uncorked the wine and set the table down by the pond. Us Brits often love to moan about the weather, but there really is very little to beat a warm, balmy summer evening. Also, one of the best things about where we lived was that most of the time the 'sound-scape' really was largely free of motorbikes, planes, ambulances and jack-hammers that are the backing-track to city life these days. Well before we moved here, the good people of Chew Stoke had also previously voted against street lights, deciding that they would be able to manage with a torch just as effectively at night, when necessary. So as we tucked in, the only background noises audible beyond our quiet chat were that of the soft 'chook-chook' alarm call of the blackbird preparing for bed, a few half-hearted bars of a robin's song and the quiet hiss of the bat detector lying alongside my glass of wine, as darkness descended, and we waited for the first bat of the evening to make an appearance.

Bat detectors are very clever bits of kit that give us the most marvellous insight into a world that would otherwise be quite literally well off our radar – the high-frequency world of bat echolocation. As the bats emerge from their roosts at dusk to hunt for insects through the night, echolocation gives them the ability to navigate and feed at a time when there are abundant insects out and about, less competition for this food and also hardly any predators around to prey on the bats themselves. Working similar to sonar, echolocating bats make calls as they fly, and by listening to the strength and time for the echoes to return they are able to build up a sonic map of their surroundings. Personally, the easiest way I have found to understand this is if you think that we humans create 'pictures' of our surroundings with light-waves, which are received by the eye and interpreted by the brain; the bat effectively does exactly the same thing, only with soundwaves. These returning soundwaves are gathered by the ear (or more specifically a flap of skin in the ear called the tragus), before being organised by the brain again into a constantly changing three-dimensional map of astonishing accuracy. Human beings are generally only able to hear across a range of frequencies from 20Hz (cycles per second) to 20,000kHz, and bat calls are usually pitched at far too high a frequency for us to hear naturally – and so this is where the bat detector comes in.

Now to be honest I don't understand exactly how these detectors work, and if you require more technical detail I'm afraid you might have to consult a sound engineer, but in a nutshell bat detectors shift the bats' ultrasound signals down to an audible frequency that we can pick up. With all our bats echolocating at frequencies varying between 20kHz and 115kHz and each species tending to have its own specific frequency range to suit its environment and prey type, this should theoretically mean that by tuning the detector into a particular frequency (like you would with the tuning dial on a radio) we could identify which bat was flying past. In practice, however, with the exception of the lesser horseshoe, which has the highest frequency calls (between 105 and 115kHz), and the noctule bat, which echolocates at the other end of the spectrum (20 to 25kHz), most of our 16 other species call in the congested middle-range wavelengths of between 40 and 60kHz. So this essentially means that identifying the species, at least with the type of detector I have, is often little more than guesswork. So rather than telling you precisely which bat you are looking at, perhaps bat detectors are best used for simply alerting you to their close proximity, so you know exactly when to look up!

The best time for bats to emerge is generally shortly after sunset, which this evening was due at 9.21pm, and this gave us more than enough time to finish the chilli, polish off at least half the wine and run inside for a couple of sweaters to keep midge bites down before the action would start. Suddenly, at 9.32pm, the detector kicked into action, picking up its first bat, which was interpreted as a series of chaotic clicks and wet-sounding slaps. As we both looked skywards there was still enough residual light for us to pick up the bat's silhouette, as what looked to me like one of our smaller species traced an arc across the sky, passing directly over our heads before heading down towards the brook.

As we watched the bat pass by, a quick one-handed fiddle of the frequency dial on the detector, the other hand being already occupied with a glass of wine, seemed to indicate that the clearest and least distorted signal had been produced at around 55kHz, which, when combined with the bat's dimensions and habitat preference, suggested the most likely candidate was a soprano pipistrelle. Most people think of the pipistrelle as the archetypal small bat, and with pipistrelles being considered the commonest and most widespread of all our bat species, up until 1999 they would probably have been correct in their assumption. It was not until the mid-1990s that bat researchers made a remarkable discovery, realising that the pipistrelle bat was not one but in fact two distinct species. With both the bats looking virtually identical in the hand, they could be separated by analysing their calls, with the original species, now called the common pipistrelle, echolocating principally at around 45kHz, as opposed to the new bat, the soprano pipistrelle, which was recorded a few octaves higher at 55kHz.

With the two species so difficult to separate, however, it is only now becoming clear from extensive survey work that the soprano pipistrelle seems to be as widespread as its closely related cousin, tending to favour feeding in wetland habitats, and along tree and hedge lines – all features which were so proudly incorporated in our garden. Quickly on the heels of the first bat, the detector then suddenly picked up another individual, and as we listened to the series of chaotic clicks, they were briefly interrupted by what sounded like someone blowing a raspberry right in the middle – a feeding buzz! This wonderful sound is always a bonus to hear and indicates that the bat has just honed in on something edible. As the bat closes in on, say, a mosquito or moth that comes up on its radar, it suddenly massively increases the number of calls by up to 200 per second, and, by listening to the rapidly returning echoes, is then able to gain a sufficiently accurate picture to snatch the moving target out of the air. This feeding buzz indicated that the bats were not just using the garden as a conduit from A to B, but were also feeding above it too: yet more justification that the insects in the meadow we had created would not just be useful for the flowers that needed pollinating.

As peak bat emergence began, we enjoyed a ten- or fifteen-minute period during which the bat detector emitted a constant cacophony as what seemed like two or three bats at a time of possibly the same species could be heard, and sometimes seen, whizzing around our heads. Then the sound on the bat detector instantly changed, to a much louder but distorted call. Quickly retuning to around 25kHz, we were treated to 'chip-chop, chip-chop' – a familiar sound which I always think resembles the noise a guitarist would make whilst slapping out a funky base line, and is diagnostic of one of our largest bats, the noctule. Powerfully built and with a wingspan of about 14 inches, the noctule is an impressive beast, and as we looked up into the gloom we could just make out its long wings as it crossed our garden at some height and speed. This B-52 bomber of the bat world was after the bigger beetles and moths, preferring to leave the small fry to the diminutive pipistrelles!

As darkness descended the bats slowly began to disperse into the surrounding countryside to feed, and the detector eventually fell silent. Two new species of mammal for the garden was an excellent return for the evening's work, and all we had to do now was to find our way back to the house. Without either streetlights or a torch and after half a bottle of wine each, this was not as easy as it sounded. Where was that bloody pond now?!

Accepting Christina's offer of a lie-in after a few busy days of filming, I gratefully closed my eyes again as she went to clean out April, May and June. She couldn't have been gone more than a few minutes before I heard her trying to rouse me. 'We've got a problem,' she said, 'the eggs have been smashed!' 'What?' I replied, having heard perfectly well what she'd said, but opting to use my selective hard of hearing as a stalling tactic whilst I desperately tried to engage my brain. Apparently Christina had walked out into the garden, flushing a small flock of jackdaws out of the coop, with the chickens standing around as mere bystanders while their food was

systematically raided. On this one occasion, the proceedings had then taken a sinister turn. When she opened up the coop, as per our daily ritual, to remove the eggs and mess, Christina had been shocked to find two of the three eggs smashed inside the laying loft, with part of one of the shells having been disdainfully tossed down the ladder steps and into the run below. Losing some of the girls' food could be taken on the chin as an acceptable loss, but not the eggs.

Throwing on some clothes I immediately went out to investigate. Just occasionally, the girls laid eggs with particularly thin shells, and, if this were the case, the chickens themselves could conceivably have accidentally broken them, but the shells looked perfectly normal. Furthermore, they'd been smashed and eaten in the loft rather than removed from the coop intact, indicating something with a beak and feathers rather than teeth and fur. And because the eggs are usually laid early each morning, the culprit was an early riser rather than a nocturnal visitor. It had also taken quite some nerve waltzing straight up the ladder and into the dark confines of the loft to smash the eggs in full view of the chickens, all three of which obviously knew exactly who had perpetrated the crime, but for obvious reasons were unable to give vital witness statements.

If I were a betting man, I would say it was 'odds on' that the jackdaws were guilty, as only recently they had been caught red-handed for the lesser crime of pinching the chicken's food. However, it wasn't an entirely open-and-shut case, as magpies were also regularly reported in the garden just after dawn, and this is a species which, let's not forget, is also renowned for being an opportunistic predator of eggs and chicks in the wild. Irrespective as to who was actually guilty, the only cast-iron solution to ensure it would only be us that continued to enjoy the eggs, rather than the wildlife, would be to once again lock up the chickens each night.

I trudged back inside for a shower, and I must still have been staring absentmindedly out of the bathroom window when I saw an animated flash of yellow and green in the meadow. I dashed out of the bathroom and around the corner down to the landing-hall window, where my binoculars were now permanently stowed. My initial guess had been correct: it was our second species of wood-pecker! Having already recorded the great spotted woodpecker on at least a couple of previous occasions in the oak tree, I had been hopeful that a green woodpecker might make a visit at some point, especially since Christina had told me that she thought she had heard their characteristic yodelling 'yaffle' when I had been away filming the previous week. Of course, with typical birding snobbery, I had assumed she had been mistaken, but not for the first time had I underestimated how knowledgeable she had become.

I called her up from the kitchen, and we watched with fascina-tion as the green woodpecker hopped around the meadow enjoying the early morning sunshine. Through the binoculars, the absence of a red streak running through the middle of the 'moustache' mark identified the bird as a female, and as I pointed this feature out to Christina, she was lucky enough to be looking through the binoculars at exactly the same time as the bird stuck out her tongue. For those who've never seen a green woodpecker's tongue, it has the appearance of a long, sticky bootlace, and in fact it is so long that the only way for it to be properly housed when retracted is by curling it around the skull. The tongue is not just adhesive, but to aid in the food extraction process it is also armed with small barbs at the tip, making it the perfect tool of the trade for relieving an ant nest of its ants. As the summer proceeded I had already noticed a number of black garden ant colonies in the meadow, and these had obviously also been located by the woodpecker too, as we watched it happily feeding away.

The largest of our three native woodpeckers, the green woodpecker is the species that spends probably the least time in woodland, being more regularly encountered in parkland, pasture or even, very occasionally, lucky people's gardens. And then in a flash, with her appetite satiated, she was up and over the beech hedge in a couple of wing-beats, revealing that vivid yellow-green rump as she powered across the playing field and out of sight on her characteristic bounding flight. The meadow had memorably delivered once again. Not content with just being the place where we would be able to catch up with the wild flowers and attendant butterflies, it had also kindly decided to take on the responsibility of providing a round-the-clock dining service for everything from bats to woodpeckers.

Despite have been preoccupied most of the week on a very exciting project filming an underwater chalk-water reef in Norfolk, it was also tough to have torn myself away from the garden at a time when there was just so much to see and do.

In the space of just six months in the house I had become fascinated with all the subtle changes throughout the year, and, feeling keen to re-immerse myself into the rhythms of the garden on my return, I decided that an incredibly early start the following morning was necessary to reacquaint myself with what was coming into the garden and when. So with my alarm clock rudely awakening me at 4am, I grabbed my binoculars and a coffee (in that order) before taking my seat in the outhouse with the window open – the equivalent of the front row of the theatre stalls – for what I hoped would be a fascinating morning.

04:28   A Song thrush starts singing.

04:31   Bats are still flying around the garden.

04:34   A blackbird begins singing.

04:45   Andy and Lorraine's cat strolls through the garden like it owns it.

04:46   A male blackbird flies through the garden.

04:48   A distant nuthatch is calling, which is a FIRST for the garden and a NEW bird!

04:50   A song thrush is seen in the meadow; could this be the snail smasher?

04:55   A wood pigeon begins its monotonous call.

04:56   The first bird on the caged (hawthorn) feeder is a robin!

04:58   Potentially the same individual robin is back for more.

04:59   A collared dove begins calling as a herring gull flies over the garden from the direction of the lake.

05:01   A female blackbird is seen pulling out a huge worm down by the wood.

05:03   The jackdaws begin flying around the garden and the call of a bullfinch is heard.

05:04   The robin comes to the cage feeder again.

05:07   The jackdaws are still very noisy.

05:12   Next door's cat sits down by the pond as two magpies fly into the rowan tree, which is full of berries.

05:14   The same robin (?) makes its fourth visit to the caged feeder.

05:18   Two juvenile great tits fly from the wood to the caged feeder.

05:20   The first blue tit, a juvenile, is seen on the feeders.

05:21   Two juvenile great tits, followed by a blue tit in quick succession, come in to feed, and a male great spotted woodpecker is both heard and seen calling from the oak tree.

05:22 A steady stream of both juvenile blue and great tits is now visiting the feeders.

05:24 A single magpie flies in again and sits on the oak bird table overlooking the chickens.

05:25 The first greenfinch (female) is seen on the bell (rowan) feeder.

05:27 A whole combination of tits and finches is on both feeders.

05:30 A temporary break to let out the chickens.

05:42 A greenfinch is seen and heard singing from the birch tree.

05:44 Abundant numbers of juvenile greenfinch, blue and great tits are on the feeders.

05:46 A juvenile jackdaw is on the cherry oak bird table.

05:47 Three female blackbirds are demolishing the rowan berries.

05:49 The same (?) territorial robin is back on the cage feeder.

05:50 A male blackbird joins the females in gobbling rowan berries.

05:51 The first bird on the ground feeder is a female chaffinch.

05:52 The first adult great tit noted on the feeders.

05:53 The first chaffinch (a female) observed on the feeders.

05:54 A wood pigeon underneath the bell feeder is cleaning up the spilt food.

05:58 Another juvenile jackdaw flies down to the oak bird table.

06:00 The first sunlight hits the garden, in this case the beech tree.

06:02 A steady stream of mostly juvenile blue and great tits coming to the feeder.

06:04 A male sparrowhawk appears over the beech hedge, but misses all the birds on the bell feeder! The feeders then unsurprisingly go quiet.

06:14   A male blackbird cleans up scraps from below the feeder.

06:17   The birds slowly return to the feeders, with three great tits in quick succession. A wren is seen on the sleepers in the vegetable patch and a male blackbird perches on the runner bean canes.

06:20   Two male blackbirds are feeding around the raised bed.

06:23   A robin feeds from the ground feeder.

06:43   A male and female bullfinch push the greenfinches off the caged feeder!

06:44   Blue tits, great tits and greenfinch are feeding in the cage simultaneously. There are a minimum of three to four birds in the cage at any one time.

06:48   Three jackdaws fly into the coop.

06:50   A female chaffinch and female house sparrow (an unusual bird in the garden) are under the feeder collecting scraps. At least eight jackdaws fly into the chicken enclosure but are prevented from stealing food or smashing eggs.

06:52   The same female house sparrow and a greenfinch are inside the caged feeder.

06:53   Two female chaffinch are on the ground feeder, with a robin on the back of one of the garden chairs!

06:54   Birds are piling into the hawthorn to wait their turn on the caged feeder.

06:55   Two female chaffinch are inside the ground feeder, whilst a male bullfinch is sitting on the top.

06:58   Two jackdaws and one wood pigeon are seen drinking from the pond.

07:00   I fall asleep!

Eventually waking up and hauling myself inside for a cup of coffee, I was surprised at how informative and insightful my morning had been. Usually watching the garden birds had been an activity that I'd confined to snatched, five-minute chunks, but by watching systematically over a longer period a few clear patterns had emerged.

The first conclusion I was able to draw was that it seemed to be only the multi-brooded birds such as the song thrush, blackbird, wood pigeon, collared dove and greenfinch that were still singing. Being keen to maintain their territories, this must have meant that all these species either still had chicks or were keen to raise more broods. This behaviour contrasted sharply with that of the blue tits and great tits, which, being species that are (mostly) single-brooded, had no need or desire to hold a territory with their breeding season having already been wound up.

Additionally, a clear chronology also seemed to have appeared as to when different species began coming to the feeders. The robin is a renowned early riser, so perhaps it was not a surprise for this to be the first bird recorded taking food from the feeders. The robin was then quite clearly followed by both species of tit, with the green-finch being the first member of the finch family to make an appear-ance, with the chaffinch and bullfinch finally bringing up the rear. It is generally considered that primarily insectivorous birds like robins and the tits are up early, as this is the best time to catch the worms, spiders and caterpillars before their prey withdraws during the heat of the day – which would explain the phrase 'the early bird gets the worm'. Life is not so frenetic for the seed-, fruit- and nut-eaters, such as the greenfinch and bullfinch, as their food actually needs to be harvested rather than caught, allowing them a later start. But with competition for a slot on the feeder severe during the busy times, and such an established pecking order amongst the species, it was also conceivable that the robins and tits were simply trying to feed as much as possible earlier on, knowing full-well that when the feeders became busier they would be monopolised by the bully-boy finches.

Scientists always say during research work that a negative result is just as important as a positive one, and following on in the same vein, it was for me equally interesting to see which birds hadn't turned up to the feeders that morning. Only seen in the garden during hard winters, I didn't expect the reed buntings to have made an appearance, as they would probably still be preoccupied with the tail-end of the breeding season over in the lakeside reed-beds, but I was surprised by the complete absence of coal tit, long-tailed tit and goldfinch, as these were three species that I had considered reasonably common in the garden. The flip-side of this was that the house sparrows were coming to the feeders more regularly than I thought. The street claimed a colony of house sparrows, at the junction where we met the main road, and they were also regularly seen on the roofs and guttering of our neighbours' houses, but for some reason they very rarely seemed inclined to pay our back garden a visit.

Based on my own observations of the jackdaws flying into the coop, I'd stopped taking bets on them being the 'eggers' and as far as I was concerned they were as good as guilty. I only hoped that our new regime of locking the birds up at night would continue to be successful in preventing a return to such antisocial behaviour in the future. Finally, it's not until you properly invest a considerable amount of time watching the garden that you maximise your opportunities to catch up with those 'blink and you'll miss it' events, such as the sparrowhawk attempting to catch his breakfast at 6.04 am ... and, come to think of it, the nuthatch wasn't bad either!

A few years ago, I presented a local series for ITV called *Wild Gardens*, where I encouraged various West Country gardeners to take small steps to encourage wildlife into their own gardens by, for example, putting up nest boxes or planting nectar-rich flowers, and in one of the programmes I persuaded a couple in the Forest of Dean to build a 'bug hotel'. This consists of a series of discarded wooden pallets, with a rudimentary roof to keep the rain out. The pallets were then crammed with everything from sticks and hay to plastic bottles containing rolled-up cardboard, all designed to provide homes for the innumerable different types of invertebrates. By the time we'd finished filming the bug hotel's construction, I have to say it looked fabulous. With so many nooks and crannies, the hotel was not just ideal for all manner of invertebrates but it also had the potential to offer quarters for everything from overwintering toads and newts to a hibernating hedgehog. Now that at last we had enough space, I'd been determined from early on that a bug hotel would not only make a fine addition to the garden but would also enhance the diversity of habitats, ultimately making it much more attractive to a wider range of species.

Early in my television career I worked as a researcher on the series *Wild in Your Garden* with Bill Oddie, which many people now consider the precursor to *Springwatch*. The series featured the various wild goings-on of a suburban street in Bristol, and the undoubted stars of the show were of course the foxes, badgers, hedgehogs and a small selection of garden birds. But of course these 'sexy' animals that made the programme so watchable represent less than 1 per cent of all the animals that can be recorded in an average garden, with the overwhelming majority of species being the far less glamorous beetles, millipedes, spiders, bugs, worms and woodlice. If you have a particularly large and varied garden, or it is situated in a great location, it may play host to around half a dozen mammals and maybe 30 or 40 species of birds (if you include ones seen flying over), but most gardens should quite literally house thousands of different species of invertebrates. So vital are all these creepy-crawlies to the functioning of the garden that, in addition to pollinating the plants, breaking down leaf litter and keeping other pest species in check, many will also ultimately go on to provide food for the charismatic 'fur and feather brigade', that we are so desperate to see at the top of the pyramid.

While identifying anything other than the birds, mammals, amphibians and the easier invertebrate groups (such as butterflies, moths, dragonflies and bumblebees) was frankly beyond my ability, I was aware that a rich invertebrate fauna would not only be the best indicator as to the health of the garden, but would also make it a much more fully functioning ecosystem too. So with this in mind, over the previous weeks I had steadily managed to scrounge half a dozen pallets to provide structure for the bug hotel. Christina had also entered into the begging, stealing and borrowing spirit around her parents' outhouses and managed to recover some pieces of old plastic drainpipe, broken tiles and bamboo canes. When these items were added to the sand and gravel left over from building the pond, and some plastic pop bottles I'd been hoarding, this collection of booty was more than enough to commence construction.

After much debate, we decided that the best position for the bug hotel would be between the rowan tree and the beech hedge we'd just massacred. Placed here, it would be partly in the shade and also tucked away to provide a quiet refuge for any invertebrates keen to take up residence. I had learnt from my previous error with the compost bins, and we first ensured that the pile of pallets would be sitting on level ground, and only then, with the structure set on firm foundations, did we begin with the roof. The roof was the only part of the bug hotel on which I'd decided to spend some money, and so the previous week I had dropped into a reclamation centre nearby to purchase some lovely old roofing tiles. Operating a bit like the pieces of a jig-saw puzzle, without of course the picture, it took a while for Christina and I to work out how they slotted together to ensure the rain would properly run off, and to also realise that when tiling a roof you have to work from the bottom up. By attaching a wooden batten to the top pallet we also managed to create a sufficiently angled pitch to allow the rain to be shed.

Having sawn up the plastic drainpipe into sections, these were then slotted into the gaps between the top and the bottom of each pallet, which effectively represented a different floor in the bug hotel. The drainpipes were then filled with chopped up bits of bamboo canes, the hollow centres of which would potentially provide holes for solitary bees to use, instead of where they had previously tried to nest in the garden, i.e. in the half-constructed walls of the pond, back in the spring. Being excellent pollinators to a huge variety of plants, solitary bees were one group that I was particularly keen to encourage to the garden, and any tubes occupied would provide the perfect place for a female solitary bee to lay an egg on a bed of pollen (as sustenance for the larva), before finally sealing the entrance with a plug of mud.

A mixture of sand and gravel was then placed in the centre for various invertebrates to be able to burrow into, or use as hibernation sites, before we stuffed several of the pallets with dead wood, using the brash previously removed from the beech hedge. It can't be overestimated how important a habitat dead wood is, and as we fussily 'over-tidy' the countryside, where fallen trees are often considered either unsightly or a potential danger to our health and safety, it has also unfortunately become a far scarcer habitat too. It has been estimated that more than 1,700 species of British insect depend on dead wood for at least part of their life cycle, and 300 of these species are either so endangered or so rare they are presumed to have already become extinct. The presence of this 'habitat' is particularly crucial to many woodland beetles, such as Britain's largest terrestrial insect, the stag beetle, with its wood-boring larvae entirely dependent on dead wood. There are also plenty of other invertebrates that are either reliant on the wood itself, or prey on those very wood specialists themselves, and I'd be very surprised if a well-rotten pile of logs, when prised apart, didn't reveal an abundance of centipedes, millipedes, earthworms, slugs, snails, bugs and flies, in addition to a healthy population of ground and rove beetles. Crucially, dead wood also supports a whole variety of fungi which will play a vital part in breaking down the woody material.

With the light fading, half of the floors of the bug hotel now fully furnished and being exhausted after my early start, we decided to finish off the hotel later in the week. We were delighted at how much we had achieved in such a short space of time; building a hotel from scratch, and without planning permission, all in a day was what I call progress!

Those who know wildlife well, appreciate that to successfully track it down often involves ridiculously early starts. I had been staying down in Dorset in order to rise at 4am so as to give ourselves the best possible chance of seeing and filming otters on the River Stour.

Arriving at the river just before 5am, and gearing myself up for a very long wait, it was one of those fabulous (and rare) days when the wildlife had obviously decided that it would be rude to keep us waiting. We had barely been given the opportunity to set the camera gear up before otters were located through the gloom, and then for most of the next two hours put on the most marvellous show, seemingly unfazed by our presence just a few yards away on the bank. It was quite simply the best view I'd ever had of otters, but by no means was it the most memorable – when you've had an otter in your own back garden you become terribly spoilt!

The other advantage of wrapping up the filming so promptly was that it freed me up to return home early, and in view of the fact that the following day I would be away again for a week's filming, it was absolutely vital I used this small window of opportunity to get my garden fix. I had arranged for Christina to put the moth trap out for me the night before, so on arriving home and as soon as my bags were unpacked and lunch consumed, I was straight out to see what delights had been caught.

With the weather set fair, rather than taking myself off to my normal moth identification location of the garage, I took the trap instead to the garden table in preparation for a very pleasant afternoon moth-ing. As I lifted off the light and funnel, my eye was immediately drawn to the hugely distinctive outline of a hawk-moth sitting, like a jewel in the centre of a brooch, on the uppermost egg box – a very good sign! Unbelievably it was another hawk-moth with which I wasn't familiar, and although it didn't possess the most striking pattern on its huge forewings, it more than made up for this with a black and pink striped abdomen, which when bisected with a dark central line running the length of the abdomen looked for all the world like a backbone and a set of ribs!

The largest British moth is the infamous death's-head hawk-moth, with a wingspan of around five inches, and this moth looked a similar size – it was simply huge. With the number of hawk-moth species fairly limited and the abdomen so distinctive, only a cursory glance in my 'Skinner' was necessary to confirm that I was looking at my first privet hawk-moth. With the majority of my moth-trapping having been conducted in North Wales it was no surprise that I had not previously come across a species which Skinner described as 'widely distributed, but not common in the southern half of the British Isles'. Nearing the end of its flight period of between June and July, it was not surprising that this individual was already showing signs of wear and tear and, being a male (identified by the small comb of hairs along his antennae), it was to be hoped that he had been lucky enough to catch up with a female, so enabling his genes to be passed on to the next generation of privet hawk-moths. Despite an absence of privet hedges in the garden, I was also interested to read that the caterpillars were capable of feeding on lilac, ash and holly. With all three of these being found in my garden, it perhaps should not have been a surprise that he'd made an appearance.

With each egg box holding a variety of different moths it became immediately obvious that it was both a large catch and an almost entirely different composition of species to when I'd last run the trap. True, there were still a few of the ubiquitous heart and darts hanging on, but now the catch was joined with high-summer species like buff arches and common footman as well as moths capable of rearing a second brood, such as ruby tiger and the imaginatively titled nut-tree tussock. With a couple of other species I'd not seen before, including the magnificent large emerald, and the plain golden Y, it was the most diverse catch of the year, totalling 60 individuals of 26 different species. Talk about an easy way of bumping up your garden species list!

It wasn't just the moths that were peaking in diversity, either; the meadow was looking mighty fine as well. So, replacing my moth book with my plant book, I thought I'd use what was left of the afternoon to compile a botanical inventory. To any gardener who prefers their flower borders immaculate and their lawns a verdant monoculture, the flowering plants in the meadow read like a 'Who's Who' of invasive weeds. In amongst the large stands of white clover and dandelion clocks could be seen common ragwort, herb Robert, rough sow-thistle, petty spurge, enchanter's nightshade and greater plantain. But the weeds' shady reputations patently didn't seem to bother the insects and the meadow was humming with hoverflies and honey bees. A further hands-and-knees inspection in amongst the dominant plants also revealed a few surprises, in the form of American and square-stemmed willowherb, crow garlic and that lovely denizen of many a manicured lawn – self-heal.

In fact it was not just the meadow that was looking terrific, as the two main herbaceous borders by the garage and around the pond must have contained close to twenty different flowering species each, and for the first time I was finally able to appreciate that all those visits to the garden centres had been time and money well spent. Not everything was quite going to plan, though, as the algae in the pond was again becoming problematic and I could only hope that it was going through that tricky process of trying to balance itself out. Nevertheless, lending the pond a helping hand wouldn't do any harm, I thought, as I got back down on all fours in an attempt to lift out the worst of the long, filamentous algae. With each clump removed I could see a surprising number of aquatic creatures embedded in the algae, so by placing the weed on one of the stones to the side of the pond, I gave these invertebrates the opportunity to wheedle their way out and back into the water. As I stood up to admire a now clearer pond, I suddenly felt a touch light-headed from all my exertions and decided it was time for a nap. It had been a very early start after all!

Whenever I go away filming, the experience is so engrossing, all-encompassing and incredibly enjoyable that sometimes I feel slightly guilty for scarcely thinking of my other life with Christina back at home. The other weird aspect of these intense trips is that when you take yourself away on location, in this case the Outer Hebrides and north Scotland, you can be so caught up in the moment that it quickly feels as though living in hotels is the norm.

Of course the trip was only a week long, but forgetting about the garden for this duration had done me good and I was able to return home refreshed and brimming with ideas as to how we could improve it even more.

I only have the opportunity to see my ten-year-old nephew and eight-year-old niece, who live in west Ireland, maybe two or three times a year, and each time we meet up I always feel they have changed immeasurably since I last saw them. This is because I only see the step-changes, and even after just a week spent away I felt exactly the same way with the garden too. In the space of this week, a number of flowers had finally gone over for the year and were busily setting seed, whilst for other plants, such as the clematis, crocosmia, buddleia and sweet peas, now was their time to shine. Taking advantage of my absence, Christina had also (surprise, surprise) managed to slot in a visit to the garden centre and carried out the impressive trick of finding space to plant a new rose ('Ferdinand Pichard'), a tree peony and a yellow bearded iris into borders that I thought were already simply full to the gunwales. It wasn't hard working out where Christina's priorities lay either, as I noticed and then couldn't help remarking on the fact that both the bell and cage feeder, having been emptied during my absence, hadn't been re-filled. She responded by quickly pointing out that the feeders were my responsibility, and if I wanted them filled so badly then maybe I should do it myself while she prepared dinner – a bargain I was only too happy to strike.

Replenishing the feeders from my rodent-proof storage containers in the garage was no more than a five-minute job, enabling me to have a closer look at the large white fluttering around the raised vegetable patch before dinner was ready. Not having seen large whites in the garden for a few weeks suggested that I was now looking at the butterfly's second brood, and on closer inspection, the subtle differences in wing markings of this second-generation female were particularly apparent from her darker wing-tips and more pronounced black wing spots. The Savoy cabbage around which she had been fluttering had indeed borne the brunt of our non-interventionist approach, and certainly the outer leaves were beginning to resemble a string vest. It didn't take me long to find the fruits of her labours either, as on the underside of one of the cabbage leaves was a little cluster of eggs, grouped together like tiny yellow milk bottles. Even if the female hadn't just given the game away, you could tell they had only recently been laid as they quickly turn a rich orange colour once ripened and I, for one, didn't have the heart to remove them even if the cabbages would suffer as a result.

With dinner ready and the evening beautifully warm there seemed little point in eating inside. However, with the nights already inexorably drawing in, and dusk now falling thirty minutes earlier, which was a touch depressing (I so adore the long summer evenings), this at least meant we wouldn't have to wait too long before we could see the bats appear – and the detector was standing by!

I picked Christina up from work, as she'd managed to get a half-day off, and we drove home luxuriating in the fact that we had the whole weekend ahead of us; with most of it to be spent – if we had our way – in the garden. Quickly checking on the chickens as soon as we arrived back, a habit we had developed as our fondness for them had grown, we were both slightly worried to see that there was some kind of problem with June. Not only was she seemingly limping but her bottom seemed to be pulsating, and it was incredibly messy and marked with blood. Further investigation revealed more blood in the coop, and then we noticed that both April and May were making the situation worse by constantly pecking at her bottom. Having not had a single problem with the chickens up until now, with the exception of when they escaped from the garden, of course, it was inevitable that at some point a health issue would arise which would need our intervention.

Catching June was never easy as she was by far the most jumpy, and she was often scared of her own shadow, but eventually we cornered her in the coop long enough for me to grab her. As I kept a firm hold of her, Christina washed the whole of her rear end and the surrounding feathers with warm, soapy water, making her derriere look like that of a plucked turkey. Although admittedly not vets, nor qualified in any way to make any sort of diagnosis, neither of us thought that it looked terminal, and by locking June alone inside the coop, this would at least separate her from the two wicked sisters in the enclosure. This measure, we hoped, would at least ensure, in the short term, that there would be no further pecking to exacerbate the problem before they all went to roost. Not having been locked in on her own before, June simply couldn't understand why she had been singled out for temporary quarantine and even cracked her head several times on the side panel trying to get out, before giving up to sulk in the corner.

There had been no rain for a few days, so Christina decided the garden needed a good dousing, and as she set about watering the beds, I had a general tidy round, which inevitably entailed clearing up some of Christina's mess from her most recent planting session. Throughout the whole afternoon the kingfishers could be heard making a constant racket as they whistled up and down the brook, but it only became apparent why they had been so active when a kingfisher suddenly bolted up into the garden before proceeding to perch on the garage roof! I sprinted inside for my binoculars, and fortunately the kingfisher stayed long enough for me to have a good look. Immediately I could see by its duller plumage and hint of a yellowy gape that this must be one of the recently fledged juveniles! Quite often a settled pair of kingfishers with good feeding habitat will attempt to complete two or even three broods during the course of the summer, which means that any recently fledged birds that seem incapable of cutting the apron strings have to be chased off. With the parents fiercely guarding their territory due to the brook's fish being a finite resource, this youngster had obviously been unceremoniously and brutally booted off to find its own stretch of water elsewhere – talk about 'tough love'!

In fact it would prove to be an afternoon of surprises, with a large frog noticed under the stone-edgings in the pond, and not for the first time since we had added water I found myself fervently hoping that the pond would be graced by frogspawn the following spring. I was also excited to see at least a couple of backswimmers coming up for air too. Perhaps better known as greater water boatmen, and differentiated from their close relative, the lesser water boatman, not by size, but by the fact that they swim on their backs, the backswimmers are also fiendish predators. Any hapless insects caught in the surface film are grabbed by the backswimmers from underneath (providing they arrive there before the pond skaters, that is), and then dispatched in a most heinous manner by the back-swimmer's needle-sharp proboscis, which is used to suck the victim dry. This beak is so strong and sharp, in fact, that it is one of the very few aquatic insects capable of giving even us humans a painful little jab – young pond dippers beware!

As dusk approached we sat outside with two glasses and a bottle of prosecco and watched the house martins feeding away on the midges and all other aerial insects some 100 or so feet above the garden. Unfortunately they hadn't been persuaded to nest on the side of our property, choosing instead some of the slightly older houses towards the centre of the village, and I had been particularly envious (but not bitter) to find out, for example, that my mate Jamie had three pairs nesting under his eaves. But even if they had opted elsewhere for accommodation this year, it was still above our garden that they came to feed! Watching them hawking for insects, I also realised what incredibly vocal birds they are, and, as we listened, the loose flock constantly trilled away like staccato canaries. With house martins often attempting two broods each summer, a large number of the birds could well have been juveniles that had just fledged from the year's first brood. Maybe they were undergoing a lesson with their parents at flying school?

With dusk finally upon us, we were just preparing to retire indoors when a tawny owl let out a full-blown hoot from the bottom of the garden, the first one we'd heard there for quite a while. Desperate for the chance of a sighting of tawny owl actually in the garden, I took out my smart phone, on which I had loaded an application with all the British bird songs and calls, to see if a return call from my phone would elicit any action. This technique is called 'playback' and works on the principle that the bird, thinking a competitor has just waltzed into its territory, will usually come in to investigate, and it has often proved very successful for seeing birds with a shy disposition. This is also a method which, it must be said, should always be used judiciously, taking particular care around rare birds, and it should never be used in the breeding season. Satisfying myself that a quick blast was justified, I played the hoot from my phone and the response was almost instantaneous. Within ten seconds of playing the recording I spotted a tawny owl fly into the ash tree above my head and then look down at me as it tried to fathom what on earth was going on. I was aware of the fact that a similar experiment had left the celebrated bird photographer Eric Hosking without an eye, as a territorial tawny is something not to be messed with, so I decided that discretion was the better part of valour, and, putting the phone away, carefully backed off, elated that the wood at the bottom of my garden was also part of the territory of the local tawny owl.

I awoke with a spring in my step after my tawny encounter, and I was up and out early to clean out the chickens and check up on June. Having probably spent most of the night preening her feathers, she was back to looking like she hadn't just been dragged through a hedge backwards, and despite what still seemed to be a pulsating bottom – which I'm not sure is a medical term, but there is no other way I know to describe it – April and May seemed to have lost their fascination with her rear (which, given the occasionally vindictive nature of chickens, was a good thing).

After a delicious scrambled egg breakfast courtesy of the girls, we cracked on with our first couple of chores. With Christina weeding the herbaceous border around the pond, my job was to crank up the mower and give our cultivated lawn the short back and sides it so desperately needed. Starting off in the front garden, I was right in the middle of creating the lined patterned effect not too dissimilar to what you see at Wimbledon or the Lords Cricket Ground when Christina came round to talk to me. I cut the motor, and she had a sober look on her face, which I immediately read as 'not good news'. Apparently she had been weeding the bed, when she had accidentally pushed a female greenfinch out from underneath one of the plants that looked incredibly sickly and obviously wasn't able to fly either.

The bird was so ill that it didn't even try to resist as I picked it up. In addition to its lethargic state, its plumage was wet and matted all around its face and beak, and the beak itself was partly covered in what looked to be uneaten or regurgitated food. With its eyes barely open it was obviously a very sickly bird, but unlike the problem with June's bottom, where I was guessing as to what the problem had been, I knew immediately what this was. It looked like trichomonosis had come to Chew Stoke, and because of the high numbers of greenfinch visiting my garden this was really bad news.

I took the bird into the outhouse, where I put it into a box with bedding, water and food so at least it wouldn't be a sitting duck for any predators passing by, and I then went onto the internet for a spot of advice. The RSPB website confirmed that I was indeed correct with my diagnosis, and it suggested that, in any gardens with an outbreak, the feeders should immediately be removed for a temporary period. Thinking this an overly draconian measure, and as so many other birds had come to rely on my hand-outs, I took both the bell and cage feeders down, throwing away any remaining seed which was potentially contaminated, and gave both a rigorous wash in warm, soapy water. After drying them carefully, I then re-filled both feeders and doused all the perches and seed hatches with an anti-microbial powder especially designed to ensure safe hygiene in garden birds. With the water bath another potential source of infection, this too was scrupulously cleaned before then being refilled. All I had to do now was to hope that I had nipped the infection in the bud before it had spread to the other birds.

With the now sparklingly clean feeders back up and servicing the birds once more, I popped back in to see if there had been any improvement from our patient in the outhouse, but it was not good news. In one corner of the box was a little inanimate bundle of feathers as the bird had already gone to that great aviary in the sky. I only hoped this was the first and last bird we'd encounter in such ill health, but I could not shake a real feeling of foreboding.

AUGUST
THE SUN-SEEKERS TAKE CENTRE STAGE

I couldn't take it any more. Over the next couple of days Christina and I discovered two more greenfinch already dead in the garden, with another one still fit enough to avoid capture, but obviously close to pegging out too. As I personally got so much from watching the birds coming to the feeders I had looked upon their removal as the last resort, but if they were actually harming rather than helping the birds, then it would have been irresponsible of me to carry on regardless. So with a heavy heart they simply had to be taken down until further notice.

Christina was at work, and I had crow-barred in a day off between filming assignments in Norfolk and south Wales, so I was determined to enjoy a quality few hours in the garden. The weather promised to be beautifully warm, and I was hoping that some charismatic insects would compensate for the now virtual absence of birds (with the exception of April, May and June, of course), as they were forced elsewhere to look for food. On the one positive note related to birds, June seemed to be back to her normal giddy self, and when I cleaned out the chicken coop I was delighted to find that the girls had delivered the first three-egg day for weeks.

Even before it had properly warmed up, it was clear that the day promised much for lovers of insects, from the instant I caught sight of a tiny wisp of silvery-blue flitting along the edge of the copse.

Knowing the butterfly well, having already added it to the garden list in April, I instantly knew it to be a holly blue, but this was the first individual I had seen of the butterfly's second generation. It is bizarre that most of the populations of this species tend to vary their host-plant according to which generation they belong to, with female holly blues from the first brood laying eggs on holly, in contrast to the midsummer females favouring ivy or occasionally spindle. With all of these three plants abundantly present in the garden, then as far as I was concerned, the butterflies were free to be as fussy as they liked!

After a late breakfast, by which time the day was warming up nicely, and still enthused by my holly blue sighting, I thought the morning would be as good a time as any to undertake my butterfly census as part of the Butterfly Conservation charity's 'Big Butterfly Count'. A number of wildlife charities have latched onto this 'Citizen Science' idea over the last few years, whereby members of the public are encouraged to take part in simple survey work. This not only helps the collation of valuable nationwide data, but should also help enthuse large numbers of people about the wonderful wildlife right on their own doorsteps, and I for one was right behind it.

The premise couldn't have been simpler; all I had to do was select a warm day between the 14 July and 5 August and count the butterflies coming into the garden over a fifteen-minute period. So assuming my position, which was seated in the middle of the garden with my binoculars so I could scan all the flower borders without obstruction, I was off …

Three large whites – check. Two small whites – check. One speckled wood – check. Two green-veined whites – check. Three more large whites – check. One gatekeeper – CHECK!

I couldn't believe it! In the exact fifteen-minute period I'd designated for my survey, a new butterfly for the garden and my first gatekeeper for the year had decided to make a grand appearance – and with only 60 seconds to go before my time was up, you'd have to say the timing was impeccable!

The gatekeeper is a smashing little insect and the archetypal high-summer butterfly throughout the southern half of the UK. It is smaller, brighter and neater than the more widely distributed meadow brown, and is typical of the 'brown' species (*Satyridae*) on being dependent on a wide variety of grass species for its caterpillars to thrive. It is also a butterfly that I associate with sunny countryside walks in August, and it can often be seen in abundance at this time of year if you happen to come across a large patch of flowering bramble that is both sheltered and in full sun. The presence of this butterfly in my garden was certainly not only able to reconfirm to me (in case I'd forgotten) that we were indeed well and truly living in the countryside now, but also that the long grass in the meadow was a fabulous habitat in its own right, without which the butterfly would have given the garden a wide berth.

Perhaps more satisfying in many ways than the recording of the gatekeeper was that owning a butterfly-friendly garden had at last enabled me finally to get to grips with the identification of all three common species of white butterfly, which, if I'm honest, I'd been fudging for years. Gauging the size of any animal is notoriously difficult when you have little to measure it against. And with the markings, for example, of both the large and small white only subtly different at best, it is only when you see the two butterflies together that you realise that, whilst the names aren't imaginative, they are at least technically accurate. Being able to quickly and definitively identify these two species by directly comparing them alongside one another also meant that I was then able to pick up other subtle differences in behaviour, such as how they flew and which flowers they preferred. This familiarisation also had the delightful knock-on effect that as soon as a green-veined white turned up to join the fray, its weak, fluttering flight and delicate appearance suddenly made it stand out from the other more common white butterflies like a sore thumb. Maybe this wasn't the first time I'd had the epiphany that owning and enjoying a garden was making me a far more competent field biologist, but it was another timely reminder that if you do take the time to appreciate and understand the common species just a little bit more, then your efforts will never be wasted.

The sun wasn't just bringing out the butterflies either, and as I transferred my attentions to the pond, my eye was immediately drawn to the biggest dragonfly to be enticed into the garden yet. Curling her abdomen around as she carefully laid her eggs on the stones by the pond was a female of one of the hawker dragonflies. 'Hawkers' (so-called because of the males' constantly restless flight as they hunt, feed and patrol their territories for females) include a number of confusingly similar species. The key to successful identification is to try and get a good look at both the patterns and the colours on the abdomen and thorax, which is often not easy on an insect buzzing around at speeds of up to around 30mph. But with this dragonfly so engrossed in its egg-laying, I was easily able to get close enough to see the green golf 'T' on the second abdominal segment and the paired green spots down the abdomen so characteristic of a female southern hawker. As I watched her going about her business, I was still slightly stumped as to why she was choosing to lay her eggs out of the water. It wasn't until I consulted my dragonfly book later that I discovered that the eggs of this species overwinter in a dormant stage, so staying on dry land throughout the winter will make them less susceptible to predation than if they were in the water. Hatching in the spring, the larvae's first job will be to crawl into the water, and only then will they be able to begin their 'life aquatic'.

In fact it was becoming a day of discovery in more ways than one, as the addition of the southern hawker, which was the fifth species of damselfly and dragonfly to have been attracted since the pond was filled, represented a stunning return by any definition. It was by no means the final tally either, as a few species could still potentially turn up later in the summer to push up the grand total a touch higher. All the considerable effort (and not to mention the considerable financial outlay of the liner) had been worth it.

After a light lunch enjoyed in the garden, I was then determined to spend the rest of the afternoon attempting to furnish the bug hotel to the stage where any tenants ready to move in could be welcomed. My first task would be the construction of some lacewing homes. Easily recognised by their transparent lace-like wings, which extend well beyond their abdomens, lacewings are surprisingly common insects in British gardens. Despite this abundance, the reason why they aren't more regularly seen can be put down to their sluggish flight; as this makes them easy pickings for foraging birds, most activity has to be confined to the hours after dark. While these somewhat delicate attributes would hardly put them in the 'world's most ferocious predator' category, it is in fact their larvae that are the real wolves in sheep's clothing. With their nickname of 'aphid-lions' well deserved, each larva is equipped with a set of pincer-like jaws, and on catching a victim will inject a secretion that both paralyses and digests the aphid's internal organs, turning it into a liquid lunch. Apparently in an attempt to avoid becoming lunch themselves, the larvae will often camouflage themselves with the empty skins of their victims – a Hannibal the Cannibal technique which seems devious and disgusting in equal measure!

Given the lacewings' abilities to polish off greenfly like they are going out of fashion, and with Christina so keen on her roses (a group of plants which, it has to be said, seem perennially vulnerable to aphid infestation), this was certainly one group of insects that I was practically begging to fraternise the garden. Of course, garden centres have also cottoned on to the huge potential of these vastly underrated insects as agents of biological control, and they now sell bespoke 'lacewing chambers' to any gardeners keen to persuade the adult insects to overwinter. But being determined to ensure that the bug hotel would be the one structure in the garden built for next to nothing, I had managed to find in one of my gardening books a clever little 'lacewing home' design that needed nothing more than a few plastic pop bottles and some corrugated cardboard.

Raiding the collection of plastic bottles that I'd been carefully stockpiling for this very moment, their tops and necks were first carefully sliced off with a Stanley knife. Next to come under the knife were a couple of corrugated cardboard boxes which had been sitting in the garage since the move. These boxes were firstly dismembered into cardboard rectangles before being rolled up and then stuffed into the bottles to create a tightly packed spiral with a large surface area. Finally, inserting a whole line of these bottles in the gaps created by the pallets with their entrances facing out, not only looked good, but had filled another floor of the hotel. It was, of course, anyone's guess as to whether any lacewings would indeed be tempted to move in, but if a few adventurous ones did so, they could then consider their rent to be paid in full – providing Christina's roses were kept aphid-free!

Turning to my trusty Black & Decker, I cut down a series of branches still kicking around from Rob the tree surgeon's work back in February, then drilled holes in one end, to provide alternative accommodation for solitary bees should the garden canes a couple of floors lower not fit their exacting specifications. Any remaining unoccupied holes could then possibly be sub-let to any woodlice and spiders still struggling for somewhere to stay. With just the top couple of floors now vacant, the remaining beech brash that had still not been disposed of was then chopped up courtesy of Marjory and Dennis's shredder and stuffed into all the remaining cavities.

Each floor was now packed with a range of residential opportunities, giving more than enough space to house thousands upon thousands of tenants, and could be declared finally open for business. On her return home, Christina thought the end product was a fine addition to the garden and, feeling like we should at least mark the hotel's grand opening, we celebrated in fine style with a stir-fry, partly consisting of some holey cabbage and half-nibbled courgettes from the raised bed.

Now that the feeders had been absent for a couple of days, the garden felt almost abandoned. With most of the other vertebrates, such as mammals (with the prominent exception of grey squirrels), amphibians and reptiles, tending to be much more introverted by nature, it was not until the birds had gone that we realised what a busy, active and incredibly visible component of any garden fauna they really are.

Although the appearance of the trichomonosis was nothing short of devastating, if it had to happen at any time, I suppose the late summer would probably have to be the least damaging period, as I consider August generally to be the quietest month for many of our garden birds. At this time of year, the nights are still comparatively warm and there should also still be more than enough food in the surrounding countryside for foraging birds to find. With both the breeding season having already finished for most species and the parents' duties towards their offspring having been dutifully discharged, many of the adult birds traditionally use this as the time to undergo a moult, whereby worn-out feathers are shed and replaced with new, strong and warm feathers to see them through the winter months. The pattern of moulting can vary enormously between different species, with migratory birds needing to complete the process far more quickly as their new flight feathers will be essential for the long journey ahead, as compared to resident species like robins and blue tits, which will probably not move far from their natal site. Either way, this essential process must also be considered a huge drain on their resources, and with the birds not able either to properly insulate themselves, or to fly well and therefore more vulnerable to predation during this period, it makes sense for them to keep as low a profile as possible.

The clever element to nature's calendar, of course, and boon for us naturalists needing a constant wildlife fix, is that at the precise time that the birds begin temporarily to retreat to the sidelines all manner of invertebrates assume centre stage. With just a couple of hours spare before I was due to go away filming, I thought the time would be well spent casting an eye over the large garage herbaceous border, which was literally humming with insects. Many of the plants we had chosen for our borders had been in the 'wildlife-friendly' category because of their ability to deliver both high quantities and quality of pollen and nectar. With insect distributions uneven across the bed, though, gauging the relative attractiveness of each plant in reality involved nothing more than a quick glance to see where most of the insects were concentrated.

Without doubt the plant that was physically and metaphorically head and shoulders above the competition was *Verbena bonariensis*. This had been one of the real success stories of the border and one of the few plants in the garden that Christina had managed to grow from seed that were now flowering. Not having grown them before, we had not appreciated how tall they would eventually reach, with the result that many of the tightly packed clusters of lilac purple flowers at the ends of stiffly branching stems had ended above head height. In terms of its pulling power with butterflies, this plant surely had to rival buddleia.

Only just pushed into second place was one of the plants that Mark had given us way back in the spring, and after the original plant had settled well to the garden, it had then been split into three large, healthy clumps. The *Sedum spectabile*, or ice plant, is a perennial that produces bluish-green rosettes of succulent foliage all spring and summer, with the large flower heads only finally opening in late summer to reveal masses of tiny reddish/pink flowers, which were already proving a real magnet, particularly for bumblebees and honey bees. Finally, the other plant which looked like it would be assured a podium position was the wallflower *Erysimum* 'Bowles' mauve'. We had planted this short-lived perennial as a single plant in the spring following an impulse purchase from a garden centre, and four months later the long racemes of mauve flowers were still proving a focus for everything from butterflies to hoverflies.

Standing back to properly appreciate the whole bed, a 30-second survey of the three species revealed the verbena to be entertaining three or four large and small whites, the wallflower a green-veined white and what looked like a worker white-tailed bumblebee, and the ice plant playing host to a small tortoiseshell, a small white, two more worker bumblebees and two honey bees.

This was a quite spectacular return for the few quid we had spent back in the spring.

Determined not to be upstaged by the flower borders, the pond also had its own retinue of insect stars, including the latest arrival in the form of a posse of whirligig beetles shooting around the water surface like crazed mini dodgems. Being such distinctive and notice-able insects, it certainly couldn't have been the case that these little black bombers had been present for weeks but simply remained unobserved, so they must have flown in under the cover of darkness within the last 48 hours – for it was only two days since I had last cast my eye over the pond. Using their short, flattened swimming legs with large hairy fringes to both propel themselves across the water and help them dive below, whirligig beetles can move like greased lightning, and, for their size, have to be one of the fastest animals on the planet. Equally impressive are their eyes, which are divided into two: the upper half to look out above the water and skyward for any potential predators such as birds, while the lower half is used to watch for any goings-on beneath the water. Looking harmless enough, for any mosquito or midge larva present in the pond the whirligig beetle is very bad news, and equally for any insect unfortunate enough to have fallen into the water and got stuck in the surface tension it would now be a toss-up as to whether it would be death by pond-skater or whirligig!

After a week spent whizzing around like a whirligig beetle myself, as I took in different filming assignments from Middlesbrough and Doncaster down to London, I was finally heading home for a much-anticipated weekend in the garden with Christina. Throwing back the duvet the following morning, from the moment the sunlight hit our south-facing bedroom I was determined the day would be long and fruitful, starting with an early-morning bonding session with April, May and June. With the feeders not yet put back out, the chickens were pretty much the only feathered presence in the garden, and on spotting me walking down the path I was under no illusions that the only reason they seemed delighted to see me was because I represented their meal ticket. Although they had access to their pellet food twenty-four hours a day, and while it was clearly both a staple of their diet and nutritionally balanced, by the way they threw it around the coop you could tell they found it only marginally tastier than shredded cardboard.

The routine both of us had developed to keep the chickens entertained as we cleaned out the coop was to give them a liberal sprinkling of something infinitely tastier then the pellets. For an animal that spends its whole day obsessed with finding tasty morsels to eat, the dried mealy worms they received first thing each morning were the poultry equivalent of manna from heaven, and as such resulted in all three powering their favourite food down at speeds that would have eclipsed a sewing machine. Having seemingly recovered from her upset stomach, June, albeit still at the bottom of the pecking order, was still just about able to get her fair share of mealy worms. April was still undoubtedly the alpha female, however, sorting out any incursions into her 'feeding zone' with an aggressive cluck and even occasionally a peck to reinforce the message that she was still in charge. Being the smallest, April was also definitely in the 'brain beats brawn' category, and was also seemingly blessed with not only the sharpest eyesight but also the ability always to be the first to take advantage of any situation which had the potential to result in an edible reward. I suppose the primary reason why most people buy chickens is for the never-ending supply of eggs, but don't underestimate how utterly fascinating they are to watch from an entertainment perspective either. I'd even go as far as to say that their constant antics were such a soap opera that they were capable of matching the best that anything on TV had to offer. If you fancy watching a real-life *Emmerdale* or *EastEnders*, get chickens!

Following on from the success of the bug hotel, I wanted to take the 'dead wood' habitat theme one step further and build a large habitat pile, and so I had arranged for tree surgeon Rob to deliver a huge pile of logs earlier in the week. Having taken on board a big enough breakfast to provide sufficient energy for humping logs, and while Christina conducted a spot of weeding, I got stuck into ferrying the logs down to the bottom of the garden. With the habitat pile best positioned in the shade, we had decided that the spot both adjacent to the bug hotel and in the shadow of the beech hedge would be the perfect location for 'Decomposition Corner', which should make it irresistible to any beetles or fungi fancying a dark and damp place to set up camp.

The logs were a nice, varied mixture of oak, beech and lime, and as such would probably take years to break down completely, but the idea would be that as they slowly decomposed I would keep throwing more logs on top *ad infinitum*, creating the perfect monument to decay. Ever the diligent researcher with a task I had not attempted before, I had read that if the lowest logs were partly buried, this would ensure they stayed damp, leading to the decaying process hitting the ground running. So before any logs were manhandled into position, I wielded the spade to create a shallow rectangular pit into which the bottom layer would sit. With the aim of creating a pyramid, the first logs were placed into the pit, with each log being selected and then, in turn, its orientation carefully chosen to ensure the pile would be stable. Interlocking all the logs to make the habitat pile as sturdy as possible ended up being like a huge game of Tetris, as the pile of logs was slowly transformed into aesthetically pleasing habitat. Unlike the pond and the herbaceous borders, which had memorably attracted the wildlife (in some cases in a matter of just a few hours or days later), the wood pile would of course be a much slower burn, as it would take considerably more time for the white-rot fungi and wood-boring beetles to establish a presence. There was no hurry, though, as Christina and I weren't going anywhere, and judging by the solidity of the pyramid it wouldn't be going anywhere soon either.

Like the bug hotel, one of the best things about the habitat pile was that it had cost me nothing to make and once I'd got my hands on the raw ingredients it had taken relatively little time to slot together. With luck, it would double up as both an interesting garden feature and a wonderfully different habitat for years to come, and if Christina the resident artist didn't think it looked a bad job either, that had to be a result in my book. It was easy, this wild-life gardening lark!

For a while now I'd been a touch disappointed at the lack of mammal sightings in the garden. Apart from the regular antics of the squirrels, the occasional sightings of foxes and hedgehogs and the frankly miraculous view of an otter, I was keen to get some kind of idea as to which other mammals were coming into the garden when we weren't around. Of course, with Chew Stoke being pitch-black at night, there could have been badgers doing the can-can out there each night for all we knew and we would be none the wiser. So to get some kind of idea as to what was happening under the cover of darkness, I'd managed to secure the loan of a special camera trap from a lovely production company I worked with. Now used frequently by wildlife film-making companies to catch footage of shy or rarely seen animals, camera traps are essentially digital surveillance cameras roughly the same size as this book. Crucially, they possess a sensor capable of detecting movement, which, upon being triggered, activates the camera into either taking a picture or some video footage of the animal, which should still hopefully be in front of the camera. The real beauty of these cameras is that not only are they equally able of filming during the day with the avail-able ambient light, but also in the dead of night using a small set of inbuilt infrared lights for illumination, which, being out of the animals' spectral range, means they won't be spooked.

Powered by batteries and recording onto a digital memory card, all I had to do was attach the camera trap to a tree or post, set it running and then simply leave it to record whatever wildlife passed in front of it as 30-second film clips. After consultation with Christina we thought that the best location to try out the camera was at the bottom of the garden near the beech hedge and facing the hole through which May and June had famously disappeared a couple of months back. With the camera turned on and ready to record, and not wanting our boots constantly being filmed as we passed in front of the camera, we then retreated to the cultivated part of the garden to admire Christina's beautiful flower beds.

With no more greenfinch deaths having been uncovered in the ten days since the removal of the feeders, I'd decided that my last chore of the day would be finally to get them back up in the garden. Having been systematically dismantled and scrupulously re-cleaned from top to bottom earlier on in the week, they were then re-filled with fresh seed before unleashing them back amongst unsuspecting greenfinches. It would be really exciting to have the birds back, as their contribution made the garden feel so vibrant and alive.

Taking five minutes for a quick spot-check of the feeders from my favourite vantage point by the landing-hall window early the following morning, the garden still looked very quiet on the feathered front. I wasn't unduly perturbed, as I would have expected it to have taken a while for the birds to relocate the feeders after an absence of over a week, and especially as they'd only been up for little more than three or four hours of daylight. It was somewhat better news following a quick stock-take of June's health outside in the chicken enclosure, though, as despite the fact that she had temporarily stopped egg-laying, she seemed to have miraculously lost the limp and her rear had fortunately stayed devoid of mess following her clean-up.

With the camera trap having now been running for one whole night down by the beech hedge in the hope of catching some nocturnal activity, the clever move would probably have been to leave it be for a few more nights, but with my curiosity now at fever pitch, I simply couldn't wait any longer and opened it up to see if it had recorded any footage. The digital display on the small screen inside the camera seemed to suggest that, despite the camera being very low on battery power, it had still managed to make three recordings.

The only way of actually seeing what was on these clips necessitated the removal of the SD card before putting it into a card reader attached to a computer, so with great trepidation, and back inside, I followed the on-screen instructions and then clicked on the first file to see what had been caught on camera. The first clip, perhaps to no great shock, did involve a mammal – me – as I was treated to a big (and none-too-flattering) 30-second close-up of my nose, whilst I fiddled with the controls. Glad at least that I'd blown my nose that morning and that the camera was fully functioning, I clicked expectantly on to clip number two. If clip one gave a marvellous close-up of my nose then clip two had another part of my anatomy covered, this time filming a close-up of my boots walking away. Clicking on the file for the final video clip, the image immediately cut to black and white, meaning that the last sequence had been filmed at night using the infrared lights. Initially it seemed that the camera had been tripped to no avail, until about halfway through the 30-second clip, quick as a flash, a mammal ran through and straight past the camera, which I almost missed until replaying and pausing froze the action.

We had only filmed Andy and Lorraine's big fat cat! Despite having drawn a blank for foxes and badgers, I wasn't too disappointed, as at least the camera looked like it was fully functioning for both day and night usage and this had been a good trial run. Now all I needed were some new batteries, and the camera would be ready for an extended period out in the back garden. Mammals beware – we were on your case! I joined Christina for brunch in the garden. It looked like another sunblock day, and with my back still sore from manoeuvring all the logs for the dead-wood habitat pile, I felt inclined to spend rather more of the weekend enjoying the garden than actually working in it. In the space of seven months we'd already achieved an awful lot and we felt justifiably proud of how we'd managed to transform the garden into something that was pulling in the wildlife left, right and centre. Since January and in rough chronological order, we'd had a diseased tree removed and the other trees managed to enhance their longevity, erected nest boxes, assembled two compost bins, added 20 yards of native hedgerow, formed a small orchard, built a raised vegetable bed, created a meadow, dug a pond, formed two huge herbaceous borders, constructed a bug hotel and assembled a habitat pile. In addition to the work creating the habitats, we'd also managed, wherever possible, to identify most things that had trotted, flown or crawled into or through the garden, and with the majority of the big construction jobs now done, we sincerely hoped the rest of the year would be composed of mostly smaller jobs, freeing up plenty of time to do the most important job of all – to enjoy the garden!

Despite August being just about the quietest month for birdsong, the wood pigeon was still calling away from the beech with its 'I'm bor-ing I am, I'm bor-ing I am' call until flushed out of the tree by a jackdaw. Capable of producing up to three broods during a long breeding season, and with eggs recorded in every single month, it is no surprise that their population has rapidly increased to over three million breeding pairs, making it one of our commonest garden birds. As I watched it flying over the garden, it then put down a marker to any other wood pigeons in the area that it was still holding territory, by flying up steeply, only to stall in mid-air as it clapped its wings above its back to produce a whip-like crack, before gliding back down. As I looked up to follow the arc of the wood pigeon's display flight, I could also see that both house martin instructors and their trainees had also returned for a continuation of their flying lessons. Then suddenly their chattering noise stopped, and, looking back up to see where they'd gone, I realised that they'd just vanished into thin air. I instantly understood why when I spotted the rakish, streamlined silhouettes of two birds that eat house martins for breakfast … HOBBIES OVER THE GARDEN!!

It was one of those classic 'right time, right place' lucky moments, as I could have stood in the garden all year looking skyward and not seen a single hobby flying over, making it the bird equivalent of the otter sighting back in May. The hobby is for me one of the most wonderful birds of prey, and as I lifted my binoculars up for a view I could clearly see the 'rufous trousers', so distinctive of this species, on one of the birds, making at least this one an adult. Along with the osprey, honey buzzard and Montagu's harrier, this is one of our truly migratory birds of prey, only spending around four months principally in the southern half of Britain, before undertaking the long journey back to spend the next winter in southern Africa. The hobby is also a species which not only prefers to catch its dinner on the wing but often chooses to eat it on the wing as well. Using a combination of its phenomenal eyesight and unparalleled manoeuvrability in the air, the hobby spends the day's warmest hours dashing across the sky, catching anything from beetles and dragonflies to inexperienced swallows and martins – no wonder the house martins had suddenly dashed for the exit.

Hobbies are commonly seen over the Somerset Levels in spring, having just arrived from the continent, and on a fine day in May it is possible to see upwards of 50 wheeling away as they refuel after their long journey. They then become much more difficult to see once they have dispersed to their breeding territories. All of a sudden the business of breeding makes them much more introverted, so to catch up with a couple of birds as they flew east towards the lake was a marvellous stroke of luck. A hobby on my garden bird list, I have to say, felt mighty fine.

By now the midsummer and midday sun was beating down on the garden, making it not only uncomfortably warm for us humans, but turning the pond into a frenetic hive of activity, as a male southern hawker dragonfly and a couple of common blue damsels were joined by another new species for the garden. Common darters are traditionally one of the last dragonflies to emerge and can quite often be seen right up until the first frosts in November. Tending to figure at the small end on the dragonfly scale, this jack russell of the dragonfly world makes up for its diminutive size by its hyperactivity, especially on those warm days when little basking is needed. The males are characterised by a distinctive orange-red abdomen, and, being territorial, are always much more obvious than the predominantly yellow females which prefer to keep a lower profile for fear of being harassed by the oversexed males. It is also a dragonfly that both likes to perch on a regular basis and is insatiably curious, and to test just how curious, I was able to attempt a neat little trick. Lying down by the pond, I then stuck out my arm over the water at an angle of around 30 degrees with my index finger additionally outstretched. With the males constantly scoping out new perching points from which to give them a better view of the current state of affairs over the pond, it didn't take more than a couple of minutes before one of the two males buzzing around couldn't resist himself and landed on my finger. After six years of dating Christina, it can sometimes be hard to impress her these days, as she is familiar with all my jokes, amusing anecdotes and party tricks, but I have to say, my dragon-taming trick definitely tickled her – there was life in the old dog yet!

With the dragonflies so active it would have been surprising for the butterflies not to be taking advantage of the fine weather too, and a quick inspection of the garage flower border quickly revealed both a couple of second-generation green-veined whites on the verbena and the unmistakable ragged outline of the comma, half sunbathing and half feeding on the sedum, which had at last opened to reveal its tiny fuchsia-pink flowers.

So-called because of the small white comma-like mark on the underside of its hind wing, the comma is certainly a butterfly of contrasts. The upper side of its wings is a vivid and beautifully coloured combination of orange hues. But as soon as the wings are snapped shut, the mixed greys and browns on its underwings suddenly turn the butterfly into a dead ringer for a partly decayed oak-leaf, with the comma-mark representing a crack in the centre where the 'leaf' seems to be breaking up. For a butterfly that over-winters in the adult form, this supreme camouflage is critical if it is to avoid detection by a hungry great tit as it hunkers down amongst drifts of dead leaves during the coldest months of the year. With many of our butterflies lasting no longer than a couple of weeks in their adult form, the commas can reach veteran ages, and in all likelihood this butterfly, which would of course have been the progeny of overwintering butterflies itself, could quite conceivably last for an astonishing 10 months. In a few months it too would be hunkering down for the winter, only finally shuffling off the mortal coil once it had successfully ensured that its genes had been passed on.

During the entire Victorian and Edwardian era the comma was considered an incredibly rare butterfly, with just occasional records across a few southern English counties, but it has since become one of the few British species that has bucked the general butterfly trend of slow and sad declines. So spectacular has the upturn in this butterfly's fortune been, that it can now commonly be seen right across southern England and Wales and is currently expanding its range north to Scotland at a breakneck speed. Dare I say, it is one of England's few successful and most welcome export stories.

Over the last few weeks, I had begun to notice a very small collection of droppings beginning to accumulate just inside the garage door, which had only become conspicuous amongst the general mess in the garage when, rather hilariously, they had begun to stand out against the white porcelain of a duplicate toilet that had been accidentally sent to us when our bathroom had been re-fitted back in the spring. Having been too busy to examine them properly, I'd ignored them until a tidy-up of the garage that afternoon brought them to my attention. Sticking my hand in the toilet bowl to fish a couple out, whilst simultaneously privately congratulating the producer of the droppings on its most remarkable aim, it was immediately obvious that they belonged to bats. Being small and cylindrical, with a powdery, crumbly texture when rubbed between the thumb and forefinger, bat droppings are quite different to those produced by mice, for example, which by contrast turn into tiny, hard pellets when dry. The droppings are not at all unpleasant as they mostly represent the minute indigestible remains of insect prey, and with a magnifying lens the tiny pieces of iridescent exoskeletons can often be noticed in some of the droppings of larger species. These, however, were pretty small droppings and so produced by a fairly small bat, and, being relatively fresh, meant that whatever had made them would in all likelihood currently be in residence!

The ramifications of this discovery were immediate: the garage must have bats; how else could they have got there? Taking a ladder to reach the loft hatch and access the false ceiling, and with Christina at the bottom, I ascended up into the space, noting immediately how cool, still and quiet it was up there. It had lain completely empty and it took me no longer than a matter of seconds to find three small distinct piles of droppings equally spaced out at the base of the central adjoining wall to Marjory and Dennis's half of the garage, with the pile closest to the door partly surrounding a small hole in the floor and through which I could see the gleaming white of the toilet bowl directly below! Would you believe it?! All of a sudden it began to make sense why, when we had been bat detecting in the garden the previous month, some of the bats seemed to be emanating from the drive. I had suspected that they were just flitting around the garage directly from Marjory and Dennis's garden, but they must have been coming out of the garage instead!

Immediately above the respective piles of bat droppings, no bats could be seen, and with relatively few bats choosing to hang freely (in contradiction to the way they are often portrayed in scary movies), but instead tucking themselves out of sight into the smallest crevices, it was no wonder that a cursory search didn't reveal any. As all British bats have legislative protection in their roosts, making it illegal intentionally to disturb them without a bat licence, which suffice to say I didn't have, I was also very eager to beat a hasty retreat before they became aware of my presence. Back down below, I was still struggling to work out where their entrance and exit point was until Christina pointed out what could have been no more than a two-inch gap between the top of the roller door and the door surround that neither of us had ever noticed before – just perfect from a bat's perspective.

The next two questions to be answered were blindingly obvious: to which species did they belong, and how many bats were roosting in there? Tackling the first question, the droppings were indeed very small, suggesting that they might have been produced by one of the species of pipistrelles, and we had, after all (and with some confidence), recently identified soprano pipistrelles among the bats picked up by the detector in the garden. As for how many bats were in there, well, by the limited amounts of droppings, clearly it wasn't a large colony, but they did suggest that we had at least three. To confirm this, of course, there was only one way to know for sure – a dusk-time vigil was needed.

Moving the garden furniture up to the patio after dinner would afford us that front-row seat from which to spot any emerging bats; and with dusk due at 8.35pm, we took our seats with the obligatory bottle of wine, glasses and bat detector to see what would happen. For an accurate count it was crucial we maintained concentration, as quite often when bats emerge from their roost site, because it's still quite light outside and as they know the exit route so intimately, they quite often don't even bother to initially echolocate. This of course meant that the bat detector could conceivably fail to give us that vital second's advanced warning to actually see the bat coming out of the garage, or even confuse any emerging bats with an individual simply flying past from elsewhere.

As 9pm approached, the light was beginning to get murky and it would soon be getting difficult to pick out any bats against the dark fascia of the garage, if any bats were in there at all, that was! Then suddenly at 9.02pm we both saw a bat drop out of the slot above the door, only to then disappear in the murk before being relocated over the garden, as it was easily picked out against the much lighter sky. Only at that point did we hear the bat detector belatedly splutter into life as the bat commenced echolocation to gain its bearings.

Realising that spotting more against the garage in the ever-decreasing light would have been impossible, I quickly adopted a technique I'd seen bat workers use when I worked as Bill Oddie's researcher on a film about bats at Lacock Abbey in Wiltshire. In order to count the number of emergences effectively, the bat workers had lain down under the roost entrance, meaning that with the sky as the backdrop the bats' silhouettes could much more effectively be picked out. Within seconds of me getting into place as I lay prostrate on the drive, a second bat was this time clearly seen dropping out of the slot above the garage door right over my head, quickly followed by a third! How many more were in there? Well, the answer to that, after another 20 minutes fruitlessly lying on my back, with neither sight nor sound of any more, seemed to be none.

My original guess, based on the piles of droppings, had indeed been correct: our roost contained three bats! But was that enough to justify a colony? Too bloody right it was!

It was my first full day back at home for eight days, and on awaking I stumbled into the bathroom before letting the girls out into their enclosure, a responsibility that Christina had taken on during my absence. With the clear glass now in the bathroom window, I got my first view of the garden from there each morning, as I dreamily and absent-mindedly gazed down towards the pond, apple trees and the meadow beyond. Looking out and half expecting to see a few greenfinch and a blue tit or two, I then saw a small blue form perched on one of the stones, which seemed to be intently staring into the water. I thought for a moment my eyes were deceiving me before doing one of those comedy double-takes and realising I was indeed looking at – a kingfisher!

With binoculars standing by the landing-hall window, we admired the adult male, easily identified by his all-black bill, still avidly watching something in the water. With no fish in the pond, the only food item he could possibly have been after was one of the newts (apparently an incredibly rare occurrence), or even an aquatic beetle or two. After about five minutes he decided that there was nothing in the pond to tempt him to get wet and he then flew briefly up into the quince for a few seconds before scooting back across the meadow to the river. 'What an amazing start to the day,' Christina said.

To be honest I was still in a bit of a daze as I shared my story with the chickens, which didn't seem in the least bit interested in what I had to say to them, but only in what I had in my hand to give them. Talk about an animal that thinks about nothing other than its own stomach! Fortunately the other garden birds seemed by now to have forgiven my removal of the feeders and were once more piling in, with primarily greenfinch visiting the bell feeder, meaning the tits and robins were relegated to the far less popular cage feeder.

Having worked at the weekend, Christina had been given the day off, so she accompanied me into Bristol to do a spot of voiceover for some *One Show* films I had recently recorded, before our preplanned afternoon visit to the aquatic shop in Bath. We had originally wanted to replace the pond lily that had not survived in the pond (primarily because I suspected I'd planted it too deep, too quickly), but on arriving there, the choice was pretty ropey, so with Christina checking out the terrestrial plants section, I busied myself admiring the stone birdbaths. I was aware that the dreaded trichomonosis could as easily be passed between birds at a communal bird bath as it had been at the feeders, so I was keen to replace the frankly rubbish old one hanging in the hawthorn standard with a brand-new bath. Immediately my eyes were drawn to the baths which were made out of concrete, but which looked just like the stone fonts you'd see at a stately home. Not sure if something as Gothic-looking as these would look out of place in an ex-council house garden, I consulted my style guru, who said she quite liked them and, hey presto, following our selection, our joint account was just under £100 the lighter – or should I say *over*, after Christina had tacked onto the bill a late-flowering gaura, a couple more sedums and a beautiful lobelia to ensure a strong flowering presence well into the autumn.

Back at home, the division of labour split along normal lines with Christina weeding, pruning and planting up a few gaps that had developed in the pond border as I stuck to my strengths, i.e. the physical dogsbody work. The first job was to manhandle the remarkably heavy bird bath into position so it was ready for action. The previous week I had ordered a product called Citrosan over the internet, having read good reviews of its abilities as a natural sanitiser, which would also help to reduce the spread of a range of wild bird diseases including trichomonosis. Extracted from oranges, it was non-toxic, which both Christina and I considered as an essential pre-requisite for use in our garden, and so following the guidelines I poured the correct concentration into the water and then placed the bird bath just to the side of the cage feeder and in between the raised bed and the pond.

My first task complete, I then undertook a massive tidy-up of the garden, starting with clearing out the water butt at the corner of the garage, which looked like it hadn't been touched for at least a couple of decades and so comprised two-thirds water and a third silt. The sludge at the bottom of the butt proved the perfect liquid fertiliser, and so this was distributed around both main beds which had begun to look thirsty after a couple of hot days.

Two new and slightly bizarre floral additions to the garage border which had shot up out of nowhere in the last couple of weeks were a couple of sunflowers, which must have become established from seeds dropped by birds raiding the feeders. With both plants now at a height close to six feet, even though they looked slightly incongruous sticking head and shoulders above everything in the bed apart from the verbenas, we didn't have the heart to remove them. Besides, we hoped in the autumn they might then go on to provide excellent feeding opportunities for some of the finches.

Christina, in the meantime, had re-stocked the pond herbaceous border so beautifully it looked like something out of *Homes & Gardens*. In addition to all the plants we'd purchased that day, she had somehow found room to plant a couple of penstemons, a philadelphus and a few candelabra primulas. By the time we'd finished, and with the light low in the sky casting a golden hue over most of the garden, I couldn't think of any other time when I'd seen the garden looking as lovely as it did that very evening.

As I'd had to go filming over the preceding weekend, the dying embers of August brought the welcome relief of a Bank Holiday, which meant at least that the Monday would be free for Christina and me to spend together in the garden before she was due back at work and I was back on the road again. With another beautifully warm day stretching ahead of us, I looked out of the bathroom window and was instantly delighted to see a couple of greenfinches already using the newly installed font-shaped water-bath for a drink. With both finches on opposite sides of the font, it looked a touch comical as they took it in turns to bow down to imbibe a beak-full of the Citrosan-infused water before throwing their heads back to drink it down, then taking their turn to ensure the coast was clear while the other bird took a drink. It must clearly be thirsty work eating primarily seeds for a living! With the birds self-medicating, I found myself fervently hoping that this would be the last we saw of the trichomonosis.

It also looked like the insects were as keen to make the most of the beautiful weather as we were, and by 10am I could already see that the battle lines had been drawn across the pond with two male southern hawker dragonflies clashing for supremacy. A common darter was also spotted well below the hawkers' radar and was busily making sure that he too would be ready and willing to chase any intruders out of his air space. The sedums in the flowerbeds were also proving rich pickings for a different suite of insects to the pond with a couple of worker bumblebee species *Bombus terrestris* and *Bombus pascuorum* both foraging for nectar for the adults back in the nest and pollen for the developing larvae. I'd been a bit disappointed not to have encountered a bumblebee nest within the confines of the garden, and with bumblebees generally not

travelling more than 400 yards from the nest I had also to confront the possibility that they had nested in another garden close by – how could they?! Interestingly enough, the honey bees which were also being attracted to the garden by the sedums were patently from a hive close by, and I made a mental note to ask around as to who kept bees in the village. Whoever they were, in my opinion it would only have been right and proper for them to donate a jar of the bees' honey to us, by way of thanks for the contribution our flowers were obviously making!

With Christina's attention elsewhere in the garden, she then made a remarkable discovery in the centre bed, which had scarcely been touched since our arrival, and which featured as its centre-piece a couple of Mr Gregory's roses. Looking at their foliage, Christina had noticed that a large number of the leaves had become disfigured by the removal of very precise hole-punch-sized semi-circles that had been neatly cut out of the leaf edges. Instantly recognising the damage, I realised that we could add another species of bee to our garden list in addition to the ones buzzing around the sedums, as we patently had leaf-cutter bees too!

Although it resembles a honey bee in size, the leaf-cutter bee has little else in common with its more famous cousin. One of the solitary bees, leaf-cutters don't use the leaf pieces as food, but instead fashion them into walls of the individual brood chambers for their larvae within the female's nesting burrow. With the rose one of the most commonly sought-after plants, the female bee straddles the edges of a leaf, and then, holding on with the claws on the end of her feet, she snips out a section of the leaf with her jaws, a process which usually only takes a few seconds. The leaf segment is then rolled up and carried along the axis of her body under the abdomen back to the nest. The nest itself is a long, tubular, cigar-like structure that can be situated anywhere in the garden from a crevice in a wall to under the eaves of a garage or a dead, hollow plant stem, and consists of a series of anywhere between six and ten cells, which are of similar size and shape to a thimble. These excised leaf sections are then used to build up the side walls and the lids between each of these cells, and are gummed together with a combination of the plant's sap and possible salivary secretions from the bee. As with the mason bees, each chamber is then provisioned with a pollen/nectar mix for the single egg before being sealed, with the same process being repeated with the next cell in line.

Astonishingly, the bees closer to the entrance are always males, and so will emerge before the females situated in the rear chambers. Virtually harmless, these bees are incredibly important pollinators and were almost certainly nesting very close to the rose bush, but unless we saw the female going in and out of a hole smaller than a five-pence piece as she provisioned the nest, it would be like looking for the proverbial needle in a haystack. On this occasion, though, just knowing that the leaf-cutters had found our garden attractive was good enough for me!

With the new water bath already needing to be refilled, I mixed up some more water from the now newly cleaned water butt with the appropriate quantity of Citrosan and then knelt down to top up our latest exciting garden feature. Crunch! Realising that I had trodden on something with my huge steel-toe-capped work boots, I promptly moved my foot aside to reveal I'd accidentally crushed the skull of another dead greenfinch which had been tucked in amongst the grass at the base of the font – the dreaded 'trich' had struck again. Really distraught that the disease had notched up another casualty, which contrasted with the large numbers of seemingly healthy greenfinch that were visiting the feeders every day, I just had to hope and pray that this represented the very tail-end of the disease, as I couldn't bear the thought of taking down all the feeders again.

To try and cheer me up, Christina suggested that checking the camera trap down at the hole in the beech hedge would take my mind off the fourth grisly greenfinch. Having finally sourced a 12-volt battery which had eliminated the power problem we'd encountered when first trialling it earlier in the month, I'd placed it back out in the garden a couple of days before in our quest for more mammal records and then promptly forgotten it was there. As usual with Christina, it was a brilliant idea, and on opening up the camera trap I was delighted to find that not only did it seem to be still working but it had filmed seven separate clips. Removing the memory card, I could barely contain my excitement as we both rushed back inside to my office to find out what had been recorded.

Sure enough, the memory card reader revealed that there were seven clips, and, deciding to watch them in chronological order, we clicked on the first one with baited breath. Shot in the daytime, the first clip showed a mammal sure enough, but the only problem was that it was domestic. A black and white cat I'd never even seen before was strolling nonchalantly through the garden before disappearing through the beech hedge and out of shot, into the playing field. Pleased that the camera and sensor were both indeed working, we moved straight onto the second clip and another file shot in the daytime produced a second cat, this time a tortoiseshell with a white undercarriage that I had recognised in our garden on a fairly regular basis and chased out on a number of occasions as well.

For the record I don't have anything against cats (or cat owners), but with so many birds attracted to my feeders I just didn't want them in my garden. It's thought that there are around eight million cats in the UK, and the Mammal Society has recently estimated that they take around 55 million garden birds a year – yes, you did indeed read that figure correctly. Quite an astonishing number, I think you'll agree.

Without further ado we clicked onto the third clip which then cut straight to black and white, meaning it had been shot at night, as we watched what looked to be a healthy fox ambling right through the shot, totally unaware that it had been caught on candid camera. What a result! Both of us had only seen a fox in the garden a couple of times each, so it was great news that it was obviously a much more regular visitor than either of us had realised. Clip four was devoid of any action, with an animal possibly having passed in front of the camera so quickly it had tripped the sensor but had avoided being filmed. Clip five then successfully captured our third cat, this time a tabby I had seen on just a couple of occasions as it too used the hole as the thoroughfare to go about its nocturnal business terrorising small mammals. With two clips left we needed something more than just a fox, and on playing the penultimate clip at first we could see nothing, until after about 10 seconds into the footage a badger's tail could just be seen on the edge of the frame. A badger in the garden! I instantly forgot about the greenfinch, because at last I had definitive proof that the hole was part of a thoroughfare used by badgers, and this had after all only been the second badger sighting in the garden, the first being Christina's brief view on 1 April. It had only taken me seven months to see a badger in my own garden. Better late than never!

The clever thing about these camera traps is that not only do they record the animal, but they also date-stamp when the clip was filmed, so I could categorically state that on 28 August 2011 at 11.20pm a badger had been in our garden! I was then elated as I opened the final clip on the computer screen to instantly reveal another badger shot taken at 2.44 the following morning. Unlike the sixth clip, where we'd only briefly seen the badger's tail, this badger stayed in full view for the full thirty seconds, snuffling around in front of the camera rather than just trotting through like the cats and fox had done. Did I forget to mention I'd sprinkled a few peanuts about, as an incentive for it to hang around?

SEPTEMBER

HARVESTING THE FRUITS OF OUR LABOURS

Following fast on the heels of the cats, fox and badger, the start of September was quick to usher in a new mammal for the garden. Normally this would have been a most welcome event, and possibly even cause for celebration, were it not for the fact that this new species also happened to be a mammal of some notoriety. I had just cleaned out the chickens, and I was sitting downstairs in the kitchen with Christina spooning down a late breakfast with one eye on the garden, when I noticed a small creature with a suspiciously long tail emerge out of the garage flower border. Cautiously crossing the couple of yards of open ground to the caged feeder, it then proceeded to mop up the food spilt by the birds above.

I raised my binoculars, even though I was already perfectly aware as to the identity of the mammal, and I was able to see the pointed snout, uniform brown grading to greyish fur on the underside and the long, naked tail of a brown rat. Originally not a native species to the UK, it's thought that the brown rat was first recorded in Britain in 1720, having slowly spread west from its origins in Russia and the Far East as the human population expanded in number and established trade routes. Forever associated with sewers, rubbish dumps, farm buildings and in fact any urban area where food is discarded, the rat has very successfully managed to make a living alongside us, as it has taken advantage of the shelter we provide and the almost limitless supply of food our 'throwaway' society produces. Of course, controlling brown rats nowadays is not just about preventing them from competing with the food we eat, as they are also unfortunately capable of transmitting both salmonella and Weil's disease to us humans.

Utterly reviled by most people, from a dispassionate or Darwinian 'survival of the fittest' viewpoint there is also something to be greatly admired about this tenacious animal. One key ingredient in the species' success is its unbelievable adaptability, with brown rats capable of surviving in just about any habitat and eating virtually anything thrown their way. Additionally, their resistance to pesticides and extreme wariness have also combined to make them incredibly resilient in the face of numerous eradication attempts.

Had I thought about it before, I suppose I shouldn't have been surprised that rats would make an appearance in the garden at some point. They have always been attracted to watercourses, and due to the frankly ridiculous number of feeders the garden was carrying, it must have been the equivalent of putting up a welcome sign in bright neon to such a streetwise and canny animal. Like the chimney-nesting jackdaws and the ram-raiding squirrels before, it once again made me realise that having made the garden as welcoming as possible for the so-called 'attractive' species, such as bullfinches and badgers, it was inevitable that a few undesirables would also turn up without invitations to gate-crash the party as well. I wasn't entirely sure what to do about the situation either, as brown rats would not exactly be as easy to remove as the jackdaws had been from the chimney. The employment of a chimney sweep to dislodge the nest (and before they had laid a clutch, for the record), had persuaded the jackdaws to nest elsewhere, but rats are past masters in the dark art of being one step ahead of us humans, and so the only thing that could be done for the time being was to monitor the situation.

With both of us having arranged a day off, we had an important morning's work ahead of us, as the following day was the Chew Stoke Harvest Home, an annual bonanza which also happened to be the biggest day of the year for the village – and as new residents we were keen to be part of the action. Having been asked to officially open the Harvest Home in 2010, in my capacity as a minor television celebrity, I knew it to be a fun day incorporating a flower and produce show, a dog parade, children's sports, a vintage car rally and more stalls than you could shake a stick at.

One of the main reasons for originally having built the organic raised bed and grown our own vegetables, apart from the obvious wish to feed ourselves, had been a desire to enter some of our produce into the Harvest Home. Neither Christina nor I had ever entered anything before into a village fete, but with the feeling that it would be a fun experience, we had put aside an hour or so to ready our entries for submission. Despite Chew Stoke being a village of marginally fewer than a thousand people, I already knew it to be a place that punched well above its weight from a horticultural perspective, and so we were not under any illusions, knowing that we'd be up against some serious competition from gardeners who had been growing home produce for decades.

We dug up the beetroot and red onions, which had been our most successful vegetables by far, and we then proceeded to harvest the best cherry tomatoes and quince before finally selecting the most uniform eggs as produced by April, May and June. Being first-timers to this type of competition, we were unsure of protocol and so were left with a dilemma as how best to present our produce, beyond cleaning them of soil (in the case of the beetroot and onions), or poo (in the case of the eggs), so in the end we just went on instinct. Having scrubbed and trimmed our two vegetable entries to remove the roots and shoots, we decided that the best presentation would be the simplest and so we displayed them on a paper plate. Our two fruit entries needed no preparatory work whatsoever and likewise would also be presented on a plate. Saving the best category to last, we really went to town with the eggs, which were placed in a small wicker basket on a bed of hay.

With all our five categories suitably prepared, I don't mind saying I felt a swelling sense of pride at the humble offerings we would be putting forward for public inspection the following day. There might be both bigger and better in the village, but would there be any tastier?

Waking up late the following day in somewhat of a mild panic as the produce had to be delivered to the marquee by 10am, I cleaned out the chickens in double-quick time before we hopped in the car, with our assorted entries, and drove round to the Harvest Home, which spread over a couple of fields diagonally across from the village shop. Earlier in the week Christina had paid the few pence necessary to register our five different entries, so we were able to go straight into the marquee – disregarding the sign which grandly stated 'Exhibitors Only', to lay out our produce.

Deciding to put out our onions first, it was only then that we realised we may have suddenly jumped in at the deep end, with nothing more than the vegetative equivalent of water-wings, when we compared our onions to the half a dozen other entries. Firstly our pool-ball sized onions were much smaller then most of the others on display, with the largest couple of entries sporting onions that I swear were only marginally smaller than Christina's head. Secondly, our presentation skills had been also left wanting when compared to the other entries, with the majority having wrapped the tops of their onions with raffia and placed them on mini-flower-pots so to display them upright and to their best effect, whereas all we had was the paper plate for them to roll around on. Flirting briefly with the idea of removing our onions entirely, we decided that we would put them in because all entries were guaranteed anonymity and it should be just as much about the taking part as the winning. Moving on to the beetroots, it was the same story, with our offerings up against bigger, more uniformly shaped and better presented vegetables. On the bright side there were only five entries in this category, with a couple of submissions not too dissimilar from our own, giving us an outside chance of a place. The same could not be said, however, of our cherry tomatoes, or quince, which we had submitted in the 'cherry tomatoes' (unsurprisingly) and 'unusual fruits' categories, with the competition here being intense. As an American once quoted to me when I had asked him to carry out a job he thought impossible, 'you've got somewhere between a "slim chance" and "no chance", and "slim" has just left town.'

The one 'chance' of Chew Stoke Harvest Home glory we thought we *did* have would be with our eggs, as they were all not only of the same size, shape and uniformity of colour, but were also beautifully presented too. As we placed our eggs in amongst the five other entries, both Christina and I were confident that, come the moment of judging, we would indeed be in the mix. Having done all we could (bar sabotage the opposition – which had been tempting), we retired home so as to enable me to carry out a very important task in the back garden, which would also have the added benefit of taking my mind off the Harvest Home while our produce was being judged.

Up until now the one habitat that we had done least with, but which in many ways had rewarded us the most, was the meadow. Throughout the spring and summer, it had not only produced a fabulous array of flowers and grasses, but also an assemblage of insects which otherwise wouldn't have come near our garden in a month of Sundays. All this had been achieved by simply letting what was present in the seed-bank grow unfettered without fear of being chopped off at the ankles courtesy of the lawnmower. As I explained in detail earlier, the key to creating an environment in which meadow-type plants will flourish is to keep nutrient levels as low as possible. The avowed enemy of the vast majority of British wildflowers is fertiliser, as enriching the soil enables the mobilisation of a different suite of fast-growing, aggressive and opportunistic plants with huge appetites that will then crowd out the very species I was so keen to nurture. So any compost would be strictly confined to the flowerbeds.

The way to manage a meadow in your own back garden is to try and simulate conditions where meadows are successfully administered elsewhere on a much larger scale. If you look at all meadows managed specifically for a rich diversity of flowers and grasses, they will at some point be grazed by animals. As to how many animals are used, of which type and when they are best placed on the meadow is not within the scope of this book, as a separate thesis of equal size to this tome could easily be written on the fine art of grazing as a conservation management tool. But suffice to say grazing carries out the vital job of keeping down those aggressive species, and as it also puts a stop to the establishment of scrub, it keeps the meadows in an arrested state of development, thereby preventing natural succession ultimately back into woodland. As we didn't have any access to sheep or goats throughout the summer, and it would probably have been too small an area to graze anyway, the next best technique is to 'simulate grazing' by cutting the meadow after the flowers have finished flowering and set seed. Cutting the meadow, and then crucially removing the dead biomass, should ensure that the meadow's soil will retain its nutrient-poor status as the cut plant material will be denied the opportunity to break down and re-fertilise the soil. The physical act of cutting the plants will also enable any seed that has already set to be shaken out (particularly for annual plants), ensuring they have an opportunity to establish a foothold for the following year.

Of course I could have simply taken the lawnmower to the meadow, but considering this method a touch draconian, and keen to emulate the way meadows had historically been cut in their heyday, I had bought a scythe on eBay. Forever associated with being the huge two-handed tool that is carried around by the Grim Reaper, the long-handled scythe was originally designed for mowing grass and harvesting crops in a pre-mechanistic era with much smaller fields than we have today, and so would be perfect for my pocket-sized meadow.

The scythe had been professionally sharpened, as they are much easier to use when razor-sharp, and it was now not just an efficient

agricultural tool but also a formidable piece of weaponry. The long wooden shaft, or snaith, was shaped with a slight 'S' curve for ease of use and possessed two small handles at right angle to the snaith to ensure that the vicious two-foot-long blade was kept parallel to the ground. The technique was to twist the body to the left, which would then move the blade in a long arc from right to left, slicing the vegetation as it went. It was also crucial to take regular breaks, not just because it was physically demanding work, but to give time for the blade to be re-sharpened, as progress is much slower when the edge becomes blunted.

Using a scythe is traditionally a skilled task that requires a degree of practice to perfect, but on giving it a go, I was delighted with my progress as the scythe made short work of the lank vegetation in a manner that was certainly far gentler than a lawnmower could ever have achieved. I raced through at least half of the meadow, but as the physical nature of the job began to affect my technique, no doubt compounded by the blade losing its edge, it quickly became apparent that it was a good job we only possessed a small meadow. I stopped to take on liquid refreshment brought out by Christina, and to sharpen the blade with a special stone I had also purchased with the scythe, and I felt a bit like an agricultural serf from the pre-Great War era – cutting acres in this fashion would certainly have made a man of you! Eventually, after an hour's solid swishing, the whole meadow had been trimmed without any major incidents. In fact, the only minor mishap had occurred when I had underestimated the length of the blade, resulting in the scythe accidentally snagging one of the apple trees, but fortunately there seemed to have been no long-term damage. Leaving the cut vegetation scattered across the meadow, which gave any seeds not yet dislodged time to fall out, I decided that the raking up could be carried out another day as our presence was needed back at the Harvest Home. We had some certificates to collect!

Arriving back at the site in a state of nervous anticipation, we made a bee-line for the produce marquee to find out our fate, only to discover it was closed for judging. Peeking through the entrance like a naughty schoolboy, I could see the judges walking around to each table (and category) in turn with all the pomp and circumstance of the judges who adjudicate at prestigious events like Crufts or the Chelsea Flower Show. With the jury still out, Christina and I decided to go for a wander to take our minds off the judging process, and we soon began to bump into all manner of people we either knew before relocating to the village or had met since moving in. My *One Show* boss, Chris and his lovely wife Natalie, who also lived in the village, were the first to greet us, and then we bumped into more village residents in the form of my good mate Jamie and his family (the man with the house martin nests), and finally Phil and his family, who'd done more to make us feel welcome in the village than anyone – it was turning into a meet and greet of the great and good! Christina and I also had a go at winning a cuddly toy on both the darts and the ten-pin bowling, but to no avail. No matter, I thought, the rewards and the plaudits would be coming soon enough.

Suddenly Jamie came over and told me that the produce tent had just been opened, which had almost resulted in close to a stampede as all the competitors had rushed in to see where their produce had placed. Entering the marquee, it seemed that each trestle table had been adorned with certificates denoting first, second and third place next to the winners in each of the respective categories. We briefly debated where to go first, and we dismissed the cherry tomatoes and quince as 'also-rans' and decided to start with the onions. With no certificate next to our plate it was immediately obvious we hadn't been placed, which to be honest had hardly been a surprise given the strength of the opposition, so undeterred we then went on to what we had previously thought might be our second-strongest category, beetroots.

We were gutted as we had only come either fourth or fifth out of five. Looking at the other entries to see where the certificates had been allocated, I entirely concurred with the judges over which had won the first and second prizes, but our beets were way better than the pokey old plate of root vegetables selected as Third Best Beet in Show. Feeling a touch deflated, we were however still hopeful, as our strongest category was next, the eggs would deliver for sure – April, May and June would save the day.

Moving quickly over to the eggs category I couldn't believe it. We hadn't been placed there either – we'd been robbed. Next to the eggs were six saucers containing a cracked egg from each respective entry, and looking at our egg, the yolk was beautifully yellow as per usual, but there was also a small amount of blood on the edge of the yolk, which must have gone against us. Since spring, when we had first bought the chickens, I must have cracked open at least 200 eggs from the girls and seen blood in the yolk on no more than a couple of occasions, so it was spectacularly unlucky. For a brief second, I was so bitterly disappointed and angry that I thought of turning over the table and storming out, as it felt like the whole of the village were saying, as of one voice, that our attempts to inculcate ourselves into a rural life had been nothing better than fourth-rate.

Since Christina knew me as well as anybody, she immediately spotted the mist descending and made everything instantly better by saying 'sod them anyway; it's two for one in the cake tent!' It made me instantly laugh and in a split second I saw how ridiculous and hilarious in equal measure my moment of petulance had been. Nevertheless, I left Christina alone to suffer the final indignity, as she went over to the 'Cherry Tomato' and 'Unusual Fruit' stands, only returning some 30 seconds later to confirm that we were indeed zero for five.

Leaving the tent, we bumped straight into Jamie with his family. 'How did you get on?' he asked, having been treated to a detailed blow-by-blow account of all our entries earlier on. 'We're obviously fourth-rate smallholders' I replied.

After a much-needed lie-in the day after our humiliation at the Harvest Home, we decided a gentle wander around the garden to take in the air would be a good way to start proceedings before we got stuck into a long list of chores. Despite the month of September being symbolic in my own mind with the beginnings of autumn, the garden still had the look of high summer, with as yet little appreciable leaf turn. Christina had noticed that the portion of the mixed-species hedgerow within the confines of the chickens' enclosure had unfortunately been given a hammering, with all the whips virtually stripped of their leaves. In fact the whole of the chickens' enclosure was so utterly devoid of any vegetation it looked like a modern-day representation of the Somme, with nothing having escaped their rapacious feet or voracious beaks! But despite the fact that they had undoubtedly ruined the hedgerow, occasionally produced sub-standard eggs, and June's bottom was looking filthy again, I still felt nothing but love for the feathered wing of our extended family.

After an impromptu and quick clean of the aforementioned dirty bottom, which thankfully seemed to reveal no underlying problem and was nothing more than just … a dirty bottom, Christina began to tidy up the garage flower border, which had begun to look a touch tired, while I initiated phase two of the meadow management. With the scything having been the only aspect of the previous day which had exceeded expectations, my next important task was to remove all the cut material from the meadow. Working systematically from the apple trees backwards, I eventually managed to rake away all the cut vegetation into a huge hay pile to reveal the lean and mean meadow underneath, which, if I'm honest, looked like it had just received a lop-sided short back and sides. On this occasion, though, temporary aesthetics would be playing second fiddle to sound ecological practice, and, with the nutrient levels driven even further down by the net removal of the vegetation (and the nutrients locked up inside) straight into the compost bins, hopefully next summer the meadow would be looking even better.

With the sun at last beginning to make its first appearance of the day, I used my creaking back as an excuse to take a rest from my physical endeavours to see what insects were currently gracing the garden. It's astonishing how, as soon as the temperature passes what must be a critical threshold, all of a sudden the garden becomes alive with invertebrates. Timing their arrival immaculately with that of the sun's appearance, a few small whites were spotted fluttering around the verbenas and erysimum, and at least twenty honey bees and half-a-dozen worker bumblebees were soon crawling all over the vibrantly coloured sedums too. With the flower borders and pond competing for my attention, a southern hawker dragonfly was once again egg-laying around the stones rather than directly into the water, and could quite easily have been exactly the same female that had been laying a batch in the pond a few days earlier. Her eggs were not due to hatch until the following spring, before then taking a further two or three years until the slow-growing larvae would finally be ready to emerge as adult southern hawkers, so it would be a long wait to see if all her efforts had been worth it. I, for one, hoped they would be, as having been lucky enough to have already witnessed the miracle of nature when a dragonfly larva emerges out of the water to transform into a winged adult in front of your very eyes, I was desperate to see it again. And to witness this spectacle in my own back garden would, of course, be even better!

With Christina having cut back a few unruly specimens, moved a few other plants to different locations and slotted in a few extra plants that had been patiently waiting for homes back up on the patio, in the space of a couple of hours she had managed to turn the bed back around to being vibrant again. Once again I was struck with how complementary our respective gardening skills were: mine as a tool-wielding labourer while Christina was the craftswoman with the secateurs or hand trowel – it was a horticultural match made in heaven. After a lunch in the garden mostly spent watching the greenfinch guzzling down sunflower hearts like they were going out of fashion, and with mercifully no more corpses having been discovered, the afternoon was spent down at the garden centre. Well, bulb-planting season was rapidly approaching, after all!

As a freelancer, my diary can often become terribly complicated when filming dates constantly have to be switched as we wait on the famously unpredictable British weather. For example, there is little point trying to film a piece on butterflies when the allotted filming day is predicted to be wet and cold; it's better to postpone to a sunny day. That afternoon was a case in point, with us still not sure even by mid-morning if the weather would be sufficiently windy for the shoot to go ahead or whether we'd have to delay filming. With my director and researcher also standing by as we all waited for that 'all systems go or stand down' phone call, I suggested that, rather than wait for the call in the office, perhaps they'd like to come out to Chew Stoke to enjoy the delights of the garden instead.

With the weather now more akin to the Bahamas than Bristol, Daz and Nick duly arrived and were invited through to the garden as we took tea and biscuits down by the pond. Almost immediately the conversation changed from speculating as to whether or not the shoot would be cancelled to that of garden wildlife, as they both remarked on what a fabulous spectator sport dragonfly watching is. Keen to know what species they were looking at, in quick succession I managed to point out a pair of common darters flying around in tandem, a single female common darter egg-laying, with a male in close attendance, and finally a female southern hawker dragonfly also egg-laying around the pond. It was dragonfly central.

Both Daz and Nick simply couldn't believe the sheer quantity of life the pond had attracted in the mere four months of its existence. Due to the warm weather, the dragonflies weren't the only entertainment laid on, as there were plenty of butterflies and bumblebees in evidence too, with the highlight being a kingfisher fly-by down by the brook, which the boys also managed to spot. Rudely interrupting our nature-spotting session, the phone then rang as Nick and I waited for Daz to inform us if the filming were indeed to go ahead. 'It's been postponed,' he said, 'not enough wind, so go and put the kettle back on, Mike, and let's see what else turns up!'

After a long week of filming, which had taken me on a whistle-stop tour of south Wales, Buckinghamshire, Nottinghamshire and Cheshire, I finally arrived back at home late on the Friday, excited that the weekend lay ahead. During the week the weather had also undoubtedly turned from being predominantly warm and dry to wet and windy, or, in another word, autumnal. As I ventured out briefly on the Saturday morning, the garden looked soggy, green and glistening, with the pond full to the brim. Additionally, the bell feeder had been blown off its hook and what looked to be wood pigeons had also been fouling the water bath as well. Welcome home, I thought. It was not just the garden that was wet, bedraggled and rather sorry-looking either, as the incessant rain had made April, May and June look more like reptilian throwbacks than the gorgeous hybrids I normally knew them to be. In response to the sustained period of inclement weather, the garden also seemed to have undergone that mental gear-shift as it too readied itself for autumn, the very first sign being that of the birch leaves which had suddenly begun to take on a buttery-coloured hue.

With the weather frankly awful to say the least, rather than getting soaked to the skin outside we decided to delay any gardening until mid-afternoon, by which time the forecast indicated that the worst of the weather would have passed. With the morning suddenly free, this now gave us the opportunity to indulge in one of our favourite new past-times – visiting farm shops. Being a townie born and bred, this out-of-town shopping experience had never really figured on my radar, but living in a rural location like the Chew Valley, it hadn't taken me long to appreciate what fascinating places they can be for killing an hour or two. As I've got older I've also been amazed at how I now seem to prefer farm-shop food to fast food, and I suppose this is because I've at last realised that the old adage 'you are what you eat' is bang on the money.

With a huge variety of farm shops in the Chew Valley, we plumped for our favourite; a particularly well-stocked one just a ten-minute drive away and with an adjoining coffee shop to maximise the fun. Although I'm the first to admit that these shops aren't the cheapest, much of the food is either produced on the farm itself or incredibly locally, so the carbon footprint for the produce is minuscule. Buying locally also helps to keep the area's economy fit and healthy too, so everyone is a winner. For someone like me who has developed an inordinate fondness for chutneys and cheeses, these places are heaven-sent, plus they also give you the opportunity to see how local vegetables should be grown. 'So that's what locally grown leeks look like,' I commented to Christina, picking up one such example which looked more like a Doric column than the pathetic excuses we'd attempted to grow earlier in the year.

With the weather having eased up from that of 'stair-rods' to what the Irish call a 'soft day', and the pair of us £30 lighter after a few impulse purchases including a slab of locally produced chilli cheese and some rosehip and passion-fruit chutney, we retired next door for tea and cake. Casting an eye across the Sunday newspapers, I kept the other to constantly monitor the steadily improving conditions. I was due to go away again the following day, and Christina would be back at work, so it was crucial that we slotted a few hours into the garden before the start of our working week. How things had changed; eight months ago wild horses wouldn't have dragged me out of the café, but since the move to Chew Stoke my whole philosophy had changed and now I was champing at the bit.

Quite often when a cold and wet weather front finally passes through, the subsequent conditions can be glorious, and as the tail-end of the cloud finally rolled away, it transformed into the most glorious late afternoon – perfect conditions for a spot of bulb-planting! The wooded bank already hosted the most impressive spring display of ramsons, but I was keen to see if it could be improved by the introduction of a few native bluebells into one or two of the bare patches.

The bluebell is surely one of our most iconic wildflowers, and it is not hyperbole to say that the world's finest bluebell woodlands are all to be found within Britain. Also native to continental Europe, where the bluebell is distributed in small clusters along the Atlantic fringe from Holland and Belgium all the way down to Spain and Portugal, only in the UK does the plant grow in such profusion that it can give certain springtime woods the impression that they have either been suddenly flooded or carpeted overnight with a deep blue shag-pile. One possible reason why our green and pleasant land is best for bluebells is our unique climate, as it seems the bluebells' overwintering bulbs infinitely prefer a typically mild and wet British winter to the cold and dry alternative offered on the continent.

When seen at its best, with possibly millions of delicately nodding flower heads turning the woodland floor into a sea of blue, it is hard to appreciate that this is a plant whose very survival is now threatened in the UK. The British bluebell is closely related to the Spanish bluebell, an imported plant whose cultivars are now increasingly being sold in our garden centres and grown in our gardens. With the resultant tipping of garden waste into the countryside, it seems that the Spanish form has not only become established but has also begun to hybridise with our native species, with fertile seeds being the unfortunate result. These hybrids not only look subtly different, but, like our hybrid chickens, also seem to be pretty tough as well, making them able to survive in a wider range of environmental conditions and ultimately out-compete our native bluebells. How serious a problem this is was not realised until a nationwide survey carried out by the charity Plantlife revealed that one in six of our bluebell woodlands contained either Spanish bluebells or the hybrid.

Some garden centres have exacerbated the problem by unfortunately selling Spanish bluebell bulbs as 'natives', and I had been particularly fastidious in confirming beforehand that the bulbs we intended to purchase were indeed both the very Best of British and ethically sourced – as there would be no point proudly planting British bluebells that had simply been obtained by illegally stripping a bluebell site elsewhere. Back at home, and with Christina concentrating on her selection of spring tulips, which were to be placed around the bases of all the apple trees, I began planting up along the base of the mixed-species hedgerow behind the beech tree.

Resembling tiny white onions, bluebell bulbs are packed with sticky starch, and historically, when crushed, were used to make glue both for binding books and for stiffening Elizabethan ruffs and collars. In our garden, however, they would be playing a far more important role in producing the next generation of flowers. Using my dibber to create a hole, each bulb was carefully placed into the ground at the allotted depth in a staggered zigzag, the idea being that the bluebells would then slowly spread to cover the bare patch of bank by the steps. With our respective sets of bulbs suitably deposited out of sight until next spring, the final batches of bulbs to be planted were those of grape hyacinth, which we planted underneath the hawthorn in the garage border, with the hope that they would provide an early boost for any insects emerging from hibernation the following April.

The last allotted job of the day was to don my wellingtons and cross the brook in order to take up the kind offer of a plant from my third neighbour. Simon and his wife were the owners of the tongue-shaped spit of land on the opposite side of the brook. Having only recently met them a couple of weeks back, following a chance encounter and a brief conversation held across the water, they had then promptly invited us over for a quick tour of the garden. Only just resisting the temptation to ask cheekily if they had would ever consider selling us the spit, it was nevertheless fascinating to see up close a garden that we had gazed across many times, but not once set foot in. Centrepiece of the more formal part of their garden, and tucked out of sight up by the house, was a beautiful pond, which despite the presence of goldfish also played host to the most enormous and incredibly vigorous pond lily. As Simon explained that it would have to be cut back before enveloping the whole pond, I suggested – being of course keen to help out a fellow neighbour whenever possible – that maybe we were in a position to take a chunk of it off his hands to replace our own pond lily which had died a couple of months previously.

So, meeting Simon back up by his pond, we eventually managed to hack off a chunk with one of his kitchen knives, and this was then plonked into a plastic bag for the short journey back across the brook to start a new life colonising our pond. All offerings are always gratefully received!

An early start was crucial the following Friday as I had much to do before the garden was fit and ready to receive its VIPs. Serving not only Chew Stoke itself but also a number of the surrounding villages, Chew Stoke Church Primary School is a lovely school for all local children aged between four and eleven. Situated just a stone's throw from where Christina and I lived, I was already familiar with the school even before moving to the village, having come to give a talk as a favour to my boss on *The One Show*, whose daughter Melissa was in the 'Owl' (or youngest) class. I was so impressed with the friendliness and welcoming attitude of the school that since we moved to the village I had been determined to invite Melissa's form – who had now moved up to the 'Kingfisher' class, to come for a nature ramble in the garden. With the form teacher Mrs Frost due to bring the 'Kingfishers' around to the house at the pre-arranged time of 2pm, it was vital that the garden not only looked neat and tidy, but that there would also be a sufficient number of activities to entertain the children when they arrived.

The first job on my list involved mowing both front and back lawns, before strimming around the edges of the flower borders and clearing up the patio to ensure that everything looked as smart as possible and, perhaps more importantly, that no one would trip over any tools carelessly left around. With the garden looking more than respectable, I then partly dug a hole alongside the communal fence we shared with Andy and Lorraine for an official planting ceremony I had pre-planned for that afternoon, and I then went to check on the contents of the moth trap set the previous evening, so at least we'd have some wildlife to show the children. The final job before their arrival had been to quickly construct and place a fish trap into the brook at the bottom of the garden, as I hoped to show the Kingfisher class what the pair of resident kingfishers had been feeding on all summer.

The main body of the bespoke fish trap was made out of a large plastic pop bottle. By cutting off the top of the bottle all around the 'shoulder' with a Stanley knife, the cut piece was then inverted so that the neck and opening were this time placed inside the bottle. By taking a bradawl to both pierce the side of the bottle and the now-inverted top, the two parts of the bottle could then be tied together with a couple of pieces of wire to ensure the neck and opening were fastened firmly inside. The whole idea behind flipping the opening upside down was to enable the 'trap' to operate just like a lobster pot with a large entrance and small exit, meaning that any fish which swam in through the wide entrance would then be funnelled via the neck into the bottle and couldn't escape. The trap was then baited with bread to attract the fish in the first place, and weighed down with a few stones in the bottle to ensure that it would sink, before placing it into the water with the entrance pointing upstream so the fish would hopefully be able to gain easy access.

As I climbed back up the slope into the main body of the garden I heard a 'tswick!' call overhead that I instantly recognised to be from a bird species which up to that point I had neither seen nor heard in the garden. As the pond came into view I was just in time to see the bird land by the pond, followed by a few diagnostic pumps of its tail. 'Grey wagtail!' I shouted, to no one in particular, as seeing a new bird in the garden after nine months of fairly intense observations was now becoming a rare event. Forever a bird associated with water, I was nevertheless surprised to see one taking an interest in our humble little pond, as I would have thought that the faster-flowing stretches of Strode brook, located a hundred yards or so away, were far more typical 'grey wag' habitat. Despite being a bird that does indeed wag its tail an awful lot, the 'grey' part of its name has always struck me as underselling what is really quite a colourful bird. True, the grey wagtail does have a mostly grey head, face and mantle, but in both sexes it is that yellow vent or bottom that invariably catches the eye – 'yellow-bottomed wagtail' would be a far more suitable name. Being somewhat more of a mouthful, however, I doubt it would catch on.

There are a number of suggestions as to why all species of wagtails wag their tails, but no one is exactly sure. The theory which I personally prefer is that the tail-wagging might help flush insects, but the behaviour could equally be used as a sign of vigilance to discourage predators, or even a form of signalling to other wagtails – take your pick. One of the lovely things about wildlife is that it often seems that there are far more questions than answers.

Waiting for the kids to arrive, and with everything ready, I felt a state of nervous anticipation, as I was keen for the afternoon to go well, and, as we all know, children can be a tough audience. If they're not both entertained and stimulated they'll soon let you know. I've never agreed with the well-worn phrase: 'if you can't do it, teach it', as teaching is not only one of the toughest professions, but it's one that also needs immense skill, meticulous preparation and limitless patience. I looked out of the lounge window, with a view up the street. I suddenly saw a luminous-yellow crocodile approaching the house as the long line of paired children in their high-visibility vests could clearly be seen following Mrs Frost as if she were the Pied Piper.

Fortunately it wouldn't be just me, Mrs Frost and 30 kids, as she'd thoughtfully brought along an extra four adult helpers to martial the troops, including my good friend Phil, whose daughter Amelia was also in the class and a good friend of Melissa's. The weather can so often make or break this type of event, but fortunately lady luck was with us in the form of a beautifully warm afternoon with no rain on the horizon. As I welcomed the class through to the back garden, I reminded the children who I was, how long I'd been living in Chew Stoke, and of our grand plan to turn the back garden into a mini nature reserve. First up, I explained, would be a mini nature tour of the garden, starting with the pond. Arranging all the kids in a large semicircle on the lawn so they could all see me standing on the stones around the back of the pond, I then began to explain how the pond had been created.

The adage 'never work with children or animals' is a phrase with which I obviously don't agree, but I'm the first to admit that 'showing children animals' can often be incredibly difficult, as most wildlife tends to be shy and reserved, making it difficult for people (with the best will in the world) who often like to be noisy and have short attention spans. Because it was such a large group, I had prepared for it not to matter even if we didn't find any wildlife at all, with the attitude that anything we did see would be a bonus, and so I was particularly pleased with the timing of a male southern hawker dragonfly's appearance as it buzzed over both the pond and the excited children's heads. This gift enabled me to talk about the amazing lifestyle of a dragonfly, which consisted of two years underwater as a mini crocodile before leaving the water and changing into an adult dragonfly, where its short life would then turn into one of fighting and mating with occasional bouts of feeding.

Keen to make it an interactive session with lots of questions, I had barely asked my first question: 'so what other animals do you think would live in a pond apart from dragonfly larvae?' when one boy immediately cut across me with 'frog!' Impressed with the quality of his answer, I responded with a 'very good, anything else?' To which the same boy shouted 'NO! FROG!' All of a sudden it became a chant as most of the children started shouting it excitedly, while pointing across the pond in the direction of my boots. Looking down, I suddenly spotted what everybody else by now seemed to have noticed, as sheltering underneath the very edging stones that I had been standing on was a large frog! Having only seen frogs in the water on a handful of occasions, I couldn't believe the fabulous timing of its discovery, which was made even more special by the fact that it was the kids who had spotted it. I felt so appreciative at that moment that I could have easily scooped up the frog there and then to give it a smacker by way of a big thank you. Having earlier stated that it can sometimes be tough to point out wildlife to kids, they do by way of compensation have the most extraordinarily sharp eyesight, and I've constantly been amazed how, for example on a fungal foray, it will always be a child who finds the rarest or most unusual toadstool.

As I moved on to show the group the flower borders, the wildlife kept coming, as I was able to point out some butterflies and bumble-bees before we quickly moved through to the meadow. I had origi-nally wanted to talk about how great the meadow, bug hotel and habitat pile were for creepy-crawlies, but by then the children's attention had been well and truly diverted away from me and in the direction of the chickens. I had made sure the electricity had been turned off beforehand, and the children swarmed round the fence demanding to know more about the chickens. Accustomed to the presence of just Christina and me in the garden, the girls didn't quite know what to make of the marauding hordes surrounding their enclosure, and so they hid around the back of the compost bins, but only until their constant eye for a tasty morsel overcame their fear of the unknown. I offered a few of the children a small handful of mealy worms to toss over the fence, and soon the chick-ens were charging back out.

For those of you who are tempted to get chickens but are unsure as to whether it would all be worth the effort, one massive benefit that you might not even have considered beforehand is that kids absolutely adore them. As we all watched the girls hoovering up the mealy worms like nodding oil derricks, the kids wanted to know the answers to three million questions, two million of which were all the same question – 'what are their names?' 'Well, you see the small brown one there, she's called April and she's the boss,' I explained, 'and the grey one there is called May,' I said, before

asking the children if they knew what the big black chicken might then be called. There was complete silence for the first time, as the kids thought about it, aware there was some kind of pattern but probably not quite old enough to fathom it out, until I heard a small voice from the back quietly say 'June?' Looking back, I noticed a hand up, which obviously belonged to the provider of the correct answer. 'Well done Mrs Frost!' I said, before going on to tell the children that they had a very smart teacher! Before we moved on from the chickens the last job was to collect the eggs. 'Does anyone have a birthday today?' I asked. While no one did, apparently one young lad had celebrated his birthday the day before, meaning he was chosen to be lifted over into the enclosure to open up the hatch on the side of the coop and see if he'd been lucky, and – what do you know? – it was one of those three-egg days! I have to say, his face was a picture as he carefully collected all the eggs. With the promise of three more eggs, he would then be able to take a boxful home to his parents as an edible memento of his day in the garden.

Next on the agenda was the moth trap, and I carefully explained how the equipment worked before passing around some of the moths that had been captured the previous night. Although it had been both quite a low catch and a little too late in the year for any of the hawk-moths, there was still more than enough to satisfy their eager minds. Another reason why moths are such brilliant creatures is that they represent the 'perfect wildlife' for large groups to look at. Readily caught the night before, and often doing nothing more than just sitting around on egg boxes the following day as they wait for dusk, they are the ideal display material to be passed around a school group so everyone has the chance of a good look. The highlight of the catch for me was the brown-spot pinion, a moth that I'd personally never seen before, but as it was one of the slightly less charismatic-looking moths it was largely glazed over in favour of the much more showy burnished brass and canary-shouldered thorn.

Gathering the children around again, I told them that now would be their opportunity to earn their keep, and I asked Mrs

Frost if she could split the class into three groups. Group one, with Phil in charge, would be responsible for planting the crab-apple tree, which I had purchased a couple of days earlier, in the hole I had partly prepared that morning, and then to follow that up by putting in a few tulips bulbs around the base of the tree. Group two, with Mrs Frost at the helm, would be planting some more bluebell bulbs on the bare part of the wooded bank to the right of the steps, and finally group three would be my responsibility as we sorted out all the bird feeders.

We took all the feeders down, and I disappeared with my posse into the garage where the bird food was stored as I explained about all the different types of food and feeders available. Getting them all involved, we then filled all the feeders bar one, which would be singled out for special treatment. Alongside the bespoke anti-squirrel feeders all year had been a wooden peanut-holder in the form of a house which had been half mangled by the squirrels trying to get to the booty inside. According to a recent RSPB press release, one way to discourage the squirrels from stealing all the food and ripping the feeder to bits in the process is to add a small quantity of chilli powder to the nuts, which seems to deter the pesky, thieving squirrels but has no effect on the birds' feeding habits. So by mixing up the two ingredients with a good shake in a plastic bag to distribute the spiciness, the chilli-coated nuts were placed back in the feeder. The children were just a joy to be with, as at this lovely age they are always keen to get involved while soaking up everything you tell them.

We rejoined the other groups back in the garden, and I could see straightaway that all the pupils had been working like troopers. Phil's team, having already planted the crab apple, were just finishing off the tulips, while Mrs Frost's little band of helpers had done surprisingly well with the bluebells, considering the ground had been so hard, and she was happy to report that every child had planted at least one bulb. An additional habitat feature (albeit temporary) which had also been created in the centre of the lawn was the most enormous pile of coats, as the glorious weather meant that most of the kids had stripped down to T-shirts and shorts or skirts. As we all took an orange squash and biscuit break to admire the handiwork of all the groups, there was one last element before they were due to return back to school – time for a splash!

I had originally planned for us all to get into the brook at the bottom of the garden before a short paddle upstream, but a quick recce the day before had revealed it to be a little too deep in places for six-year-olds, so the longer but safer option was chosen as we walked round to the playground in the adjacent street and then through the gate at the bottom down to the brook. With all the children forewarned to bring wellington boots, and with help from the adults, we eventually managed to get them all into the brook and gathered round me as I picked a few stones out of the water to point out some of the freshwater shrimps and empty caddis-fly larval tubes on the undersides. In fact the only disappointment of the whole afternoon was the fish trap, which for some reason hadn't managed to catch a single fish ... where were they all? Originally Mrs Frost had only planned to bring the class over for an hour, but having already overrun by 30 minutes it was time to take the class back to school, but not until I'd quickly shown them the hole in the bank where the kingfishers had been breeding earlier in the summer – this was the Kingfisher class, after all.

Mrs Frost thanked the class for being so well behaved and such good nature-spotters, and she then returned the compliment by getting the whole class to give me a big 'thank you Mr Dilger' in high-pitched unison, which was so lovely and heartfelt I had a lump in my throat as we said our goodbyes and went our separate ways. Back in the garden, it suddenly felt strangely quiet without the chatter of thirty excited voices looking at frogs, dragonflies and chickens. I staked the crab-apple tree to make sure it had support, since it had been planted in the centre of the garden's 'windy corridor', and I then tidied away the numerous tools scattered around the lawn before retreating inside for a well-deserved lie-down. I'd only been with them for 90 minutes and I was flipping exhausted – how do parents and teachers do it?!

Both Christina and I had a heavy work schedule looming ahead, and we were conscious that 25 September would be our last day that month to enjoy the garden in anything other than a fleeting sense. We were also only too aware for a few months now that, with the back garden in relatively rude health, the front garden had really begun to let the side down. A tidy-up was well overdue.

In the spring I had used up some whips left over from creating the hedgerow to plant a much shorter version to cover the ugly fence panels separating our front garden from Andy and Lorraine's. Unlike the rear hedgerow, where a large portion had been severely mangled by the chickens, the front hedge was looking much healthier. True, it was still some years off being that thick, mature hedge capable of providing both a nesting habitat for a whole variety of breeding birds and food for winter visitors, but with every single whip having survived at least to the autumn, it looked to be well on its way.

Having not really been touched since the whips had been planted and mulched, a fine collection of weeds had pervaded the whole hedge line, and while in the meadow these botanical opportunists would have been cherished as wildflowers, along the hedgerow they just made it look an unholy mess. In a bookshop a few weeks before, Christina had on impulse bought me a book by the gardening guru that is Bob Flowerdew. Entitled *Weeding Without Chemicals*, it was a small book that was the summation of everything Bob had learnt about this resilient group of plants, compiled from thirty years of organic gardening. I had previously looked upon weeds as being nothing more than unsightly when growing in a flowerbed, but hadn't appreciated until reading Bob's book how, in addition to weeds competing for water, air, light and nutrients, they are also capable of spreading problem pests and diseases. In other words, my hedgerow would probably be doing even better if I removed the weeds!

I had also always equated weeding to spending hour upon hour down on hands and knees as each offending plant was first dug up and then removed, but Bob was a big fan of hoeing. With the hoe, the weeds are also uprooted, but rather than collecting the weeds Bob suggested they should be left exactly where they were. Once out of the sanctuary of the soil, the weeds quickly die then rot back down in situ, enabling all the nutrients which had been locked up inside their seeds to be returned to the soil whence they came – the diametrical opposite to what I had carried out in the meadow. As I started my first-ever hoeing session, with Christina alongside weeding the border running along the front of the house with the same method, there was another benefit to using a hoe that Bob had obviously forgotten to mention – it was also a darn sight easier on the back and knees!

Due to its diminutive size, and the fact that it was surrounded on three sides by either tarmac or house, it was inevitable that the front garden would never be able to compete wildlife-wise with the rich and varied mix to be found in the back garden, but as we weeded away we still uncovered a surprise or two. Drawing my attention with a 'what's this butterfly?', Christina had only gone and spotted the garden's very first small copper as it was basking away in the autumnal sun.

The small copper is our only remaining British copper butterfly since the extinction of the large copper in the nineteenth century, and it has a pretty wide distribution across the UK's lowlands, but never seems to be abundant anywhere. In looks, it is an immaculately marked scrap of orange and is most often encountered in dry, rough grassland with copious scrub, so I'm not entirely sure what it thought it was doing in our front garden. Dinkier than the females and with more pointed wings, the male we were looking at was also quite probably a member of the year's third generation of small coppers to appear, a sign that the summer had probably been much warmer than we had initially thought. Perhaps more presciently it represented our thirteenth species of butterfly, or, put another way, one in five of all Britain's butterflies had at some point visited our garden. Not a bad haul for eight months!

OCTOBER
DEPARTURES, ARRIVALS AND RESIDENTS

With Christina away working there seemed little incentive to stay in bed, particularly as I had invited my good birding and ringing pal Ed around for what would hopefully be an exciting morning in the garden. Over the last couple of months the two of us had discussed the possibility of netting Strode brook in an attempt to see if we could catch the kingfishers. Not only would this give us the opportunity to ring them and check on their health and wellbeing, but it would also give me my first view of this cracking little bird in the hand.

As Ed pulled onto the drive at 6.30am, the weather was cold, still and overcast, or, in ornithological terms, absolutely perfect conditions for mist-netting. I met Ed with a broad grin and a hot cup of coffee, and we bundled straight through the garden and down into the brook to get the net erected as quickly as possible. With the brook spanning no wider at any point than four yards and Ed's shortest mist-net six yards in length, this problem was quickly solved by placing the poles across the brook on a diagonal slant. With both poles safely tied off to either bank and the net loops placed over the poles, we were just at the point of spreading the loops, an action which would have instantly opened the net to create the invisible 10-foot-high wall, when a kingfisher suddenly flashed straight past us. Flying upstream at such a speed had necessitated it banking around the corner of the meander, and so it had probably been as surprised to see us as we were it. This also meant that the bird only just managed to avoid Ed standing on the bank as it bypassed the pole and flew out of sight further up the brook!

It was a ridiculously close encounter that spelled both good and bad news for our attempt to catch one. Good in the sense that at least one bird was still using the stretch of brook despite the fact that the breeding season was over, but also bad in that now it had seen us down by the brook it would be much more wary about passing this stretch a second time. It was also frustrating because, had we arranged to meet five minutes earlier, by now we'd undoubtedly have bagged our first kingfisher. Undeterred, we clambered back up the bank and then put another six-yard mist-net in the garden, running from behind the left-hand orchard apple tree and past the bell feeder in the rowan, to just in front of the bug hotel and habitat pile.

Once both nets were duly erected, we retired back to the discreet distance of the patio to wait for the first birds to tumble into the nets. Even though it was only the second week of October, the autumn migration was already well under way, and as we sat there we recorded in quick succession pied and grey wagtails flying over the garden, followed by a small flock of meadow pipits, immediately identifiable by their 'tsip, tsip' call as they flew overhead. In addition to being another new bird for the garden list, the 'mipit' was one of those species that would only ever be in the 'fly-by' category, as gardens just aren't its cup of tea. The meadow pipit is a bird more commonly associated with the open country offered by moorland, heath, farmland and salt marsh, so this was nothing more than a 'right time, right place' bird.

Bird migration is such an astonishingly complex subject, and its intricacies are only slowly being revealed to us in the form of bird ringing recoveries and more recently the use of tiny Global Positioning System (GPS) trackers, which have been miniaturised to such an extent that they can now be attached to some species of birds without impeding their ability to fly. When most people are asked to give examples of bird migration, I dare say they would probably mention the huge intercontinental journeys undertaken by swallows, cuckoos or ospreys, all the way from the African tropics to Britain each spring, but migration is sometimes much more subtle than this, and it can also occur over much shorter distances.

These meadow pipits were a case in point, as they could easily have been local birds that had spent the summer on breeding territories up on the Mendips. But faced with a bleak winter up on the hills, they decided instead to pass the coldest part of the year in the far milder climate found in the coastal grasslands along the Severn Estuary. So when compared, for example, to the enormous range of latitude covered by most of our waders and warblers, the meadow pipit's yearly movements are nothing more than a gentle excursion down the hill. As for the two species of wagtails, I simply had no clue as to where they had come from or where they were going, so while we have made considerable strides in our understanding, there is still much to learn.

Following on the heels of the meadow pipits, a flock of around 20 black-headed gulls noisily squawked its way across the garden. With Chew Valley Lake so close, they were surely birds that, having roosted on the lake overnight, were in the process of spreading out to the surrounding fields to look for breakfast. As we watched them overhead, all of them could be seen sporting their winter plumage, having lost their characteristic plain-chocolate coloured hood that is so noticeable during the breeding season, and which was now replaced by a crown of white feathers with a single dirty blotch behind the eye (or on the ear coverts). From now on, as we descended towards winter, and with the garden situated no more than 500 yards from the lake, the number of gulls passing over the garden could be expected to increase dramatically, especially as Chew Valley supports one of the largest gull roosts in southwest England, which during cold snaps has reported as many as 50,000 birds roosting on the water each night.

With temperatures set to plummet, the bird feeders were still quite quiet, suggesting that there was plenty of food in the surrounding countryside to keep the local populations busy. In fact the only species coming to the feeders in any number was the greenfinch, and it was not until we had watched them flying in and out for a while without getting snared in the net, that we belatedly realised we had put the net on the wrong side of the bell feeder. With the birds preferring to enter the garden from the playing field side, the net was easily avoided altogether. We quickly fixed this by simply moving it across, and we then also checked the net down by the brook, but as yet not a single bird had been caught.

Almost immediately the repositioning of the net worked as we simultaneously caught a male and a female greenfinch. Expertly extricated from the net by Ed, they were soon both bagged and brought up to the patio for processing. The greenfinch, possibly with good reason, is not considered to be one of our most stunning birds, but if you look at the male close up, he is much more handsome than he is usually given credit for. Mostly shades of olive-green, the rump is a bright yellow-green and sets off beautifully the bright yellow patches on both the sides of the tail and the flashes in the flight feathers. Of course the best thing about both birds was that they seemed completely clear of the cursed trichomonosis, which had been the source of much angst over the summer months. As to where these two birds had originally come from to end up feeding in our garden was anybody's guess. As evidenced by the large numbers of juvenile greenfinch on the feeders during the summer, there was obviously a healthy breeding population locally, but large numbers of greenfinch which breed in Scotland and northern England will also move down to spend the winter in the milder climes of southern England, thereby boosting the number down here. Even though I had no idea where they had come from, if I could at a later date spot the bright silver rings that Ed was busily putting on their legs, one thing I would definitely know (providing no one else was ringing close by) was that our garden was attractive enough for them to want to stick around for a while.

The birds were released back into the garden, and we sat back to enjoy some visible migration (or 'vis mig' as it is known amongst birders). We were delighted to spot another small flock of meadow pipits, a single skylark, two more pied wagtails, another grey wagtail and a flock of six more skylark all moving along the same south-easterly to northwesterly route. Still with only two birds caught in the garden mist net and nothing at all in the net down by the brook, this low capture rate could have been down to the wind having picked up, which made the net more visible. Nevertheless, as the morning progressed the garden bird activity steadily seemed to increase as we were treated to a couple of goldfinch trilling away with their distinctive and delectable contact call whilst perched high up in the beech tree. In quick succession we then heard a green woodpecker from the direction of the playing field and briefly saw a chunky female sparrowhawk passing over the garden, which caused all the smaller birds to scatter like nine-pins.

A couple of magpies then graced the garden with their presence. Being a bird that probably made a daily appearance in the garden, they usually tended to arrive early, were always wary (as if subject to a persecution complex) and never stayed for long. Although magpies are undeniably incredibly common in both urban and rural gardens, and they do not enjoy the best of reputations, if you try instead to look at them objectively without this 'excess baggage', they are simply stunning birds. With the blue-green iridescent sheen to their wings and tail and their flickering white flight feathers in such crisp condition, it was obvious that both birds had just undergone their post-breeding moult and were looking resplendent as they strutted about the meadow, with their very human walking gait.

The magpie is a bird that has benefited from a considerable upswing in its fortunes over the last 50 years, which is probably due to a combination of a decline in its persecution in the wider countryside and the bird having realised that urban and suburban areas are places of great opportunity. Able to eat everything from berries to carrion and beetles to dog faeces, the magpie has gained a level of notoriety from its habit of raiding the nests of other species for their eggs and nestlings. With a population of around 650,000 pairs

breeding each summer, like both the sparrowhawk and the badger the magpie is a perfectly natural predator, and any suggestion that they are the cause of widespread declines of our songbirds is unsupported by scientific evidence and as far as I'm concerned utter hogwash. (I promise I won't mention the 55-million figure associated with cats again, okay?)

As you read this, you could be confused in thinking that Ed and I were narrow-minded birders, but despite it being true that birds (of the feathered variety) were our first love, we always had our eye open for anything else of interest, particularly when that 'anything' happened to be *another* new species of butterfly for the garden. What was perhaps even more surprising was that it was warm enough for a butterfly to be flitting around, as despite the sun having made a belated appearance, it couldn't have been any more than around 11 or 12°C.

Like a number of the birds that had visited the garden over the summer, the red admiral was also a migrant. Flying to the UK from southern Europe, the species is thought to breed in late autumn, with their caterpillars overwintering before pupating into fresh adults; it is these butterflies which then begin the long flight to northern Europe. The number of red admirals arriving here can vary enormously from year to year, depending both on how successful breeding has been and the warmth of the summer, but the highest concentrations are generally seen in Britain in early autumn. So you could say that this individual butterfly's timing was just about spot-on, as it landed on the verbena to have a slurp of nectar and catch whatever rays were around. Incapable of surviving in our British winters, the adults that have arrived here, and with luck reared a generation themselves, are then thought either to perish or unbelievably to migrate south again and back to the continent – not bad going for an insect weighing less than a twenty-pence piece.

The mist nest in the garden then began to twitch again, a sure-fire sign that we had caught another bird, which turned out to be our third greenfinch. Immediately noticeable as a male, with his intimate knowledge of the species Ed was also able to reveal that it was what's known as a 'first-year bird', in that it would have been a chick earlier in the summer. Apparently the best way to identify a young greenfinch is through subtle plumage differences that are only really noticeable in the hand, as Ed pointed out the brown colouring to the primary coverts (the small feathers covering the bases of the main flight feathers), the fact that some of the chest feathers were still in pin (emerging from their sheath), and the pointed nature of the tail feathers. It's easy when you know how!

With a grand total of three greenfinch caught in the garden mist nest and a total blank in the net down by the river, we decided to close the nets at around midday. Frustratingly, had we chosen to try and catch the kingfishers a month earlier we would probably have had more luck, as it looked like they were already dispersing in preparation for the winter. But while the ringing had been a touch disappointing, the visible migration had been an unforeseen bonus and just went to show the glorious unpredictability of wildlife. I had woken up hoping for kingfishers in the hand but wouldn't have expected to see meadow pipits flying over the garden in a month of Sundays.

We packed the nets and poles away, and, with our wellingtons still on, we decided we'd put them to good use for a quick wander up the brook to have a look at the kingfisher hole. As we passed the oak tree on the left-hand side, Ed spotted a small sprinkling of feathers littering the bank below one of the hawthorns and just off our land. Obviously the remains of a greenfinch, two bits of evidence told us that it had met its somewhat grisly end in the talons of a bird of prey rather than a mammalian predator. The feathers had been plucked out with the end of the quill still intact, which was the *modus operandi* of birds of prey, in contrast to predators like stoats, weasels or even foxes which tend to bite the feathers off. Also, the feathers were distributed over a wide area, suggesting they'd been both dropped from a height and carried by the wind. It was exhilarating to think that not only had the greenfinch probably been snaffled in my garden, probably by a sparrowhawk, but that we had also discovered where the local sparrowhawk came to eat its breakfast.

After thanking Ed by way of a spot of lunch and seeing him on his merry way, I was ready to use the afternoon to embark on phase two of increasing the garden's mammal list. Having already had a degree of success with the camera trap, and with phase one very much still ongoing, I was keen to have a look at any smaller mammals that might either be visiting or resident in the garden which hadn't yet been recorded. When attempting to survey for mice and voles, there is really only one way this can be done properly without harming the animals themselves; in other words, it was time for a spot of small mammal trapping. Not owning any traps myself, I had managed to persuade my good friends at Bristol Zoo to kindly loan me half a dozen of their traps that they occasionally used for research purposes.

The traps were of the 'Longworth' type, an incredibly well-known design to any university student of biology carrying out a research project on small mammals. Made of aluminium, the traps are strong yet incredibly lightweight and consist of two parts – a small rectangular tunnel containing the door-tripping mechanism, which slots into a slightly larger rectangular nest box holding both food and bedding. This larger section is the place where the rodent will sit out the night, until released the following morning.

Mammal trapping tends to be a numbers game, because the more traps you put out, the more animals you are likely to catch. But because the garden was in reality pretty small, I reckoned half a dozen would be more than enough to sample what was running around out there. Enticed in by the smell of the food, the mouse or vole enters the tunnel, and, by making a beeline for the food, trips a small wire which causes the trap-door at the entrance to flip shut behind it. Temporarily imprisoning the animal causes it no harm whatsoever, as it simply eats the food before curling up in amongst the bedding for the night, realising it can't escape. This technique for catching mice and voles has been so successful that in areas where trapping is undertaken regularly individual animals have been known to become 'trap happy'. By purposefully seeking out traps, these free-loaders have worked out that in addition to a free meal and an overnight bed, they'll be released the following morning totally unscathed!

In order to prep the traps each one was baited in turn with a combination of hay (from the chicken's bedding), mixed grain and the special ingredient of peanut butter – which would get their whiskers twitching for sure. The one foodstuff that I would definitely not be putting in the trap would be any meat such as cat or dog food, as I was keen to avoid trapping shrews. These little hyperactive insectivores have such a high metabolic rate that they can easily die of starvation in traps, and therefore their capture not only needs specialist training but also a licence from Natural England, which I didn't have. So once filled with the vegetarian option, and after ensuring that all the doors were set to 'open', the traps were finally ready to be set out in the garden.

The key to successfully trapping small rodents is to carefully consider the positions of the traps, and to do that you have to think like a rodent. Mice and voles are eaten by a wide array of predators such as kestrels, tawny owls, foxes and weasels, and killed in huge numbers again by cats, I'm afraid, and so by nature they tend to both be incredibly wary and never stray far from cover, so sticking a trap in the middle of the lawn would be next to useless. It's far better to place the trap along the bottom of a linear feature like a hedge, which a mouse might regularly use as a thoroughfare. Also it helps if you can try and look at your garden from the perspective of where a mouse or vole is likely to live, so close to brash or log pile would be another good trapping location, as would any place where rodent activity seems obvious, such as any entrance holes or what look like small mammal runs.

Another really important aspect to bear in mind is that it's vital to remember the location where each trap has been placed, as any lost will not only be a financial inconvenience (they aren't cheap), but any unrecovered trap which has already ensnared a small mammal inside will result in a long, slow and lingering death by starvation. As I have a brain that on a regular basis resembles a block of Swiss cheese, I find the best way to remember where the traps are is to number them, check them in strict order and draw a small map with their locations marked on it as an *aide memoire*. So starting at the garage and then working around the garden in an anticlockwise fashion, trap number one was placed at the very back of the border, underneath a small concrete lintel which ran the length of the garage. I then put the second trap along the fence line separating our garden from Marjory and Dennis's, with the third positioned no more than a couple of yards away along the edge of the wooded bank. Moving across to the other side of the garden, trap four was slotted under the beech hedge, with numbers five and six placed around the back of the dead-wood habitat pile and the bug hotel respectively. With the traps set, all I then had to do was to wait until the following morning to find out which animals, if any, had found the peanut butter simply too irresistible.

There is nothing like the hope of recording a new mammal for the garden to get you throwing back the duvet and springing out of bed, and having been cold, wet and windy during the night, the best place for a small rodent to have seen out the frankly awful conditions should definitely have been inside one of the traps! With the chickens quickly cleaned out and the eggs collected, and Christina also up very early (for her on a Sunday) to photograph any captures, we barrelled outside with my map for a quick initial sweep to see which traps had been tripped. Down on hands and knees in the garage border to inspect the first trap, I could immediately see the door was closed, meaning that the trap had been tripped. Now this didn't necessarily mean there would be an animal inside, as occasionally adverse weather conditions, a poorly set trap or an exceptionally fast rodent can cause it to be tripped, but it was nevertheless an encouraging sign. Traps two and three down by the fence were both still open and patently hadn't been visited, but I was delighted to see trap four also had its door closed. With traps five and six still open, 33 per cent was still an impressive strike rate for the first night

– providing there were mammals inside of course. I was also pleased that the two traps that might have mammals inside were also in the same locations that I thought had the best potential the evening before – thinking like a rodent was helping!

As the weather was still dreadful, we decided the traps were best emptied in the kitchen, and as we carried them carefully inside it certainly felt like trap number one was heavy enough to have captured something. As both mice and voles are astonishingly nimble, they can escape from an opened trap incredibly easily, so the standard operating equipment to ensure they don't prematurely escape is nothing more hi-tech than a large see-through plastic bag with smooth sides which they are unable to climb. I also find it best to have your arms uncovered too, as mice in particular can jump incredibly well and once onto your sleeve with your arms stuck in a bag they will be up and out like the proverbial rat up a drainpipe. So with my upper attire consisting of nothing more than a T-shirt, I put the first trap into the plastic bag and undid the catch to remove the rectangular tunnel. Removing this component from the bag, I gently tipped up the nesting chamber so that the bedding, any remaining food and hopefully also any hiding rodents would be gently encouraged into the plastic bag as gravity took hold. Sometimes it takes a few seconds to see if you have indeed actually caught anything, as it can be hard to pick them out from amongst the mass of bedding, but on this occasion I immediately saw TWO little fur balls drop into the bottom of the plastic bag. No wonder it had felt heavy!

Now I have done a fair bit of mammal-trapping over the years, but one thing I have never, ever done is catch two mammals in one trap, and so I was immediately in unchartered territory. I could only surmise that they had entered the trap either simultaneously or in incredibly quick succession. Carefully removing the bedding to get a clearer view, I could immediately see from their pointed faces, prominent ears, large eyes and long tails that they were 'mousey' rather than 'voley'. A number of key features also enabled me to discount house mouse from my thinking process. Firstly house mice tend to be mostly grey in colouration, whereas these two had sandy brown coats with whitish underparts. Next, by placing my nose up to the bag for a sniff, there was also an absence of the strong mousey smell always associated with house mice, and finally house mice are not commonly found anywhere else other than indoors with us where they prefer the warmth.

The two species most frequently encountered in gardens are wood mouse and yellow-necked mouse, but it can be difficult to separate them in the field, unless of course you happen to have them captured in a see-through plastic bag, just a few inches from your nose! The yellow-necked mouse tends to be a larger animal, but with size being a perennially difficult feature to gauge, the far simpler technique is to look at their necks. Yellow-necked mice have a distinctive yellow collar, making it look like they haven't washed, as opposed to wood mice which either have a clean white throat or nothing more than a small yellow streak on their upper chest, and by lifting up the bag to examine the undersides of this pair, a couple of clean necks meant the garden had wood mice!

Found throughout the British Isles, the wood mouse is thought to be our most common and widespread wild rodent, with a pre-breeding population thought to be around 38 million. But with breeding commencing as early as March, and each female capable of rearing four litters a year, it's no surprise that by autumn numbers may pass the 100-million mark – so if I hadn't caught any at this time then I probably never would have! Although the wood mouse is mostly found in woodlands and fields, its adaptability has meant that the only habitats that it actively avoids are those at high altitudes or those associated with water. Primarily eating a combination of seeds, nuts and fruit, they're also partial to any invertebrate prey in the form of caterpillars, worms and centipedes that they may come across during their nocturnal forays out for food – and on a personal note they're incredibly engaging little animals too! I was not keen to keep them constrained any longer than was necessary, so once their identifications had been assured they were taken straight back outside to the garage border and released exactly where they'd been trapped. As I watched them hop away into the vegetation, I was again struck by their closer resemblance to miniature kangaroos than scurrying rodents. Back inside, and with the final sprung trap also revealing another wood mouse, such a high capture rate immediately led to one inescapable conclusion: the garden was fraternised by wood mice.

Needing a sequential evening and morning to both bait and then check the traps, it would be a couple of days before I had the opportunity to continue my search for more small mammals. Attempting to mix it up a touch, instead of placing all six traps in the main body of the garden, this time I had slotted three along the wooded bank, which from a small rodent's perspective represented a totally different habitat. With Christina off to work, I too was up early to ensure that any trapped animals would not be left waiting too long, and I was delighted to find once more that two of the six traps had been tripped. The traps containing potential occupants were two of the ones placed on the bank, with the first one being placed below the hazels and alongside the large pile of garden waste that had accumulated during Mr Gregory's era, while the second one had been left underneath a pile of brambles at the base of the oak tree.

With the weather distinctly more clement than during the first trapping session, I decided that emptying the traps outside with the sun on my face would be infinitely more preferable, and so as I sat at the garden table I put trap number four into the plastic bag and with rising excitement unclipped the tunnel and inverted the nesting chamber. Vole! The strategy of moving some of the traps elsewhere had immediately paid dividends as a small gingery creature with a much blunter face, smaller ears and shorter tail than the wood mice was thrust blinking into the daylight.

Three species of vole are found in mainland Britain, and, having not seen them close up for a couple of years, it was crucial that I ran through a mental checklist to ensure that the animal was at least correctly identified. Despite the trap's close proximity to water, I was quickly able to discount water vole, as the chunkier nature of this species meant that it would probably have struggled to fit in the trap in the first place. Additionally a lack of sufficient bank-side vegetation along the margins of our section of the brook would have made this species highly unlikely here anyway. With the field narrowed down to two species, this meant that identification would have to rest on the animal's general appearance and habitat preference. Short-tailed field voles are yellowy-brown in colour and tend to favour either fields or areas with lots of rank grassland, in contrast to the chestnut-brown bank voles, which rarely stray far from bramble thicket, hedgerow and woody scrub – it was looking good for bank vole!

After a glance in one of my books to double-check that I did have my facts the right way round, I was quickly satisfied and able officially to confirm that the traps had indeed rewarded us with a second new mammal, a terrific result and a shot in the arm for the garden mammal list. Having previously recorded Britain's commonest small mammal, i.e. the wood mouse already in the traps, the bank vole is thought to be our second most abundant rodent with an estimated pre-breeding population of 23 million. It was astonishing to think that, despite their abundance, the vast majority of the human population has never seen one of these gorgeous gingery critters. Unlike the leaping and bounding wood mouse, the bank vole prefers a running and scurrying style for getting from A to B, and it can also be equally active in the daytime, provided there is a sufficiently thick undergrowth to give it cover from the ever-watchful eyes of a wide range of predators. Being almost exclusively vegetarian, the bank vole's diet consists of a wide range of seeds, berries, nuts, and the occasional fungus, but with one of their favourite foods undoubtedly being hazelnuts, and with a couple of large hazels positioned on the bank, autumn must have been like manna from heaven for this little fellow. There was also a lovely symmetry about a bank vole having chosen to make its living on the wooded bank, and, for the record, with the other trap containing a wood mouse I made it a two-species day – a result by any definition.

For the next ten days the garden was physically and metaphorically a long way from my mind as I enjoyed a ten-day busman's holiday birdwatching with a few pals in Israel, but on touching down back at Heathrow I found myself instantly making the switch and eager to find out how our beloved garden had changed. Having arrived back with little more than a third of the month now left, I was also greeted with an unmistakable chill in the air which had definitely been absent on departing the UK. Back at home, and with Christina still at work, I had time to sort out my dirty laundry and spend an hour quietly reacquainting myself with the garden and seeing it properly in its full autumnal glory before she arrived back keen to hear how my trip had gone.

Walking out into the garden, I had wanted initially to have a gentle amble around to slowly absorb the changes, but as soon as the chickens spotted their lord and master, and immediately came running across the enclosure to meet me at the fence, my attention was well and truly diverted. When I said 'the chickens', I only meant two out of three, as June was probably tucked up in the coop having apparently suddenly become broody during my absence, doubtless due to the fact she had been missing me, I thought! I hopped over the electric fence and opened up the coop to find June sitting inside the partition assigned for laying, looking both irritated to have been disturbed and rather sorry for herself in equal measure. Sitting on a couple of eggs, neither of which she'd probably laid, she was also surrounded by a pile of her feathers, which meant that in addition to a bout of broodiness she was also obviously midway through her annual moult. I'm afraid it often has to be 'tough love' with brooding chickens, so I gently lifted her out into the enclosure, leaving her to just sit on the ground in a slightly dazed and confused state while I made the coop habitable again.

As I watched June eventually get to her feet and have a half-hearted poke at a bit of food scattered in front of her, it was only then that I noticed that the enclosure itself was covered with a coating of beech mast, an early indication that a bumper season for fruits, berries, nuts and seeds might lie ahead. Looking up to where the mast had rained down from above, I saw that only a few of the leaves had made the conversion from soft green to the copper colour for which beech trees are justifiably famous at this time of year. With the chickens now clean and sated, I hopped back over the fence to carry on with my initial mission, which had been to see how the rest of the garden was gearing up for 'the season of mists and mellow fruitfulness'. Even a cursory glance across the wooded bank seemed to confirm that a fruit and nut bonanza may well have arrived already, as in quick succession I noted that the hawthorns were plastered with literally thousands of deep maroon-red berries, the ash tree had huge bunches of 'keys' festooned on virtually every branch and there were also acorns aplenty ready for the squirrels and jays to fight over in oak-tree corner.

Back in the main body of the garden, the birch leaves had by now all turned a buttery yellow and looked much more aesthetically pleasing than the sickly-looking leaves on the rowan – a tree, it has to be said, that is not renowned for its autumn colour. The rowan had fruited heavily in high summer, and there were surprisingly few berries left, as most had already been picked off by the resident blackbirds. The real surprise package, though, was the spindle, as what had been for most of the year a rather underwhelming shrub situated in the middle of the planted hedgerow and inside the chicken enclosure had suddenly developed rather striking (and highly poisonous) pink fruits in small clusters of four, which were in the process of splitting open to reveal fleshy orange-coated white seeds. The fruits were not just confined to the garden's wild plants either, as the cultivated stock also had its own booty to boast of. The three apples trees planted back in early spring had between them borne a small but delicious crop, the last of which had only been polished off by Christina while I'd been away in Israel; and despite the quince bush not having impressed the Harvest Home judges, it had delighted us with the sheer size and abundance of its fruits.

Christina had kept herself busy during my absence, and she had tidied the raised vegetable patch, with the only vegetables waiting to be harvested consisting of a few holey Savoy cabbages, which looked so unpalatable they would be donated straight to the slightly less fussy chickens, and the parsnips, which we were saving for Christmas Day. Elsewhere in the cultivated section of the garden, the verbena, sedums, erysimum, salvias, cyclamen, gaura, geraniums and a couple of roses were still in flower, but despite these plants putting on a strong autumnal showing, I couldn't help feeling that the garden had floristically peaked some weeks ago and was now inexorably fading towards winter. Likewise, although the pond was still well vegetated, it looked like the days of associated frenetic insect activity had disappeared for another year. I knelt down and fished out a huge, stringy clump of algae, which was unfortunately beginning to rear its ugly head in the pond again, and on placing it on one of the rocks watched a broad-bodied chaser nymph struggle out from amongst the stringy slime before I helped it back into the water. Activity might well have lessened above water, but it was patently still business as usual below the surface!

Meeting Christina back from work with a big hug, whom I should have said I had also missed during my birding trip, she suggested that maybe we should use the rest of the day's available light to take a stroll over to the lake via the footpath at the end of our road. I was keen to collect some blackthorn sloes to make some winter-warming sloe gin, so I thought this was a brilliant idea, and grabbing nothing more than a couple of plastic bags we set off. One of the best aspects about where we live is that no more than a stone's throw from our own doorstep there must be a least half a dozen footpaths which lead straight into the countryside. So throughout the year whenever we'd felt like a break from the house and garden, or just fancied a spot of exercise, we were spoilt for choice. We powered up the path opposite our street and within two minutes we were flanked on both sides by two of the loveliest mature hedgerows you could ever wish to stumble upon, and which ours would hopefully begin to resemble over the next few years. Being away from the road and therefore out of the reach of tractor and flail had been their saving grace; they had been allowed to grow unfettered without fear of being hacked back. As we hit the plateau of the hill, the path quickly widened out to encompass a much broader open space of rough meadow and scrub, which also turned out to be a spot where Christina had previously spied a bumper crop of sloes. As she worked the blackthorn like a seasoned forager, I suddenly realised that I could make a collection of a different kind over in the meadow. Having long since gone over, the dried flowerheads of a number of wild flowers were just begging to be harvested, which would mean I could sprinkle any gathered seeds around the meadow and along the beech hedge back at home.

The first seedheads I wanted to get my mitts on were those belonging to hogweed. Historically gathered for pig fodder, a practice from which its common name derives, I much prefer the Latin name *Heracleum sphondylium* – which believe me is best said out loud. Hogweed is a member of the *Umbellifer* family and a really familiar plant of rough meadows and hedge-banks throughout the summer. It is characterised by its large, flat and white flowerheads on long, hollow stems, which after flowering dry out and then invariably remain as a skeletal memory of summer for the duration of the winter. Not smelling particularly pleasant, the reason why this is such a brilliant wildlife plant is that it attracts legions of insects to its flowers, and in particular one fascinating species of soldier beetle, nicknamed the hogweed bonking beetle. This name is well earned because when found on hogweed flower-heads it is almost always, well, copulating! And who wouldn't want to see hogweed bonking beetles in their garden next summer? Extracting the seeds couldn't have been easier, and simply involved scrunching up the dried flowerheads between my hands over the plastic bag until the flat, winged seeds tumbled out.

The other plant that I had spied and whose seeds I was also keen to redistribute belonged to common knapweed. Less than half the height of the hogweed, knapweed is a tough perennial found in all types of grasslands and looks superficially like thistles minus the prickles. It is also adored by a whole raft of butterflies and bumble-bees in high summer and is definitely a species that would add a certain *'je ne sais quoi'* to the meadow. Chafing the bullet-shaped dried flowerheads between my thumb and forefinger allowed me to tease out a good number of the somewhat smaller seeds to add into the mix.

Meanwhile, with the light fading fast and Christina's bag full of sloes (with plenty still left for the birds), we headed back down the hill for home. After all, we did have some seeds to sprinkle and sloe gin to prepare …

As I peered out of the curtains first thing, I was delighted to find the morning cold and clear, which after two days of near incessant rain was some relief. The garden looked a soggy mess, and with the first leaves having already fallen, this was the first indication that the rake would soon be the busiest tool. With the sun progressively closer to the horizon with each passing day, it was now not until at least 3pm that the half of the garden closest to the house received any direct sunlight at all.

Showered and clothed, I grabbed the chickens' food and proceeded down the path as I contemplated the fact that we were now well and truly on the long, inexorable descent to the winter solstice. I must have been drifting away in a world of my own when I was suddenly jerked back to the present by a flash of action in the meadow out of the corner of one eye. Whipping my head around, I was treated to the sight of a startled female sparrowhawk lifting off from the ground like a Harrier jump jet and execute a 180-degree turn before flying off in the direction of the wooded bank. It was only then that I saw something clutched in the talons of her right foot that had obviously just been nailed in the garden seconds before I had blundered out. From the moment I first caught the action to watching the sparrowhawk disappearing through the trees couldn't have lasted any longer than three or four seconds, but the sequence felt like it had been seared onto my retina as I replayed the thrilling event in my mind's eye.

Wondering which species of bird had met its maker in the meadow, I walked over to the spot from where the sparrowhawk had been flushed, and it was only as I ducked down for a closer look that I noticed two freshly plucked feathers belonging to the victim nestled in the grass. The first was one of the primary wing feathers, and from the yellowy-green leading edge I could tell immediately that it had belonged to a male greenfinch. The second was a tail feather, and by recalling what I had learnt from my tutorial with Ed on ageing greenfinch earlier in the month, the feather's rounded edge also meant it had come from an adult male – what wonderful evidence feathers could be!

Saturday was clear of commitments, so at last we had a window to spend making the front garden a touch more presentable and capitalising on the weeding carried out the previous month. After a quick breakfast the first task involved mulching the beds with some well-rotted manure I had purchased locally from a man with a van, and which now needed transporting around to the front from where it had been stored on the back patio. I was in the process of humping a particularly heavy bag of steaming, smelly muck, when my Spock-like ears instantly picked up a 'pssst, pssst' call I hadn't heard for at least ten months but instantly recognised. As I craned my neck for a view of the birds which had made the sound, I accidentally dropped the bag of manure and it split open as it hit the ground and spilt its contents all over the drive. Of course I didn't care a jot that I was now covered in horse shit, as I'd just recorded my first winter migrant of the year and a new bird for the garden list to boot – redwing. It was a small price to pay for a seminal moment in the garden!

Redwing breed in tiny numbers – perhaps only 20 pairs, or even fewer – in central and northern Scotland, so the vast majority of British birders only ever really think of the redwing as a winter

visitor. The birds that choose to spend each winter in Scotland and Ireland tend to be of Icelandic origin, and these contrasted with the small flock of half-a-dozen birds that I had watched fly overhead, and indeed with most of the redwing across southern Britain, which would have come from as far away as Finland or Russia. Whenever I see flocks of redwing flying, it always looks to me like they are at the mercy of the wind, as rather than flying toward their destination, they always seem to 'be blown' in the direction of the prevailing wind. It is also one of a small cast of birds that makes that descent into winter just a little bit more bearable, as the sight and sound of a flock flying overheard during their constant search for hawthorn, pyracantha and cotoneaster can lighten even the darkest and coldest of days. There were plenty of berries still up for grabs in the garden, and I was also hopeful that as the weather sharpened and the food became scarcer they would be persuaded not just to fly over the garden but also to drop in and pay us a visit.

I changed into clean(ish) apparel and shovelled up the mess on the drive, and we then covered the bed with manure to fulfil the triple whammy of providing nutrients, locking in moisture and keeping the weeds down, before Christina began to sprinkle the bed with all the foxgloves and lupins that she had lovingly cultivated from seed throughout the summer. As the basal rosettes of the foxgloves and lupins were currently far from showstoppers, the bed was made a touch more presentable in the form of a splash of colour from some recently purchased and late-flowering asters and an *Abutilon* 'Kentish belle', the latter having been my favourite flowering plant at the old flat. Finally, one of the old geraniums in the centre bed of the back garden, which had outgrown the space available for it, was divided and relocated into the border at the front to give any passing bees the option of feeding in either garden the following summer.

Despite the fact that November was only just around the corner, a couple of red admirals were still flitting around the verbenas in the back garden, and not for the first time I was left contemplating what a wonderful addition to the garden this plant had been. We were just putting the last touches to the front garden when we received an impromptu visit from one of Mr Gregory's daughters, who had popped by to say hello to Marjory and Dennis and couldn't resist asking for a quick peek in the garden.

Jane had been born and brought up in the house and, having not visited the back garden since April when I'd last given her a tour, was keen to make sure we were still behaving ourselves and that we hadn't decided to change the garden into a pay-and-display car park after all. I enjoyed taking her round, as she always came up with a few nuggets of information about the garden that I hitherto hadn't been aware of. Because the weather had recently been so wet, and because we'd only been able to spend a limited amount of time in the garden over the last few weeks, it did look a touch messy around the edges, making me feel bizarrely that I had to half-apologise to Jane.

We wandered around the garden as I justified all the alterations we had made, and the subject soon came on to the beech tree. Jane explained that it had been planted during the 'Plant a Tree in 73' government-sponsored campaign, which was designed to encourage the population to plant more trees, and in part to counter all the elm trees which at the time were being lost in the wider countryside due to Dutch elm disease. I was flabbergasted that the tree was only around 38 years old, for I had previously thought it to be much older than me, when in reality it was the other way round. In fact, with a four- or five-year head start, I must have been running around in shorts before it had even been a seed! The other tip that I wisely took on board was not to dig too deeply around the base of the beech hedge and behind the bug hotel, otherwise we might suddenly begin unearthing a whole generation of family pets which had been buried there. Fortunately, with no plans for this area beyond letting the meadow do its own thing, I was delighted to inform Jane that letting the animals rest in peace was the least we could do. Satisfied that her heritage was still safe in our hands, she then made her excuses, leaving us to crack on with big job number two.

Having moved in on the last day of January, there was only so much that we had been able to achieve on the wooded bank before spring had sprung, meaning that the basic woodland management we had originally wanted to carry out would have to wait until the end of the year. It's safe to say that, prior to our purchase of the property, the wooded bank hadn't really been touched for years and was desperately in need of some remedial work to revitalise and rejuvenate overly mature shrubs and tired-looking trees. It's a commonly held misconception that as woodland effectively represents the climax (or final) state, in terms of natural succession, their management should consist of little more than sticking a fence around it and leaving it to get on with it. However, many conservation organisations found to their cost in the 80s and 90s that if your aim is to maximise the woodland for the maximum diversity of wildlife, then a degree of intervention in the form of coppicing and tree removal is crucial to ensure that the 'light and shade' is, quite literally, perpetuated for everything from bugs to butterflies to thrive.

A couple of the hazels with a lot of standing dead wood were looking in a particularly sorry state, whilst other branches desperately needed to be coppiced to make way for fresh material. Cutting much of the wood back would not only enhance the longevity of the hazels but would also bring more light onto the woodland floor, encouraging in turn the flowering of plants in the seed bank that had been patiently waiting for their chance to shine. As we worked systematically across the bank, the presence of every shrub and limb in turn was debated as we made life-and-death decisions as to which bits we could earmark for the chop over the winter as opposed to what could be salvaged for the long-term health of the habitat. Following in the now tried-and-tested tradition of attempting to carry out most of the work ourselves wherever possible, I was keen to try and do all this coppicing myself – but only after I'd learnt to use a chainsaw!

With certain shrubs given a safe passage, while the Sword of Damocles hung over others, the last chore before we retired was to put out the small mammal traps one more time to double-check that I had indeed trapped the full complement of rodent species visiting the garden. I was hopeful once again that the traps and peanut butter would combine to come up with the goods, and I selected three locations in the garden and three along the wooded bank. I was just putting out the last trap in the fading light when I noticed a few bats flitting along the brook. Whether they had come from our garage was hard to tell, but despite the steadily dropping temperature these individuals patently weren't quite ready for hibernation just yet. The same could be said of autumn too, which also still had a few weeks left before finally relinquishing the reins to winter.

I hate it when the clocks go back. Okay, there is the tiny bonus of an extra hour in bed, but this in no way compensates for the abrupt end to our evenings in the garden after work, as all we'd now want to do would be to scurry inside instead. However, with both the chickens and any trapped rodents unaware that British Summer Time had just been brought to a shuddering halt, they would both need attending to, so, like the martyr I was, I hauled myself out of bed and into the garden.

By the time the chickens had been cleaned out and I'd quickly checked the traps, to find three shut, Christina had joined me to have another attempt at photographing anything we caught. With trap one un-tripped, I carefully placed trap two, which had been under one of the hazels on the bank, into the plastic bag back in the kitchen. Sure enough, a bank vole tumbled into view. I gently grasped the vole by the scruff of the neck with the thumb and fore-finger of my left hand (being cack-handed), and my other hand was then used to hold the body softly but firmly whilst Christina snapped away. With the evidence documented, the vole was then taken straight back to where it had been captured and released under the hazel.

With traps three and four both drawing blanks, the beech hedge along the playing field again came up trumps as the fifth trap produced another wood mouse. Using the same technique to grasp the mouse by the scruff, I lifted it out of the bag to take it outside to be photographed, but I was suddenly aware that my grip wasn't as firm as I would have liked so I attempted to readjust it in my hand. Ouch! In a deft move the mouse rotated its neck and got a good, solid bite on my finger, causing me to drop it onto the table as I recoiled back in shock. Hopping away like a kangaroo rat, in just two leaps (and as many seconds) it then jumped from the chair to the floor, before bolting under the pipe-work emanating from the radiator, right up against the skirting board.

It wasn't just the mouse that had been hopping that morning; Christina was hopping mad too when she found out that I had acci-dentally released a mouse into her kitchen, and demanded it be immediately recaptured, but as with the chickens in the summer, the only question was 'how'? With the mouse unable to go anywhere that didn't first involve running across the 'open ground' of the floor, to get even close to it we first had to clear away a mobile set of shelves and all of the food it housed. Then remembering what I'd learnt from the chicken recapture, I re-set the trap it had only just come out of and placed this against the skirting board. Then by using a combination of the brush to prevent the mouse from entering the kitchen proper, and the mop handle to encourage and gently poke it along the skirting board I finally reduced the mouse's options down to two: either make a bid for glory over the top of the brush, or go into the nice, dark rectangular tunnel which looked remarkably familiar. Fortunately it chose the latter.

We were almost hysterical with relief: I because I hadn't killed it and Christina because she wouldn't have to kill me, and both mouse and trap were taken outside for the rodent's instant release. It was definitive: the garden had wood mice and bank voles, and, perhaps even more importantly, the house had neither.

NOVEMBER AND DECEMBER
THE TEMPERATURE DROPS BUT THE ACTION HOTS UP

They were back. Having barely made an appearance over the last couple of months, due undoubtedly to the surfeit of food at their disposal in the wider countryside, as temperatures had started to spiral down the squirrels began to return. The visits were currently nothing more than early-morning forays to clean up spilt food from the bird feeders, but I was under no illusions that they had also come back to probe the defences with a view to exploiting any signs of weaknesses amongst the various food dispensers. And being the smash-and-grab types, they wouldn't easily take no for an answer.

As I exited through the back door into the garden on the first weekend of the new month to clean out the chickens, a couple of squirrels spotted me and spun on their heels to beat a hasty retreat back to the sanctuary of the wooded bank. The usual escape route for any squirrel caught in no-man's land, i.e. in the middle of the lawn, was to sprint to either the rowan or birch tree. Bounding up either of these, they were then free to access the aerial walkway of interconnecting branches in the canopy, as they tightrope-ran their way between the trees before making the final leap to freedom between the birch and one of the hazels on the bank. Once in the hazels, these Olympian gymnasts disappeared like smoke amongst the asymmetric bars.

While their bully-boy tactics and domineering presence in the garden irritated me beyond belief, part of me admired their unbelievable resilience and adaptability to what was after all a foreign land. Maybe it was my persecution complex but they seemed to enjoy sticking two fingers up to the species that had brought them here in the first place, in other words, us humans. Despite numerous attempts to halt the spread of greys with extensive culls, in the long term these have had little or no impact, and so, like it or not, they are here to stay. With the squirrels' breeding season just around the corner as well, I suspected their activity in the garden would only continue to increase, but it was a battle I would relish!

With June still broody, moulting and having (to our knowledge) not laid an egg for at least a couple of months, it was another two-egg day courtesy of the ever-reliable April and May, who were at least repaying their keep. In spite of her general hopelessness, June was secretly still my favourite, and this was not just down to the fact that she had originally been my pick, but also because she was so marvellously entertaining too. After all, how could you not adore a chicken that made strange noises all day, was scared of its own shadow and was also a sandwich short of a picnic?!

Like the squirrels, the other birds were slowly beginning to leak back to the garden too, and as we sat up by the patio to have our morning coffee we were soon alerted to the presence of a great spotted woodpecker in the vicinity by its distinctive 'tchick!' call. Knowing where it was most likely to be hanging out, I then spotted the perpetrator investigating a couple of dead branches on the oak tree in the hope of winkling out a beetle larva or some other juicy grub. It was immediately identifiable as a male, due to the small crimson patch on the back of his head. This was one species that has expanded its population in recent decades and which has also become a much more regular visitor to garden feeding stations. In fact, with all the food on offer in the garden, I was surprised we hadn't encountered the species more frequently than just the handful of sightings that we had noted throughout the year.

Coal tit was another of those species that I had, at best, only seen infrequently in the garden, but I hadn't been quite sure why, until we watched a couple of coal tits nip quickly in to grab a single sunflower heart each from the caged feeder, before quickly scampering. Coal tits, being the lightest and the most timid of the 'true' tits, have always been at the bottom of the pecking order, but I hadn't realised until then how heavily this inferiority complex affected their feeding habits. With the feeders currently receiving certainly no more than one or two visitors a minute, this small window of opportunity probably represented one of the few times during the year when they were able to feed in freedom without the monopolising effect of the greenfinch or the discriminatory tactics of the great tits or blue tits. As soon as concentrations of birds built up at the feeders they would again be relegated to watching from the sidelines, which in reality meant being forced back out into the countryside to find food.

With just the morning available to fritter away in the garden, after breakfast we split into two task forces. Christina had been keen to take hardwood cuttings of a couple of the roses and a dogwood, rather than take the more expensive option of simply restocking from a garden centre, and I wanted more mammal sightings! I dismantled the camera trap from the hole in the hedge where cats, foxes and badgers had all been recorded, for I was keen to see if anything could be enticed in front of the camera if I put it down at the bottom of the wooded bank by the water's edge. Having had a degree of success by baiting the trap with peanuts, I was intrigued to see if any aquatic mammals could be encouraged to make an appearance if they were given a fishy incentive. I had heard from a wildlife cameraman, who was a good pal of mine, that by baiting the river bank outside his house with fish he'd managed to have otters waltzing around in front of his remote cameras, and I was eager to know if the otter sighting back in May had been a ridiculously lucky one, or whether, as I suspected, they were passing through far more regularly than we imagined. And did the brook also have mink?

I tied a smelly piece of pollack to a stake in front of the camera-trap, set it running and left it to its own devices, while I went to see how Christina was getting on. Having wielded her secateurs like a composer would a baton, she had chopped up a few rose and dogwood stems into small sections, which were then dipped into rooting powder and planted out in a line in a small, empty section of the central bed. What with growing her own plants and taking cuttings, Christina was rapidly becoming the Carol Klein of Chew Stoke. I might be the garden's professional naturalist, but I was under no illusions as to who the real gardener was out of the two of us!

The following day was my last before I hit the big 45. I was away early on my actual birthday to track Scottish wild cats down for work, so Christina had arranged that, on just this one occasion, like the Queen, I would be able to celebrate two birthdays: my official one with her, and my real one the following day with my filming pals up in a pub on the Ardnamurchan Peninsula. The weather on my official birthday was so gorgeous that we decided to take my favourite breakfast of smoked salmon and scrambled eggs in the garden – the latter an early birthday present courtesy of April, May and June.

The chickens hadn't seemed in the slightest shaken up by the huge village fireworks display courtesy of Guy Fawkes that had passed the previous evening no more than a couple of hundred metres away from their coop, and already sated from their own breakfast, were now wandering around their enclosure, pecking at anything vaguely animate with their dagger-like bills as we tucked into the fruits of their labours. Even though Christina knew that I generally don't like to be fussed over on my birthday, she is one of those few people who genuinely seems to enjoy giving more than receiving. So on this occasion she felt justified in flagrantly disregarding my feelings, announcing with great pomp and circumstance that once breakfast was finished it would be present time.

I expected a small, immaculately wrapped present to be placed in my outstretched hands, but Christina told me to stand up, take her hand and close my eyes, with express orders not to open them until given permission. Following her command to the letter, I felt myself turned around and led in the direction of the wooded bank, passing what should have been the beech tree on my right before I was stopped in my tracks at what must have been the top of the steps down to the wooded bank. 'Okay, you can open your eyes now!' she said, with more than a hint of rising excitement in her voice. Generally speaking, I'm not massively keen on surprises, with the phrase 'I know what I like, and I like what I know' tending to be more applicable than I care to admit, but on opening my eyes, all the build-up had been worth it as I gazed down upon a wonderful wrought-iron bench for two people on the flat plateau at the bottom of the steps.

It had a swirling plant pattern on its backrest, a lattice seat and wonderfully ornate armrests, and I adored it instantly, and I also adored Christina for her thoughtfulness and ingenuity. 'But how and when did you get it down there?' I asked, aware not only that it must have been heavy, but that I had been down on the bank the previous morning to set up the camera trap, so arranging for the delivery of the bench in such a small window and without my knowledge had been no mean achievement. 'None of your business!' she replied. One thing was for sure, however: kingfisher-watching had suddenly become a whole lot more comfortable!

Once more as work came in a flurry, it was a week before I had another chance to properly park my posterior on the bench down by the stream. We had earmarked the Sunday as the day when we would attempt to initiate the restoration of the hedge in the chicken enclosure, which was being slowly nibbled to death by the girls. After a fair amount of debate, we had decided that the only solution would be to fence the whole hedge line off from the rest of the enclosure until the whips had an opportunity to become re-established. The disadvantage of this course of action would result in a reduction in the size of the enclosure, but it was either that or have the hedgerow reduced to little more than a line of sticks, which meant all the time and money planting them in the first place would have been wasted. Starting off at the DIY store, we purchased a roll of chicken wire and some stakes, and then almost made it to the checkout tills without adding any impulse purchases before Christina threw in a small bag of winter aconite bulbs, which would hopefully give us a late-winter splash of colour in the flower beds.

Back at home, after placing the stakes along the line we wanted the fence to follow, we then rolled out the chicken wire into position and used fencing staples to secure it to both the stakes and the wooden fencing panels at either end. Even though I had made distinct progress during the course of the year in refuting my supposed inability to tackle any practical jobs requiring more than a hint of technical ability, I was still far from perfect. One manifestation of not being innately gifted in this department often resulted in me getting irritated and irritable during the work when it didn't go exactly to plan. Christina, who it has to be said would have probably done a much better job than me had she not instead project-managed the installation, wisely chose her words carefully on the slightly wonky and skewed finished fence line when she diplomatically stated that 'as long as it keeps them out, it doesn't matter how it looks'.

Taking a break for a cuppa at our new favourite seated location in the garden, which was down by the brook on my birthday bench, I was just gazing skyward thinking how the view through the canopy had suddenly cleared since most of the leaves had dropped when I spotted the unmistakable bowed wings of a large bird flying over the brook in the direction of the lake. Like the meadow pipit that we had observed in the process of migration the previous month, it was highly unlikely that we would ever get a grey heron in the back garden, particularly as the pond had no fish to entice herons down, but even 'flyovers' were gratefully added to the list. After a quick count of all the bird species recorded either in or over the garden since we had first arrived in January, I made the heron our 53rd bird

– not bad for a piece of land that was only marginally more than a tenth of an acre!

They say buses come in threes, well maybe I should create the phrase that 'birds often come in twos', as we had barely taken a couple of sips of tea following the 'heron fly-by' when I heard the unmistakable tones of species number 54 for the garden. The fact that I couldn't see them was irrelevant, as the immediately distinctive 'chack-chack-chack-chack' call of a small flock of fieldfares passing overhead was as familiar to me as the sound of a foghorn to a ship's captain. The fieldfare was the second half of the thrush double act which comes to visit Britain each winter. Along with its close friend and congener the redwing, close to three-quarters of a million fieldfares often form nomadic flocks as they scour our orchards, hedgerows and fields for berries, apples and any tasty invertebrates. Reaching northeast Scotland in early autumn, which is the part of the British mainland closest to their Scandinavian breeding grounds, it is not until at least mid-October that the fieldfares find their way down to southern England. As soon as areas become stripped of berries the birds will move on, but with the strong tradition of cider-making having resulted in a large number of orchards in the West Country, this part of the world would certainly be keeping more than its fair share for the winter, until the rising temperatures eventually triggered their departure back to the continent.

I often consider November to be one of the quieter wildlife months, but when the sun came out the garden did its best to dispel this myth as we were treated to a red admiral floating around the garden. This butterfly's final journey would go one of two ways: either it would kick the entomological bucket with the first frosts in the UK, or it would make the remarkable journey over the English Channel and across to continental Europe, to head south for warmer climes.

After lunch we decided that the afternoon would be best spent trying to further improve the lot of the beech hedge separating our garden from the playing field. Having lopped off the tops of the saplings back in the summer, this seemed to have had some success in encouraging the formation of adventitious buds up the stem. The hope now was that these buds would eventually go on to form horizontal branches the following year, helping work towards the ultimate aim of forming a lush, dense hedgerow. What the hedgerow now needed after the 'stick' that had been applied by the loppers earlier in the year was a bit of 'carrot'. So having weeded around the bases of all the saplings to keep down any competition for those vital nutrients, we then treated the whole hedgerow to a good mulch of horse manure and bark chippings to encourage the horizontal branches to shoot out with confidence.

After a couple of hours on our knees paying homage to the beech hedge, we'd done all we could, and now it was up to the beech saplings to repay our efforts. As we stood back to admire our handiwork, we watched a large flock of as many as 50 jackdaws fly east over the garden, while simultaneously making a racket with their 'ky-ow' calls as they headed off to their communal roost. This jackdaw squadron told us that not only was dusk on its way, but winter was too, as these most gregarious of birds always choose the coldest months of the year to be at their most sociable. So averse is the jackdaw to spending the nights alone that it will even go as far as inviting other noisy neighbours, like rooks, to while away the nighttime in their company. No doubt those extra pairs of watchful eyes help to ensure there are no nasty surprises during the night, even if an entirely peaceful night's sleep might be sacrificed in the process.

With the month already slipping away, I rose out of bed, ready for my early-morning interface with the garden while cleaning out the chickens. One of the other things that I liked so much about the chickens was that because they needed attention on a daily basis, the essential ritual of sorting them out each morning ensured that even on my busiest days I would need to spend, at the very least, five minutes in the garden. Through the very act of being out there at such a lovely time, I'd already forgotten the number of times I'd seen 'firsts' for the garden or noted some interesting behaviour that I would otherwise have missed had my day commenced with the more conventional bedroom – bathroom – kitchen – car – work routine.

After what had seemed so far to be a comparatively mild autumn, I was somewhat surprised to find that the first ground frost of the season had formed overnight, giving the lawn the impression that it had been dusted with icing sugar and producing a wafer-thin layer of ice across the pond and bird bath. Despite the arrival of the season's first sub-zero temperatures, there were still an admirable number of flowering plants in the garden in the form of a couple of roses and individuals belonging to the salvia, verbascum, geum, gaura and erysimum genera. But at this time of year there was a somewhat smaller cast of attendant insects buzzing around their flowerheads, as the vast majority of the invertebrate world had by now either given up the ghost or been persuaded to enter hibernation. Those leaves still hanging onto the trees were few and far between as well, with the base of the birch now surrounded by a halo of yellow. The majority of the beech leaves had fallen too and could now be seen in an Andy Goldsworthy-esque concentration gradient, with the copper colour most intense closest to the tree, before becoming steadily more diluted with each step away from the majestic iron-grey column of the tree's trunk.

With the chicken-poo bucket in one hand and the trowel in the other, I opened up the coop to let out the girls and I ran through my normal routine of extracting any No.2s from the roosting compartment that had been produced overnight. Being hugely beneficial as compost accelerant in the process of decomposition, every few days this waste was usually added to the right-hand compost bin, along with the household vegetable waste, to be turned into next year's fertiliser.

The bucket was finally ready to be emptied, so I lifted up the compost-bin lid to add the manure to the rich and vibrant mix merrily decomposing away, only to spot an animal quickly bolt down a specially dug hole it had created in one of the corners. The bloody rat that I'd seen back in September, and which I'd conveniently forgotten about, had found the combination of warm decomposing vegetable matter and chicken poo too good to refuse and had patently moved in. This was not good news. Not only would I have to use gloves near the compost heap from now on, due to issues associated with disease transmission, but I had to consider the fact that the rat might also have been pilfering the chickens' food. Promptly taking a garden fork to the compost bin, I then proceeded to turn over the heap so as to at least temporarily evict the rat while I thought of a more permanent solution. I suppose that, from a rat's point of view the compost bins were warm, safe and had takeaway food available close at hand 24 hours a day, so they must have represented the perfect 'des res'. Good news for the rat and the complete opposite for us.

Although, from an astronomical point of view, winter does not commence until the winter solstice (and shortest day of the year) on 21 December, from a meteorological perspective, and indeed from my own point of view, the season had already begun on the first of the month. To paraphrase Shakespeare rather crudely, I wouldn't exactly go as far as to say that winter was our 'season of discontent', but it has always been my least favourite time of the year. For much of the wildlife it is a time of death and dormancy, and of departing and delaying until the good times can roll once more the following spring.

In the space of just a week, and after several more frosts, we could see the garden stripped back to the bare bones of its architectural framework. With the loss of the last of the flowers we were instantly able to see that certainly in the garage herbaceous border we had made the somewhat green gardening error of purchasing both a few too many herbaceous perennials and not enough evergreen shrubs, meaning that any element of structure had at least temporarily disappeared. This could simply be corrected by a few additions over the next few months, and could be forgiven by the fact that we were still relative novices at this gardening lark. Having been overshadowed by showy flowers for most of the year, the bay tree by the water butt and the euonymus behind the pond had at last come to the fore. Also, the two yews we had planted in the spring and then promptly forgotten about were at last repaying us handsomely. And down on the wooded bank pretty much the only plants that seemed to be still registering a pulse were the perennially evergreen ivy and the hart's tongue ferns.

With most plants having shut up shop, the invertebrates virtually nonexistent, reptiles and amphibians hibernating and many of our mammals either comatose or keeping a lower profile, the saving grace for anyone needing a wintry natural-history fix in their back garden had to be the birds. Generally, the colder the weather, the better gardens are for birding, and even though the temperatures had yet to plummet properly, the activity around the feeders and any bushes still containing berries was beginning to 'hot up'. With this in mind, and after having been away for a week filming winter spectacles as far apart as north Wales and Norfolk, I was interested to see what was now on my own doorstep.

Taking my position on the patio with a mug of steaming coffee early the following morning, I was determined to see what would be fraternising the garden during an hour or so of intense observation:

07:45   Two male blackbirds guzzling hawthorn berries on the standard by the garage and a blue tit on the caged feeder. The blackbirds have just finished their moult and are looking terrific. Two fieldfare then fly east over the garden, possibly bound for Chew Valley Fruit Farm.

07:50   A male and a female blackbird feeding in the hawthorn, a goldcrest in the bay tree and a female chaffinch on the feeder. A song thrush is also singing, an indication that the weather is still relatively mild for the time of year.

07:55   Around 30 black-headed gulls leave their roost at Chew Valley Lake and fly over the garden as the first squirrel appears.

08:03   Two collared doves flying around the garden, four more fieldfare and a couple of feeding blue tits on the caged feeder.

08:30   After a break to clean out the chickens, a female chaffinch and two blue tits are noted on the caged feeder. The tits grab a seed each before eating it in the hawthorn.

08:33   A wren looking for morsels of food in the garage guttering.

08:35   A robin perched on the chicken coop, a goldfinch singing from the beech and a MISTLE THRUSH flying over – a NEW bird for the garden!

08:35   A male greenfinch, female chaffinch and great tit all visit the bell feeder in quick succession. A robin is also singing from the wooded bank and a female mallard is calling from the brook.

08:40   The jackdaws have woken up, with around 40 flying over the garden.

08:43   A female greenfinch lands on one of the sunflower heads and eats five seeds!

08:50   A female blackbird lands in the hawthorn and eats seven hawthorn berries in quick succession before flying off.

08:55   Three starlings observed flying over the garden followed by a grey wagtail.

08:55   Breakfast!

In the space of an hour and a quarter I'd managed to see sixteen different species of bird, with the highlight being the mistle thrush, which also represented the 55th species for the garden. The other totally unexpected bonus had been the behaviour of a female green-finch feeding on the rogue sunflowers that had grown up in the flower borders. Standing on the rim of the sunflower head, she'd then reached round to extract a seed, still in its husk, which was then adeptly manipulated in the bill until the ultimate prize could be extracted. This neat trick was observed five times before she took off. The take-home message from my birding minutes was clear: taking time out to stop and appreciate your garden is time well spent!

From my occasional wanderings up and down the brook and my more recent time spent on the new bench watching the water babble past, for some while I'd begun to worry about the levels of litter that I'd been encountering. Some of the larger pieces strewn along the brook had patently been there for years, but possibly due to the increased amount of rain washing rubbish down from elsewhere upstream, I'd also noticed an increase in the number of plastic bags and bottles floating past and I wanted to do something about it.

I spoke to the contractor who had been building a small housing estate in the village, some of whose properties were situated close to the north side of the brook, and I managed to persuade them to deposit a couple of skips in the strategically important positions next to the village shop and alongside the badger sett. Next, I phoned my good pal Phil – in his capacity as village socialite, I asked if he wouldn't mind sending a round-robin email to all his contacts, as a call to arms to anyone interested in helping out with a Strode brook litter pick to turn up at the village shop on Sunday 4 December at 10am. With sufficient participation from a number of stalwarts of the local community I thought that in a couple of hours we might be able to relieve about half a mile of the brook of its rubbish. Aware that there was no such thing as a free lunch, I wanted to provide exactly that, by rewarding anyone who had bothered to turn up with some hot grub and mulled wine in our garden afterwards by way of a thank you.

Whenever you organise these types of events, you can never be sure whether a good number will turn out or apathy will take over, but with Christina back at home sorting out the food to be served later I walked round to the bridge by the shop in my chest waders and with a massive roll of industrial-strength plastic bags, assorted gardening gloves and a wheelbarrow to see who would turn up. Meeting Phil first, I shouldn't have worried as I was then steadily introduced to a whole 'stream' of people from around the village who had offered their services in the full knowledge that they would in all probability be getting both dirty and wet. By the allotted start time the clean-up posse had swelled to an impressive number, and, in addition to myself and Phil, also included Nick, Carl, Mary, the Lovedays, the Manvilles, Phillip the farmer and my wildlife camera-man mate Jamie, with the promise of more to come from Bristol later, in the form of a few of Christina's friends.

With everyone looking at me and ready for instruction I suddenly realised that they would be expecting leadership too! Having had a brief dip into the brook the previous day for a recce, I knew where most of the litter was located, the depth of the water (for health and safety) and also the physical effort that would be necessary to remove some of the pieces, and so had at least given some thought as to where the manpower should be best deployed. Firstly I thanked everyone for responding to the request and giving up part of their Sunday to help out, and I explained that I was looking for no more than a couple of hours' help, reiterating that afterwards food would be served in our garden with the additional offer of a free tour should anybody want one!

Trying to walk the delicate line between being terribly assertive yet friendly and grateful, I then split the posse up into three groups. Group one was delegated to pass through the gate at the bottom of the playing field, which ran alongside our garden, and clear up the large section of bank on the south side of the brook, opposite where the kingfisher had been breeding, and also where a few of the local youngsters obviously liked to disappear for a quick smoke or a few cans of cider. Group two would then walk round to the new housing estate, from where they could access the north of the brook down by the badger sett to clear a huge amount of debris on the banks there. Finally Jamie, Carl, Nick, Phil and I would jump into the water and sweep along in a broad front collecting litter as we went.

While for the first group the rubbish consisted almost entirely of bottles, cans and discarded cigarette packets, the second group on the north bank was soon pulling out, from either the stream or the adjoining bank, a whole array of fly-tipped items, which included a toilet, a dog mess bin, an old pram, some metal sheeting and a number of old car wheels. With Jamie and I sweeping ahead to pick up the numerous smaller plastic rubbish, the majority of which was snagged in tree roots, this left Carl, Nick and Phil free to remove the somewhat heavier items which included a bus-stop sign with concrete post still attached, the obligatory bicycle, another pram and countless random components from a car which must have been dumped upstream and then slowly washed down.

With Christina's friends Laura, Clare and Nature Chris joining group two on the north bank, by 11.30am most of the debris that could be reached had been ferried back and thrown into the skips, which were now nearly two-thirds full. I waded back to our garden to prepare to receive the troops, and I was delighted at how much cleaner the brook looked – many hands had indeed made light work. With the provision of a number of baked potatoes in addition to the huge bowl of chilli I'd prepared the night before, a small vat of mulled wine and the year's first raft of mince pies, it soon turned into quite the village get-together as the food and drink worked their magic. Although I would not wish to denigrate city living any more than I may have done already, it seemed that, in addition to the rural wildlife being far more sociable, the surrounding folk seemed incredibly genial too, and I sincerely hoped this would be the first of a number of garden parties we'd be holding over the next few years.

I then took half a dozen around who had expressed an interest in the tour, and treated them to a potted history of the garden and a brief summary of the animals that had graced us with their presence over the preceding ten months. Part of the reason for my being so assiduous in explaining all the changes that we had made since moving in was to deflect attention away from the house, as the exterior hadn't changed a jot and was now beginning to look shabby and vaguely embarrassing when compared to the properties on either side. With their eyes on the garden it would be their backs to the house, a technique which seemed to work admirably! And there was always next year to remedy our living quarters – we were starting out and working in!

As I looked out of the bathroom window the following Saturday it was obvious that it had been the coldest night since our arrival, with the entire garden taking on the appearance of a frosty winter wonderland. To help the birds through the sub-zero temperatures I'd hung a couple of fat blocks out in the garden a few days previously – fatty, calorific food which would be a dieter's nightmare, but perfect for any small birds attempting to survive the freezing conditions. The block in the quince was being demolished by a squirrel that had obviously needed to replace the fat reserves burnt off during a chilly night in its drey. But the squirrels weren't having it all their own way, as the other fat block, suspended from the hawthorn standard by the garage, had been modified by surrounding the housing with an excess piece of chicken wire left over from fencing the hedge line in the chicken enclosure. So effective had this measure been that it was now just being used exclusively by birds bullied away from feeders elsewhere, and I watched entranced as a flock of six long-tailed tits took it in turns to pop through a couple of slightly widened holes designed to give access to the life-saving booty.

Not too dissimilar from cotton-wool balls with a cotton bud sticking out at a tangent, there can be few more engaging garden birds than the long-tailed tits. They are surely one of our most sociable birds, as throughout the winter they form small parties consisting of the parents and their young, together with related birds from previous breeding seasons and even any other adults that failed to raise a brood during the breeding season. With many of the birds being related, they operate as a joint taskforce to defend a winter territory from neighbouring long-tailed tit flocks, and in this case their territory included the fat block in our back garden. Because they are such tiny birds they tend to be incredibly susceptible to cold weather, but they use their sociable nature to good effect by also huddling together either in the middle of a bush or along a branch to share bodily warmth and conserve heat each night. Even accounting for this ingenious and endearing strategy, particularly cold winters can knock back the population by as much as 80 per cent, but like most of our small birds, with their large brood sizes they are quickly able to bounce back from such setbacks. They are nowhere near as abundant as blue or great tits (and to which they are only distantly related as well), but recent surveys nevertheless suggest that long-tailed tits are happily on the increase, thanks no doubt to the recent run of fairly mild winters over the last decade and their ability to cash in on food provided by gardens like ours.

I was slightly envious that Andy and Lorraine were proving somewhat more successful than me in attracting goldfinch to their garden with their niger feeder, so I reinstated a similar feeder, which up until that point had been lying redundant in the garage. Niger seed is a fine, black and oil-rich seed which originally hails from Ethiopia and in recent years has been found to be a real hit with goldfinch, often attracting them in the space of a week to a garden that might never have recorded them previously. With my niger feeder now up and running in one of the apple trees, the competitive, sneaky streak in me was also delighted to see they'd been encouraged back over the fence and I was two-nil up on the goldfinch front. What could I say? Well, they were obviously birds of immaculate taste!

As I slipped out into the cold to clean out the chickens, my appearance suddenly flushed a surprisingly large number of birds out of the garden, including half a dozen chaffinch, three or four greenfinch and a couple each of goldfinch, blackbirds and blue tits. Even in the space of a week, the much sharper weather had forced so many more birds into the garden to feed that the four perches of the bell feeder were now being more or less permanently occupied all day long. Unsure as to exactly how far temperatures had plummeted the night before, it had certainly been cold enough to totally freeze the water in the bird bath. In anticipation of a cold snap a couple of weeks back I had placed a tennis ball in the water, which I hoped, by constantly moving in any breeze, would keep a small amount of water ice-free. But with the ball frozen lock-solid I would have to resort to the boiled kitchen kettle to ensure the birds were still able to drink.

Also frozen over, the pond ice was so dense that it would probably have supported my 175lb weight had I been foolhardy enough to try, but as I didn't want to risk damaging the butyl liner just in case it was not quite as thick as I had thought, quite unusually (for me) I managed to refrain. In contrast to the bird bath, where I would have to melt the ice to provide drinking and bathing water for the birds, the frozen pond would be left to its own devices. Historically the received wisdom was that pond owners should break a hole in the ice following sub-zero nights in the garden to allow the all-important oxygen to reach the water, but new research by the charity Pond Conservation has shown that a non-interventionist approach is much better.

The researchers discovered that, rather than oxygen levels quickly decreasing in frozen-over ponds, they will in fact often rise, benefiting all the aquatic creatures still living and breathing below. As ponds freeze from the surface downwards, it would have to be astonishingly cold for the whole pond to freeze completely, meaning a large amount of freshwater is still left under the ice, within which animal life is free to move around. As the ice is no barrier to the underwater plants photosynthesising, they will continue to produce oxygen which will then in turn become trapped in the pond causing the oxygen levels to be elevated. So the only time interference might be deemed necessary during the winter would be to brush away any snow from the pond's surface, as this would block out the light, thereby halting photosynthesis.

Over the previous few days we'd also begun to become slightly worried about April. On at least a couple of occasions she'd somehow ended up inside the fenced-off enclosure we'd created to protect the fledgling hedgerow from the girls' marauding beaks, and, having managed to get in, she patently couldn't get out again. Now this wouldn't ordinarily have been anything more than irritating were it not for the fact that she was then unable to access either food or water or put herself to bed on the odd occasion that both Christina and I were away for the night, putting her at a considerable risk in the process. What was even more annoying was that we had no idea how she was managing to access the off-limits area in the first place, and had speculated that she might be flying in via a leap of faith from the top of the compost bins a couple of yards away, and, once in, was incapable of achieving the necessary height to be able to flutter back over.

As I released the chickens into their enclosure that morning, I went through my normal routine of cleaning out the coop and removing the eggs before they were finally fed their treats. On pulling my head out of the coop, the chickens usually took this as their cue to jockey for position around me as they waited to be fed, but unusually not only was April not in her regular spot at the head of the queue, she wasn't in the queue at all! Looking round, almost unbelievably she was in the fenced-off area, having somehow accessed it in the thirty seconds during which my back had been turned! I was perplexed and cross in equal measure, as I then had to climb over to retrieve her, muttering away to myself that the fence was useless if this was going to happen on a regular basis. Like the ongoing rat issue, this was a problem we were going to have to solve, otherwise the fence would have to come down and the hedge sacrificed.

With my garden chores completed, I had planned the rest of the day to involve lots of the boring life-admin-type jobs that I had been procrastinating over for weeks but couldn't put off any longer. One of the reasons for buying the house in the first place, apart from the sensational potential of the garden, was that the extra space offered by a three-bedroom house provided both a study for me, where all my books could at last be put up on shelves, and a painting studio for Christina. Due to my huge collection of books, it made enormous sense for me to use the downstairs front reception room, which had shelf space, while Christina took the third bedroom, which had less storage space but much more uniform light for painting and the added bonus a fabulous view over the back garden.

This meant that when we were both working away in our respective rooms Christina was often the first to see anything of note in the garden, which of course she always took great delight in telling me about, or 'gripping me'. Slightly frustrated by my inferior view, which included nothing more than our pocket-sized front garden and the street, I had recently bought a bird table to give me some 'wild fix' whilst carrying out unspeakably dull tasks at my desk, such as filling out my tax return. Having taken a few days for the birds to locate the food, it had then quickly begun to pay dividends in terms of sightings.

Without the traffic levels of the back-garden feeders, I liked to think that the birds visiting the front were more quality than quantity, and with the table relatively quiet at least it meant that it wouldn't be a *constant* distraction from the mountain of emails I had planned to respond to. As I worked, I found I had soon perfected the technique of glancing up for a couple of seconds whenever flickering movement caught my eye, giving me the chance to both briefly rest my eyes from the screen and identify whatever had flown down, before returning straight back to the email in hand.

'Dear Mr Smith, thank you for your email last week regarding coming to give a [coal tit] talk to your local RSPB group on the subject of my work as a television [coal tit] presenter on *The One Show*. I can confirm that I would be delighted [house sparrow] to come down to Kent next November and will need to make sure you have a [dunnock] DVD projector as well as speakers, so I can give a ... BLACKCAP!

I'd already become accustomed to the fact that the table in the front garden seemed to be attracting a different suite of birds to the feeders a mere twenty yards away in the back garden. In the ten months of watching the feeders behind the house I had not seen house sparrows or coal tits feeding there on more than half-a-dozen occasions, but these two species were now the commonest visitors to the front. For the coal tits, it hadn't been too much of a surprise, as they often found the competition for food a touch too intense in the back garden, and likewise the house sparrows were much more abundant in the street than in the back garden, but blackcap by any definition was a stellar winter visitor regardless of where it had turned up!

Relegating the emails to the sidelines for more than a few moments, I watched entranced as a female blackcap wolfed down a few beakfulls from the fat-balls hanging from the table. So-named 'blackcap' due to the colour of the male's cap, it could be argued by certain people who like to debate this type of thing that the species' name is inherently sexist, as it doesn't take into account that 50 per cent of the blackcap population (i.e. the females) have a cap that is actually reddish-brown. Irrespective of the inaccuracy of the black-cap's name, it was still a very exciting record for the garden. Up until 30 years ago the blackcap was considered nothing more than a summer migrant to the UK, arriving here each spring from its wintering grounds in southern Europe and West Africa, and having heard the song back in April I had suspected that a pair had indeed bred across the brook from our garden. This migratory route of our summering blackcaps is not believed to have changed, but now a small but increasing number of blackcaps that breed in Germany and northeast Europe are choosing to spend the winter in the UK. With this population estimated to be at around 3,000, I was natu-rally delighted that just one of our continental cousins had chosen to visit our front garden – even if it was interfering with my work productivity!

Christmas was just around the corner, and, following on from the mini-freeze earlier in the month, the weather seemed to have turned comparatively mild again, meaning Bing Crosby would have been disappointed to hear that a 'white 25 December' was by now looking increasingly remote. In addition to temperatures that had to be considered positively balmy for the festive season, it had also been incredibly wet, meaning that the chickens' outdoor area once again looked more quagmire than grassy enclosure.

Although less broody, June still looked the most dishevelled chicken in Christendom, and with Christina having been worried that the others were back to their pecking tricks again while I'd been away, we decided that she needed a hands-on inspection. I spread some oilseed rape bedding around to try and dry out the worst of the mud in the enclosure, and June proved easy to catch as she was always the last to leave the coop. I had recently purchased a bottle of gentian-violet spray, which poultry keepers use as a mild antiseptic to both treat minor injuries and (being foul-tasting) discourage pecking by other birds. However, on closer inspection it seemed that June was much healthier than we had previously suspected. All her rump and tail feathers, which had fallen out during the moult, were all re-growing and 'in pin', which meant that she would soon start looking markedly better. Nevertheless, to ensure that her rear end wouldn't be hassled during the sensitive developmental stage of her new feathers, Christina sprayed the affected area, trying in the process to avoid spraying me, as the liquid can permanently stain both skin and clothes. Five minutes and a ruined pair of jeans later, June was released back into the mud to join the other two, looking none the worse for wear – and with a purple bottom to boot!

The blackbirds continued steadily to strip the hawthorns of their berries, with the occasional help from a few redwings, and the only non-avian wildlife that had been keeping us royally entertained was the squirrels. Now that their breeding season was rapidly approach-ing, the males began to chase the females up and down the trunks and across the tree canopies, a spectacle that could easily be seen due to the absence of leaves. But it was not just sex that they had on their minds, as both Christina and I had recently begun to notice a single-minded obsession amongst a few individuals which were determined to break into the bell feeder.

A couple of days previously I had noticed out of the kitchen window one particular squirrel attempting to tackle the feeder from above, with hilarious consequences. Starting on the branch, it had then shinned down the steel rod holding the feeder to the tree before landing onto the plastic inverted dome – but that had been the easy part. Like a parachutist jumping out of a plane, it had then spread its body and limbs flat across the dome, as it tried to use both fore and hind paws to gain purchase before trying to flip around the rim and onto the perches, giving immediate access to the food. But as it attempted the last and most difficult manoeuvre, it suddenly lost its footing and in a fraction of a second was off, and tumbling to the ground much like the contestants on *Total Wipeout*! Of course, for an animal as light and agile as a squirrel a 6-foot fall was nothing more than the equivalent of a trip over the kerb for us, but it wasn't half funny!

After we had attended to June, I then retired to my office to get some work done, while Christina retreated upstairs to her studio to carry on with the preparation for an up-and-coming exhibition of her work. All of a sudden, my concentration was broken when I heard her raised voice from the stairs imploring me to come up to her studio quickly. I sprinted upstairs and she immediately directed my gaze to a squirrel sitting on the small stub of a sawn-off rowan branch, at the same height as the feeder some two yards away along a branch. Christina had apparently just seen it leap across the divide, and it had just failed to grasp any of the perches in the process, before tumbling to the meadow below. And by the look of the animal quivering just like a coiled spring, it was obviously contemplating another attempt.

Suddenly deciding it was time to put up or shut up, the squirrel sprang like a frog towards the feeder. In that split-second I found myself almost rooting for the squirrel to make it, as it flew through the air before crashing straight into the feeder. Unfortunately for the squirrel, which had overestimated the length of leap needed, the feeder was instantly shoved further out of reach like a pendulum before the squirrel had an opportunity to grasp the now moving target. With nothing to grab and gravity taking over, the only way for the squirrel to go was downwards. Hitting the ground, it was of course only the squirrel's ego that had been bruised but it was quite possibly one of the funniest things I had ever seen. Tears were rolling down my face from the hilarity of the moment, and I was too busy crying with laughter to notice in the meantime that, undeterred by failure, it had climbed back up the rowan for another shot at the title. As a result, only Christina saw the perfectly measured leap, and by the time I had wiped my eyes all I could see was the squirrel perched on the feeder whilst it swung merrily away as its contents were plundered. Unbelievable! On any other occasion I'd have been outside like a shot to shoo it away, but this squirrel had earned its meal; and sawing off the stub to prevent any further incursions could wait until the following morning.

Christmas Day was upon us, and despite having been together for six years this was the first time that Christina and I could actually spend it together at home. I received the day's first presents early on with the wonderful gift of three eggs from the girls, meaning that, after a 'lay-off' of at least a couple of months, June was finally back in business. Not only was she back laying again, but the broodiness seemed to have gone completely and with the emergence of new tail and rump feathers, she was *almost* back to her beautiful best. Christina had been so right to persuade me to get chickens. To say I adored them would have been an understatement, and it might sound a bit soppy to say it, but just watching them go about their daily business made me feel enormously happy. I also felt justifiable pride that I had gone from being someone who was a complete novice with chickens to somebody who could now talk poultry with the best of them.

As I opened up the compost bins to add the accumulated chicken poo and hay waste from the bucket into the mix, I was brought straight back down to earth with the discovery that the rat

which I thought I'd evicted the month before had returned like a thief in the night to the sanctuary of his illegal squat. Storming off to the garage, I returned with the garden fork, and, rather than just giving the compost a couple of jabs to turf the rat out, I decided instead to remove the front slats and upend his accommodation. By turning over huge forkfuls of compost I was pleased to see how well all the vegetative material was composting and I also quickly uncovered what must have been the rat's lair, which was lined with leaves and what seemed a larder of pilfered chicken pellets!

Turning the compost was not just to encourage the rat to move elsewhere; mixing it up and aerating it would also enable the heap to 'breathe', thereby speeding up the decomposition process. I turned around to see what the chickens were up to during this process and I was surprised to find them right behind me avidly watching the whole proceedings, no doubt having calculated that my forking of the heap could turn into a terrific opportunity for food. I had barely stood back a pace before eagle-eyed April, having seen the woodlice, spiders and worms aplenty, was into the bin like a shot, closely followed by May and then June. As they piled in, and began digging up various tasty morsels with their feet, it felt like the most wonderful impromptu Christmas present from me to them, and, if you'll pardon the vulgar pun, they were like pigs in shit!

As it had once again been mild the night before, I decided on a whim that checking the moth trap on Christmas morning might also be a fun activity. Of course, moth-trapping is mostly carried out between spring and autumn for good reason, because this is when the vast majority of moth species are on the wing. But there are a tiny minority that can be trapped even in the depths of winter, and I was keen to see what other wildlife had been out and about in addition to Santa's reindeer!

319

I was aware that there was a distinct possibility that we might not even catch a single moth, so I began by lifting off the light and the funnel, before then carefully checking each egg box in turn to make sure nothing was tucked away in their numerous nooks and crannies. About three-quarters of the way through, I was just beginning to think that we would draw a blank when I noticed what looked like a moth tucked into the deepest recess on the underside of one of the egg boxes, and by tapping the box against my hand, I was delighted when a moth dropped straight into my palm.

The December moth could be described as a medium-sized species with charcoal-coloured wings and a couple of creamy-white squiggly lines which run across between the leading edge and the trailing edge of the forewings. But it would be disingenuous to describe the moth in just these terms, as the outstanding feature to anyone who hasn't ever seen this species before is what must surely be the hairiest body in the British moth world. In fact, the thorax and abdomen are covered in such dense, black hair that the moth looked like it had wrapped itself up in a miniature mink coat to keep out the cold! It flies primarily between late October and late December in southern Britain, and I was delighted to read in my moth book that it was 'most numerous in woodland, but also frequent in scrub, hedgerows and established gardens'. Yes, only in *established* gardens – like ours! With one December moth duly recorded, I had then hoped to find maybe a mottled umber or winter moth – another couple of cold-weather specialists – but unfortunately that was it. Despite the sum total of the catch being one individual of one species, I was nevertheless delighted, as I had at last recorded some wildlife in the garden during the month that wasn't either a bird or a grey squirrel!

Before plonking the turkey in the oven, Christina had engineered enough time for our presents. After the frankly beautiful present of the bench for my birthday only six weeks earlier I had expressly forbidden her to spend too much on Christmas, but as she placed two beautifully wrapped presents on the garden table in front of me I had the distinct feeling that this plea had been ignored.

I did have some idea as to the identity of the smaller of the two packages, as I'd asked for an outdoor thermometer, and was chuffed on opening it to find she had sourced a posh one with minimum and maximum values, so I could keep track (temperature-wise) of the highs and lows of the back garden.

I pulled out from under the table my present for her, and she declared herself over the moon with the ridiculously expensive pair of left-handed secateurs I had purchased for her, complete with a leather holster to keep them stored safely, so she would be able to prune away to her heart's content over the coming year. It was my turn again and I ripped away the packaging of the larger present to reveal a beautiful handmade gardening trug for collecting our vegetables prior to preparing them for entry into the Harvest Home next year! It shouldn't have come as a surprise that all the presents were linked in some way with spending time in the garden – it had become our joint passion, after all.

Delighted with the careful consideration that Christina had (as ever) put into my presents, a sudden realisation hit me like a ton of bricks that we hadn't had a proper argument for months. Quite simply, the move to the country had been the best possible tonic for both of us, stale from an urban life in a one-bedroom flat. While the house had given us some much-needed physical space in our relationship, it was the garden that had metaphorically brought us closer. I had been worried that, with my love of wildlife and sport, clashing with hers of art and literature, that we simply didn't have enough in common, but the difficulties of turning a house into a home and the hard work associated with converting the outdoor space into a beautiful garden hadn't been the breaking of us, it had been the making of us …

As I cracked on with preparing the turkey, Christina went back outside to dig up the parsnips we had been saving for our special day, and she must have only been in the garden for five minutes when I heard her breathlessly rushing back in. As I turned round, with one of my hands firmly placed up the turkey's innards, I saw her come into the kitchen complete with my new trug which held a couple of bizarrely shaped root vegetables, before announcing to great fanfare, 'I know how April is getting into the hedgerow!'

JANUARY

A BOX, WITHIN A BOX, WITHIN A GARDEN

Like a large proportion of the adult population, I woke up on the morning of 1 January slightly the worse for wear after a night of revelry, which entailed both seeing out a wonderful year and hopefully ushering in an even better one. Surely there had to be no finer way of blowing away the cobwebs than spending a day out in the back garden, I thought – the fresh air would do me the power of good. The weather over the festive period had been both very wet and also incredibly mild, according to my shiny new thermometer that had not dipped below 5.6°C since it had been put out by the back door on Boxing Day. New Year's morning was such a case in point, with the thermometer reading a positively tropical 10.1°C as I slipped out for my early-morning meet and greet with the girls to compare and contrast notes from the night before.

Since Christina had spotted how April had been managing to access the fenced-off hedge line on Christmas Day we'd quickly been able to remedy the situation, resulting in no further incursions. Being the smallest (and smartest) of the chickens, April had discovered and then exploited a small section of the chicken-wire fence butting up to the main wooden fence panel which hadn't been properly secured down, and so accessing the cordoned-off area had entailed nothing more than squeezing under the peeled-up section. Having entered by this means, she couldn't then leave this way as the ends of the chicken wire, which had curled up on the inner side like a set of spikes, formed an impassable barrier, making the journey a one-way ticket. Now that we had finally worked out that she hadn't in fact gained access from an aerial leap of faith via the compost bins, a couple of fencing staples and a hammer were all that was necessary to prevent any repeat offences.

During the festive season the rodent situation had taken a turn for the worse, with the rat having managed to tunnel under the chicken coop, thus gaining instant access to the girls' food. This disturbing turn of events had necessitated a change in our routine, with the chickens' food now having to be removed each night on putting them to bed. This had the knock-on effect that if we didn't up get up early each morning to release them into the enclosure the girls would be ravenous by the time we were out. I chatted to Dennis next door about the problem, and he kindly lent me a couple of rat-baiting stations that had previously worked to good effect in his own garden. These consisted of a strong, weatherproof box into which only rats were able to enter to feed on bait blocks laced with a rodenticide, and I came to the difficult conclusion that this draconian measure would have to be attempted. On closer inspection of the baiting stations that morning, however, it seemed that the poison had not been touched, meaning perseverance would have to be the order of the day.

The period between the beginning of Christmas Day and the end of New Year's Day was also one in which I traditionally took part in a competition coordinated by the BBC Natural History Unit (NHU) in Bristol. Famous for making everything from *Life on Earth* to *Planet Earth* and the *Deadly 60* to *Springwatch*, this arm of the BBC is world-renowned for its wildlife documentaries and was also responsible for employing me to file many of the wildlife reports for *The One Show*. Slightly less well-known was that between midnight on Christmas Eve and midnight on New Year's Day each year, the

Unit organises a fun contest for employees to see who can record the highest number of different bird species during this period. Offering a number of different categories, the most kudos and stiffest competition has always been attached to that of Overall Champion, where entrants compete to see or hear the most species anywhere in the UK in the allotted timeframe. However, with little time available to go gallivanting around Britain racking up a huge species list, I was nevertheless keen to enter the recently added category of Highest Garden List for less mobile or busier birders.

With this in mind I had been carefully compiling a bird list of each bird either seen or heard, both in or flying over the garden during this period. So far the species tally had been a disappointing 26, primarily because the weather had been so mild, but hopefully with a full day in the garden a few more would be added before the end of play.

We had scheduled 4 January to be a red-letter day in the life of the wooded bank, as this would be when the long-planned coppicing of all the hazel would take place. This practice could only ever have taken place in winter when the trees are dormant, as cutting at any other time would either have seriously damaged their re-growth, or, worse still, have killed them entirely. Also, taking a chainsaw to trees at any other time than between when the leaves have fallen and the buds have reappeared would potentially both disrupt any nesting birds and cause the trampling of any sensitive ground flora. I had wanted to coppice the wooded bank soon after we had moved in, but as so many other big projects were competing for my time earlier in the year, and due to coppicing being so time-sensitive, an executive decision was made early on that this would be one job that would simply have to be delayed.

So by way of preparation for 'coppice day', it was important beforehand that we guaranteed that the wooded bank would be a safe environment in which power tools could be operated, especially as it would be me using them! The first job I was keen to tackle was to re-cut the steps down to the stream to ensure that the whole area could be more easily accessed without either constantly slipping over or trampling across any more areas than was necessary. While I got to work with the spade, Christina, who, having not drunk the night before, was irritatingly as fresh as a daisy, tackled the worst of the brash pile that had been left over from Mr Gregory's days, when the bank had been more dumping zone than wooded copse.

There is something about good, old-fashioned hard labour in cold weather that is immensely satisfying, and as the physicality of our respective jobs began to take its toll we were soon dispensing with our clothes like streakers at Twickenham. As I slowly removed spadefuls of earth in order to reshape the steps back to the aesthetically pleasing geometrical shapes that they must have originally been, I could see that the green shoots of spring were already beginning to materialise. Either side of the steps the first snowdrop leaf-tips were breaking free of the soil, making me think that this would be the first plant since moving to the country that we would be able to see through its second complete cycle. The plant's appearance also flagged up the fact that not only was our first anniversary in the house only just around the corner, but from now on the flower would also be used to mark every future anniversary too. As I descended further down the bank, the spade occasionally and inevitably cut through a few of the wild garlic (or ramsons) bulbs just below the surface, producing that instant 'garlic' hit that had been reminiscent of our bank back in the springtime.

After I had superficially searched for any juicy worms or slugs as treats for the girls, the excess spoil was then tipped out of sight behind the quince. While I improved the bank's accessibility, Christina made great strides with the brash pile, most of which she'd managed to drag up to the meadow, before feverishly lopping the new pile into manageable sizes for burning once dry. With my work complete, it definitely proved the right decision to help Christina out, as in the open of the garden I was soon able to add a 'fly-by' pied wagtail and a distant singing song thrush to my NHU bird list, making a slightly more respectable total of 28. With the garden now finally ready for the chainsaw and the weather beginning to deteriorate, we beat a hasty retreat indoors as we had lunch to prepare for some pretty important visitors.

My older brother lives in the west of Ireland with his wife and two kids, so I don't get to see him and his family anywhere near as much as I'd like, and when they do come over to the UK, the list of people they have to catch up with is so long that they can usually fit in little more than a flying visit to the 'Bristol Bumpkin' arm of the family. My brother Paul and I are in many ways 'chips off the old block' and share a good number of familial traits. I suppose in summary we could both be described as follicly-challenged extroverts with a sunny disposition and garrulous nature, which means that whenever we meet up the banter usually flows. Main topics of conversation tend to centre on either family matters or sport – two big areas of common interest – but one subject on which we're poles apart and which therefore rarely comes up is wildlife. Put bluntly, Paul doesn't give two hoots about nature!

No sooner had Paul pulled up the drive and applied the handbrake than both rear car doors suddenly shot open simultaneously like a bird preparing for take-off as my nephew Oisín and niece Béibhinn spilled out and charged over to greet me. I had not seen them for at least six months, during which time they'd patently grown substantially, and I only just managed to lift them off the ground, signalling that their joint age of 18 meant my days of 'double hugs' might soon be over. Paul seemed on terrific form too, and everyone was delighted to see Christina, who suggested that while she finished preparing lunch and before the gathering storm-clouds hit Chew Stoke, maybe I should take them down to see both the garden and the chickens.

The proud owners of a couple of bantams themselves, the Irish Dilgers were also avowed 'poultry-philes' and the instant we moved into the back garden my nephew and niece made a bee-line for the chicken enclosure to become acquainted with April, May and June. Without going into too much detail for fear of boring my brother, I then took him on the ten-cent tour around the pond, herbaceous borders and meadow, before finally ending up down on the wooded bank by the stream. Having seen the garden just after we'd bought it, he seemed genuinely impressed by the sheer amount of work we'd undertaken. The kids joined us down on the bank, as for them the water was the only item of real interest in the garden apart from the chickens, and we then had a quick game of Pooh sticks. Looking up, Oisín, who had always been wise beyond his years, tugged my arm and said 'I think it's going to rain, Uncle Mike', and following the direction of his gaze upwards I could see the most enormous cumulonimbus cloud towering above the garden, followed by the almost instant increase in wind speed ahead of the gathering storm.

In a matter of seconds the storm was upon us as hailstones started pelting through the trees, with us located at the furthest possible point from the sanctuary of the house. I turned back to the garden and, picking up Béibhinn in one fell swoop, sprinted back up the steps followed by Paul and Oisín, with the feeling that we were almost running for our lives. Pea-sized hailstones were pelting down and I instantly took hits left, right and centre as they pinged off my head and stung my ears while we hurtled through the meadow and back into the kitchen. Making it inside safely without any loss of personnel, we all then began to laugh hysterically as we turned round to see what looked like the world's largest pile of polystyrene packing beads that had just been dumped on the garden. 'Just my favourite type of nature ramble,' said Paul, '… one lasting no longer than five minutes!'

With the kids watered, fed and back off to spend the night with Paul and their doting grandma in Bristol, the awful weather meant that any more work in the garden would be futile, so Christina and I were forced to spend the rest of the day indoors carrying out a whole variety of chores we'd been prevaricating over for weeks. Christina was delegated to clean the bathroom, and I was left to tackle the vacuuming whilst simultaneously contemplating the anonymous quote 'God made rainy days, so gardeners could get the housework done'. In fact the only time I stuck my nose outside for the rest of the day was to lock up the girls and remove their food. But, as ever, the capricious garden often liked to reveal little surprises when they were least expected, and the trip outside in frankly appalling weather would not prove to be a wasted one. With a torch in one hand and my other hand shielding my eyes from the driving rain, I stepped over the electric fence into the quagmire of their enclosure and mid-straddle suddenly recorded my 29th and final species for the NHU garden bird race as a tawny owl's hoot managed to cut through the wind and rain. The list hadn't included cold-weather specialities like reed buntings, bullfinches or siskins, which were birds that I would normally have considered certainties for the week following Christmas, but it was still respectable. But the question was, would it be enough?

Having already delivered the most intense hailstone blizzard I had ever seen, the New Year then continued its bizarre meteorological start by ushering in some of the windiest and wettest days I could remember since the Great Storm of October 1987. During filming only a couple of days later, I received a worrying text message from Christina saying that the wind had knocked down the fence between our garden and Marjory and Dennis's. Paranoid that this would enable the chickens to escape into the Chew Stoke countryside, never to be seen again, I immediately rang back to find that the only thing that had prevented them from getting out had been the unsightly chicken-wire fence that we had only just put in place to protect the hedgerow.

In fact the village's weather had suddenly become national news, as a lady driver crossing Strode brook's ford just west of our house during the worst of the weather had underestimated the depth of the water and promptly stalled in the middle, before the water (the level of which had been swelled by the accompanying rainfall) then picked up the car and whisked it off downstream. It appeared that the only thing preventing her and the car from sailing past the bottom of our garden was an upended willow tree straddling the brook further up, which had managed to wedge the car in its tracks.

Fortunately for us, due to the brook being ordinarily so far below the level of the garden (and the house), it would have needed to rain for 40 days and 40 nights before we would be contemplating sandbags. However, as we stood on the bank at the bottom of the garden, it was astonishing to see how the tinkling brook had suddenly been transformed into a potentially dangerous torrent. With all the extreme weather we had been experiencing since the turn of the year, I was more than a little worried about whether or not the following day's big event in the garden would even be able to take place, as it was one of only a handful of projects that had been months in the planning. However, waking up on the morning of 4 January, I needn't have worried, as a quick glance out of the curtains told me we had arrived at the calm *after* the storm.

I was keen to attempt the coppicing of the wooded bank, where possible by myself, and back in November I'd attended a two-day course on operating chainsaws run by a local tree surgeon I'd found on Google called Tim. Learning the basics on the course, including maintenance, health and safety and basic chainsaw techniques, it wasn't difficult to guess who the dunce of the class had been. Having been around chainsaws for much of my conservation career, I'd been mistaken in thinking that a couple of hours would be more than enough to learn a sufficient amount in order to operate them safely, but I had underestimated what technically and physically demanding bits of kits they were. I felt like I was back at school again as I tried to get to grips with the difference between the 'chain gauge' and 'chain pitch' and where on the chainsaw I would find the 'heel' and 'toe'.

Suffice to say, with substantial help I managed to scrape a pass from the course and was deemed competent to be let loose in my back garden, but feeling like I would only achieve my aims with considerable on-site help and guidance, I persuaded Tim to bring his chainsaw over and act as Consultant Operative. I needed both to sort out the chickens and prop up the blown-over fence in the back garden until it could be properly replaced. Tim duly arrived, and after a meet and greet from both Christina and me with a cup of coffee, he unloaded his gear and came to look at the work we had planned.

Tim was a tall, rangy chap, who was close to my own age and had been wielding a chainsaw longer than he cared to remember. His humour could best be described as dry, and his worldview was one that could be summed up as 'glass half empty'. His tuition on the course had been nothing short of outstanding and if he was able to instruct muggins how to use a chainsaw, he could have taught anyone. In addition to using Tim to monitor my technique, I was also keen to canvass his opinion on best coppicing practices too. As I showed him round the garden, he was first keen to know whether we were worried that the house might have 'concrete cancer' before saving the worst news for the beech tree. The beech had always consisted of a large fork with two seemingly co-dominant stems emanating from the top of the main trunk, and as it had not yet reached its fortieth birthday, I had always considered it not only to be the best-looking tree in the garden, but also one of those in the best nick as well. But pointing to a hairline crack, Tim's highly trained eye had spotted a fatal flaw in the tree's architecture, which up until that point I hadn't even noticed myself, and which ran from where the two main stems or branches diverged, for some 12 inches down the middle of the trunk. 'I hate to be the bearer of bad news,' he said, sounding suspiciously like he was in fact relishing it, 'but this tree has an occluded fork.'

'What's one of those?' I dumbly asked, as Tim went on to use the analogy of a pair of throw-away wooden chopsticks to explain that the two diverging stems hadn't properly formed a union and the crack was indicative that the considerable weight of each was slowly tearing the tree apart. On asking him how we could sort this out, his response was nothing short of devastating as he explained that in the short term we should monitor the crack to make sure it didn't get any wider, and even though both stems could potentially be braced to offload some weight as an interim measure, ultimately the tree would have to be cut down. Although drastic, bringing in tree surgeons to remove the tree would be infinitely more preferable than letting gravity take the matter into its own hands, as just a glance to the right revealed that the garage would not escape a direct hit should the tree suddenly not be able to take the pressure from more strong winds.

I was simply gutted that the days were suddenly numbered for one of the principal features of the garden and my favourite tree, and, loving trees as much as I do, I was pretty inconsolable. 'Look,' said Tim, 'it's not going to fall down any time soon, and today is your chance to make sure that the others avoid the same fate.' It was just the tonic I needed and a surprising ray of sunshine from the bearer of bad news, and I determined from that point that I would just have to put it to the back of my mind and concentrate on the work that needed doing that day.

Tim handed over his chainsaw for me to conduct all the essential pre-operation safety checks, even though I'd only been on the course five weeks previously, and I suddenly had that panicked feeling of old that I couldn't remember a single thing about what to do next. Tim must have seen the look of confusion and embarrassment on my face and kindly took it upon himself to step in and take me on a mini-refresher course which involved checking the brake for chain-creep on the guard bar, making sure there was sufficient oil and that the on/off switch functioned effectively. Having purchased chainsaw trousers, a helmet with visor and goggles and special gloves for the course, the only item I had to borrow from Tim were chainsaw boots, and so with the saw ready for action, I was too.

The first active combat the chainsaw would see was on the multi-stemmed hazel nestling behind the birch tree and alongside the oak in the corner. The stems would be removed via a technique called the 'step-cut', which involved cutting a small notch out of the under-side of the stem and then using the chainsaw on the upper side and slightly back from the notch so that, as the cut widened, the chainsaw wouldn't get pinched as it cut through. This technique also had the benefit of enabling the stem to be felled in a controlled fashion. To start with, I was making small mistakes all over the place, such as not putting the brake on after each cut, forgetting to put my visor down and generally rushing at it, but after a while I began to make steady progress. Trying to shape the coppice stool like a mushroom, I quickly began to generate a lot of cut wood, which Tim and Christina kindly dragged away to form an ever-increasing pile along the beech hedge for disposal at a later date. With the first hazel quickly cut down to size, I then made short work of a strange shrub which had not passed muster all year, before tackling the middle hazel we'd identified for remedial work.

Coppicing the hazel proved a much more difficult proposition, as a number of the stems were all bound up with the ash tree above by long, sinuous stems of honeysuckle and ivy, meaning that, once cut, they were not able to fall freely, but instead left dangling some-what precariously in the wind. I then began to find out how experience in just this type of situation is paramount, as Tim stepped in to help out and with a combination of brute force and some judicious use of loppers was able to take these branches out of the air and out of the equation.

As I tidied up the coppice stool on the middle hazel I realised how physically exhausting chainsaw work was too, as despite the fact that it was bitterly cold (5.3°C, in fact), I had in the space of less than an hour stripped down to nothing more than a T-shirt and thin jumper in a bid to give the accumulating sweat an opportunity to escape. In many ways the far more time-consuming activity than the chainsawing itself was the disposal of all the cut material currently piling up. The logs would be cut to the right sizes for use in the wood-burning stove we had just had installed in the lounge, but the brash would have to be incinerated *in situ*. As ever, one job being tackled in the garden only succeeded in creating a couple more tasks further down the line!

The third hazel to the right-hand side of the bank and alongside the steps was the biggest job of the lot, due to being the most mature and having some stems easily the thickness of my thigh. Rather than coppicing the whole lot, Christina and I wanted to keep some of the height but cut back four huge stems reaching out over the water that shaded a substantial part of the bank. Tim advised me to take these big heavy branches out with a 'birds-mouth' technique, which entailed removing a wedge from the underside of the branch in the direction you want it to fall, before making a horizontal felling cut on the upper side just above the 'birds mouth' to create a hinge, which would dictate the direction of fall. Once the branch had fallen, the remaining coppiced stump was then cleaned up to create a nice, tidy finish and to prevent water accessing the cut and opening up the possibility of infection. Once felled, each branch was then cut into stove-sized logs and by the time I'd removed and sawn up all four of these branches I was so exhausted I could hardly stand up.

The final chainsaw job was to lop off a large and ugly bough from the rear of the ash tree on the bank. However, because the bough being was about 6 feet above ground (making it a difficult cut for a novice), and given my weary state, I asked Tim if he wouldn't mind doing the honours. Observing him take this huge branch down quickly, safely and with consummate ease was a marvel, and I can only liken it to watching an artist with a paintbrush or a surgeon with a scalpel. With all the technically demanding work then completed, the chainsaw was then passed back over to me to section up the felled bough. Of all the firewood we had generated that morning, the ash was the most highly regarded, as it is one of our few native woodland species which burns well even when green, meaning this was the wood that would be keeping us warm indoors for the rest of the winter.

We stood back to admire our work, and the bank looked radically different. Christina and I were delighted that the work seemed to have successfully achieved our main aims. Christina was much happier that not only did the bank (at long last) look much tidier, but with more sunshine now streaming onto the woodland floor it also felt less gloomy. I too was delighted that, despite the removal of a lot of wood, the bank had still managed to retain the feel of still being in essence a woodland, and that all the coppicing would hopefully now be able to give the trees a new, and much needed, lease of life. To help celebrate a tremendous morning's work, Christina then prepared one of her famous beef stews, which all three of us demolished in the garden, before thanking Tim profusely for his help and bidding him farewell.

With the afternoon still ahead of us, we decided to keep the momentum going by a quick visit to the DIY store to purchase a garden incinerator. Resisting the temptation to add a few plants, we quickly scurried back to the garden as I began chopping up the brash whilst Christina was the delegated fire-starter. Pretty soon we had an incredibly efficient production line going with me cutting the brash into manageable sizes as Christina continually fed the flames until bad light stopped play some two hours, and half of the brash pile, later. Throughout the afternoon the wind had steadily picked up once again, and with strong gusts forecast overnight, the last job, before retiring indoors to rest my aching back, was to check that the temporary posts which I'd been using to hold up the blown-over sections of fence would last another night.

Having asked for the thermometer for Christmas to try and get more of a handle on how the temperatures would affect the garden and its wildlife, it seemed like a rain gauge and anemometer would have been far more illuminating meteorological instruments, as the next few days were mild, yet very wet and windy. Fortunately, in one small window of opportunity amongst the almost incessant battering by a westerly wind cutting across the garden, Marjory and Dennis were able to engage the services of three of the street's residents, who also happened to be builders, to replace the fence between our properties which had been flattened for good following a particularly gusty couple of nights. Running in a north-south direction, this fence would always be in the 'wind-zone', but with the slatted wooden fence panels now held in place by concrete posts, this meant that the chickens, having been confined to barracks for the best part of a week for fear that they might escape, could at last be released back into their enclosure.

With the obvious exception of the feeders, the garden during this time was as quiet as I'd ever seen it, but despite still being firmly in the grip of winter, the first signs of spring were slowly beginning to emerge too. Once again the snowdrops had delivered memorably, and on the sections of the hazel that had avoided the wrath of the chainsaw, the lambs' tail catkins were already beginning to form. After having passed the last few months in full-on hibernation mode, the meadow was also showing signs of a 'heartbeat' in the form of the kidney-shaped leaves of lesser celandine appearing alongside the basal rosettes of primroses – surely more clues that spring would soon be elbowing winter out of the way. As W. E. Johns wrote in his interwar gardening book *The Passing Show*, 'one of the most delightful things about a garden is the anticipation it provides', and I too felt as excited as a child on Christmas Eve at the prospect of what a second spring would bring to the garden. Which plants had survived the winter? Would anything nest early in the garden? When would I see the first brimstone butterfly? So many questions!

Just when I was beginning to despair that a proper, cold winter would never materialise to replace the unrelenting wind and rain that we'd been served up, the weather suddenly changed, presenting me with the perfect opportunity for an expedition I'd been keen to carry out ever since I'd taken the children on the back-garden nature ramble back in September. Surprised that I hadn't managed to catch a single fish in my plastic pop bottle fish-trap, this had also made me realise that in fact I hadn't even spotted so much as a single fish in the brook since our arrival. Given that the kingfishers had successfully managed to raise at least two broods during the summer, fish must be present in places along the brook, but that wasn't good enough for me – I wanted to find out where!

With Christina confined to her studio, I managed to enlist the help of my good friend Jamie in the village. A wildlife cameraman of some standing, Jamie had shinned up the greasy pole of television with relative ease, garnering along the way a reputation as a man who always came back with the goods. Constantly in demand to film anything from wolves to whales, he had a CV that would make any aspiring cameraman weep with envy, but more to the point, having worked with his good mate Charlie on the famous 'Natural World' of *Halcyon River*, he knew the habits of kingfishers as well as anyone – and he was also at home on one of his rare breaks in between shoots!

Kitted out in my chest waders and with the temperature hovering around zero, but with warmth promised later thanks to a cloudless sky, I met him at his house, which looked over the brook a couple of hundred yards upstream from our humble abode. Aware of the fact that during his limited time at home his priorities lay with being a husband and father, I also brought half a dozen eggs (courtesy of the girls) for his wife Sarah, as a thank you for kindly allowing her husband to come out and play for a couple of hours. Despite living around 150 yards from where the kingfishers had nested, the fact that he saw them passing his house most days led him to suspect that, while nesting closer to my house, they might be fishing nearer to his. So after a quick cuppa we hopped in the water and headed upstream.

Opposite Jamie's, the water was clear, fast flowing and very shallow, meaning that silt had been given little chance to build up, which in turn was able to reveal that the brook's bottom consisted of either gravel or huge slabs of bedrock. This contrasted hugely with the appearance of the brook passing my garden, where its deeper, more sluggish nature had resulted in quite a silt build-up. Despite winter not being the optimal time to go looking for freshwater fish, the simple act of lifting a few small rocks upstream from his house soon paid dividends, as we both quickly located the unmistakable broad head, wedge-shaped bodies and spiny dorsal and pectoral fins of bullheads. Hidden away during the daytime for fear of being predated, these relatively small fish are much more active at night-time when they emerge to feed on insects, crustaceans and fish eggs. Bullheads were also firmly on the menu for kingfishers too – no wonder they were keen to keep their heads down! Under another boulder I was lucky enough to find the larva of a beautiful demoiselle dragonfly, the adult form of which I'd first recorded flitting around our freshly filled pond back in May. Looking more praying mantis than dragonfly larva, it was hard to believe that this alien predator would be making the transformation next summer into one of our most graceful and dainty insects.

As we passed the ford in the west of the village which had been responsible for whisking the car away in the heavy rains earlier in the month – but which had since dropped considerably – this was also apparently the location where Jamie had seen brown trout parr earlier in the summer. I had already been tipped off by a number of locals that the brook had historically been well known for its brown trout, but I was worried that they might have since disappeared due to a variety of pollution issues or predation by the introduced American mink, but Jamie's sightings proved that they had at least hung on in a few paces – good news for both the brook and its resident kingfishers!

We left the village behind and entered farmland as we continued to wade upstream, and, from the difficulty in negotiating several parts, it became obvious that no one had attempted to navigate the brook in this manner for years. Wearing chest waders, I was usually able to find a way through, but in several places Jamie's thigh waders were insufficient, necessitating a quick scramble up the bank on the deeper sections before he was able to clamber back in again. By now the weather was nothing short of glorious and the best it had been so far all month (and year), and, with the sun still so low in the sky, any catkins and snowdrops we encountered were bathed in the most glorious golden light. Kingfisher! I was slightly ahead of Jamie, and I waded round a corner only to see a kingfisher sitting on some tree roots as it contemplated breakfast. I didn't know who was more surprised to see whom, and in a flash, having decided my intrusion was an unwelcome one, it was up and off further upstream like a speeding blue bullet. Only I saw it, but Jamie, having seen them thousands of times before, was not unduly bothered, but instead more interested as to why the bird was so far from its core range near my back garden. He was very familiar with mapping these birds' territories, and the only conclusions he was able to draw were that this bird was either an ousted youngster from the breeding pair downstream or that it represented a bird from another territory. Did Chew Stoke have more than just a single pair of kingfishers? It was a tantalising thought!

The brook then divided into two and Jamie suggested we take the right fork as it would end in a surprise that his family had been delighted to uncover earlier in the year. By now the effort of scrambling over, under and around fallen trees and carelessly placed barbed wire was beginning to tell, and so we took a quick pit stop as we caught our breath and enjoyed the sun's warmth on our faces. Ahead of us I suddenly picked up the sound of a robin singing from one of the alder trees along the bank as if it too were revelling in a quite glorious day.

To those who ask me how they can learn birdsong, my answer is always the same, 'learn one species at a time, starting with the common species, and once you know these intimately, then the more unusual ones will begin to stand out'. If you do attempt this technique, then surely one of the first you should try and learn belongs to the robin. For starters, with close to six million pairs, it is not only one of our commonest breeding birds, but as one of our most widespread species it can be found virtually throughout Britain. Perhaps more pertinently for dawn chorus beginners, it is the bird that sings more often throughout the year than any other species, only giving its voice a rest in mid- to late summer during the post-breeding moult, and the reason why both males and females carry on singing right through the winter is because it is one of the few British species to hold a territory all year. Successfully holding its own piece of robin real estate can often mean the difference between life and death, and so its territory will always be pugnaciously defended against any other red-breasted intruders.

I was not aware as to how potentially aggressive territorial robins could be until a few years ago, when, while working as a researcher on *Springwatch*, we put out a stuffed robin in the middle of another robin's territory. To spice it up a little we then played a CD recording of another robin's song, and it proved the equivalent of waving a red rag to a bull. With the infuriated incumbent fooled into thinking that an intruder had not only entered his territory but was singing in an attempt to claim ownership, the resident robin attacked the inanimate imposter so viciously that he almost ripped its head clean off. However, as we sat there listening to the robin's varied and melodious song I would like to have thought that on this occasion maybe this bird wasn't just singing as a warning for other robins to stay clear. Maybe it was also singing because it was a beautiful day, or because it had at last stopped raining, or just because it liked singing.

I had heard that there was a waterfall west of Chew Stoke but hadn't realised that's where we would end up as we waded round a meander to be confronted with the water cascading over a 18-foot rock platform down into a plunge pool below. It was thrilling to think that this was the same water that would soon be flowing straight past both our back gardens a couple of miles downstream. Even more importantly, the brook looked in great condition, and even though we hadn't located many fish, the indication of a second possible kingfisher territory suggested that a healthy fish population was indeed present, meaning that hopefully the brook would continue to remain an attractive proposition for kingfishers for many more years to come.

Retracing our journey, this time by footpath, I took my leave of Jamie at his house and returned home to find Christina out in the garden and staring over the garden fence. 'There's been another murder,' she said on my arrival, pointing in the direction of Andy and Lorraine's lawn where a dead wood pigeon could be seen lying on its back with its feet stuck somewhat comically up in the air. Sure that our neighbours would be thanking me for removing carcasses from their garden, I hopped over the fence, with an idea that this wood pigeon would now not mind in the slightest if its body were to be used in the advancement of science. To put it bluntly, the camera trap down by the river had been a dead loss, and despite having been left down by the water for a few weeks it hadn't caught anything on film apart from Christina and I taking it in turns to watch an increasingly smelly piece of pollack slowly decomposing.

Guessing that the otter either hadn't passed through during that period or smelt it, I hit upon the idea that we might just have more success with the camera in the garden if we used the pigeon as bait. Tying the pigeon to a stake, to ensure that any animals visiting the garden wouldn't be able just to whisk away the food in an instant, it was then placed back by the hole in the beech hedge with the camera once more placed a few yards away, ready to catch any action. If a tasty plump-breasted wood pigeon wouldn't pull any predators in during this time of hardship, nothing would.

As the clear skies from the previous day had stuck around, causing the temperature to plummet as soon as the sun dipped below the horizon, it was no surprise that on looking out of the bathroom window the following morning I found we had woken up to another widespread frost. Both the pond and the bird bath had re-frozen, the feeders were suddenly back in demand, and, with the help of my binoculars retrieved from the landing-hall windowsill, I was able to count four greenfinches on the perches of the bell feeder and a further twelve chaffinches scouring the meadow in quick succession for spilt food below. At the back of the meadow where we had sprinkled a number of apples past their sell-by date, I spotted a few redwings tucking into their favourite food.

As I scanned my bins elsewhere around the garden for other action, I noticed a robin perched on top of one of the woodpiles that had been temporarily created as a result of the coppicing, and which seemed to be behaving strangely. I wasn't sure why until I noticed another robin just on the ground no more than a couple of yards from the woodpile. The 'woodpile robin' had his head thrown back, resulting in the maximum amount of red breast to be displayed to the robin on the ground below, and he animated this posture with some sideways bobbing of the head, making him resemble more of an animatronic puppet than a real live robin. The meaning behind this posturing was abundantly clear; it was an explicit threat to the 'ground robin' that if it didn't leave immediately, it would be in line for a bit of featherweight aggro. In such cases it is usually the resident robin that wins the day, with the higher perch helping to assert dominance, and such was the case here too, as I then watched the 'ground robin' turn tail and fly off, hotly pursued by the resident robin who was patently keen to complete the rout.

Outside in the garden a temperature of –2.5°C represented the coldest day of the winter so far, and when I checked out the wood pigeon before cleaning out the girls, it was also unfortunately and immediately obvious that the carcass hadn't been so much as sniffed at by anything during the night. I wasn't unduly fussed by the lack of action, as surely such a tasty meal wouldn't remain undiscovered for long. With the girls fed and their water defrosted, Christina and I only had a short while to idle, sitting in our down jackets up on the patio before our guests arrived, but as we sat there, me of course with my binoculars virtually glued to my face, it proved long enough to make a remarkable discovery. As I watched the birds toing and froing, I suddenly noticed a male greenfinch on the bell feeder with a silver BTO ring on his right leg, and, excluding the small possibility that it could be a bird that had been rung in another garden, the only conclusion that I could draw was that it must have been one of the two male greenfinch that Ed and I had rung in the garden during the course of the year. It was a most welcome sight, as it undoubtedly meant that, for any passing greenfinch, coming in to

feed in our garden wasn't the potential death sentence it had once been. I was so pleased that, had it been a little later than 9am, I would probably have been tempted to uncork some champagne there and then!

The first anniversary of moving into our house was now rapidly approaching, and Christina and I had arranged for a final visit that morning from our horticultural consultant and dear friend Mark, who had been persuaded to come around with his partner Ian (and the offer of lunch) to give an honest assessment of our progress thus far. We were particularly keen for his opinion as to how to capitalise on our good work and ensure that our herbaceous borders would be in the best condition next summer. When they arrived we bundled straight into the garden and got straight down to business. It would be a fair summary to say that while I had been the driving force on both the big construction jobs in the garden and the biological recording, it was Christina who had been the heart and soul behind the flowerbeds. This meant that, despite Mark having been my friend for over 25 years, when it came to the subtleties of getting the best out of the various cultivars, he soon realised that his remarks were better directed towards Christina.

The group of four quickly fractured into two groups of two, as the horticultural heavyweights began chatting away about best mulching practices for the borders and when and where to wield the secateurs in order to rejuvenate certain plants, whilst Ian and I followed mutely behind playing conversation tennis. As we worked our way around the garage border, Mark and Christina then became particularly animated when they began discussing which plants had delivered memorably during the year as opposed to the others that had been a let-down. Zoning out temporarily, Ian and I turned away to look down the garden as he asked me when I'd last seen the … crash, bang, wallop! He didn't even have a chance to finish his question as the two of us suddenly saw a sparrowhawk flash into view, which must have flown over the newly erected fence between our garden and Marjory and Dennis's, before flying straight at the bell feeder. In the blink of an eye, we both watched – Ian probably with his mouth still open – as the sparrowhawk then executed a barrel roll, and while still inverted shot out a talon to pluck a hapless greenfinch off one of the bottom perches. Having snaffled the bird, the sparrowhawk then needed to both quickly right itself, while simultaneously pulling out to prevent a collision with a conifer in Andy and Lorraine's garden positioned on just the other side of the fence. Any accident suitably averted, it then flew off with its prey along the line of the beech hedge and out of sight, presumably down to the plucking spot that Ed and I had uncovered back in the autumn down by the brook.

It was a two- or three-second spectacle of quite stunning aerobatic agility, combined with a brutal efficiency, and having seen cheetahs catch gazelles in Tanzania and ospreys catch fish in Scotland, what Ian and I had just witnessed, in my opinion, was right up there with anything the natural world could offer anywhere in terms of an interaction between predator and prey. It had also happened in our garden! Turning around to see if the other two had seen what we'd witnessed, the obvious answer was a resounding no, as they still had their backs turned and their noses in the flowerbeds. 'What was it you wanted to ask me?' I said, turning round to talk to Ian, but he was in no position to respond with his mouth still open.

It was equally frosty the following morning, as I blundered bleary-eyed through the back door and stumbled down the back garden for my morning constitutional with the chickens. As usual, on spotting my approach, they began to go ballistic at the thought of being let out and fed, but on this occasion my attention was diverted elsewhere as my presence must have flushed a large bird out of the brook. The all-white plumage, heron-like appearance and long, trailing black legs with yellow feet meant only one thing – Christina had been right! I must explain that while I'd been away filming a couple of weeks back, Christina had told me on the phone that she thought she had flushed a little egret out of the brook, but I'm afraid to my shame I'd dismissed the record as being that of a misidentified gull – and once again I'd been wrong to have doubted her.

The little egret's recent colonisation of Britain is remarkable given that around 25 years ago this species was nothing more than an infrequent and exciting visitor to our southern estuaries. But following an influx, probably from France in 1989, their numbers steadily increased until they finally bred in Dorset in 1996. Now numbering over 600 breeding pairs at a whole host of sites, and with estimates of overwintering little egrets put at around 4,500, it is astonishing how quickly they have made themselves at home here. So common are sightings of little egrets these days that in just a couple of decades they have gone from being considered to be of real rarity status to barely warranting a mention by many birdwatchers. However, seeing a little egret on the Severn Estuary or Chew Valley Lake would never be quite as big a story as spotting one paddling around at the bottom of our patch, especially when it represented the 56th bird species for the garden!

With the chickens sorted and my hands desperately needing to be thawed around a hot mug of coffee indoors, my last job was to see if anything had visited the wood pigeon, and, fully expecting it to be untouched, I was shocked and stunned to find that all that remained were the feet that had been used to tie the pigeon to the post and a few bits of the wings! I was immediately down on my knees to extract the memory card, and I was chuffed to see that the camera had recorded fifteen clips for my viewing pleasure! Rousing Christina, we both perched ourselves in front of the computer as I impatiently waited for the card reader to reveal what had been filmed.

I was concerned that the clips would consist of a series of all the neighbourhood cats waltzing through the garden during the day, but I needn't have worried as the first clip cut straight to black and white, meaning it had been shot at night. Fox! We watched enthralled as a big fox came in from camera left – or the side with the hole in the fence – and proceeded to first sniff and then tug at the wood pigeon. All of a sudden, distracted by a barking dog, the sound of which had been picked up by the inbuilt microphone, the fox looked up and past the camera in the direction of where the noise had come from, and we could instantly see from just a single eye shining in the light – it was a one-eyed fox!

This injury was a reminder that foxes' lives can often be short and brutal, with an estimated 90 per cent of those living in rural locations not even making it to their fifth birthday. Being hit on the road, shot, trapped, snared or contracting mange are all high up the list of a whole raft of daily hazards by which Britain's foxes can meet their maker, but a surprising number can also be killed in disputes with their own kind. With the size of the fox indicating it was prob-ably a male, and fox mating season at its peak in January, in all likeli-hood this injury may well have been caused by fighting with another male either for a piece of foxy real estate or over access to a foxy lady. Whilst undoubtedly a shame for the fox, the loss of the eye didn't seem to be hindering him in the slightest, and as he returned back to feast on the wood pigeon, we could clearly see that apart from his diminished vision he looked in otherwise excellent condition.

With the video clips running for a minute in length, and then programmed to take another minute's break before the camera was able to record again, we were able to scroll through the clips in chronological fashion as the wood pigeon was slowly dismembered by 'one-eyed Pete' in front of our eyes. But then after six clips, and a couple of hours later that same night, a smaller-looking fox with a longer, thinner tail appeared from the other direction, and on lifting its head we were clearly able to see a double eye-shine, as the infra-red light was reflected back off the *tapetum lucidum* (the reflective surface at the back of many animals' eyes), making it categorically a different fox! This individual was much more timid, and so the first few clips involved nothing more than a wary sniff of the wood

pigeon before hunger eventually overtook fear and it too tucked in to the free meal.

By the time we had watched the fourteenth clip there was hardly anything left of the wood pigeon, having been so thoroughly disposed of by both foxes, and interestingly at no point did we see both individuals appearing together – one was obviously company and two represented a crowd. As we opened the fifteenth and final clip, we fully expected to see the smaller fox finishing off its supper, but as we were unable to see anything immediately in shot we thought nothing had been filmed, until halfway through the recorded minute a badger suddenly shuffled through the shot. What a result – double mammal action!

Before closing my computer down, a quick check of my emails revealed one message which had just arrived courtesy of the organiser of the BBC Natural History Unit Birding Cup with the results. As I trawled quickly through the various categories I could see that the winner of the main competition was a good pal of mine called Rob, with a very creditable score of 99 species of bird recorded around the whole of the UK between Christmas Day and New Year's Day. As far as I was concerned, however, this was nothing more than a side issue when compared to the real deal of the 'Highest Garden List' category. Taking the results in reverse order, like they used to with the Miss World beauty competitions, in third place was a chap called Jon with seven species recorded in his garden, followed in second place by my BBC drinking buddy Colin with sixteen, before streaking out in the lead and pulverising the competition was yours truly with 29 species! If only! Having forgotten to send in an email with my score, unfortunately I wouldn't be receiving the plaudits, the cup or the bouquet of flowers. But the moral victory was mine!

We'd planned 31 January to be a very special day, as it marked the end of our first year in Chew Stoke, my first year living out in the country and the first anniversary of the garden under our steward-ship. Christina had arranged to take the time off so that we could enjoy the whole day in the garden together, and I left her upstairs with a cup of tea on the bedside table as I slipped out onto the patio to see what was knocking about in the garden before sorting out the girls. Having hovered around freezing during the night, the clear blue sky indicated that as soon as the sun had risen sufficiently above the horizon the temperature too would begin to improve.

The previous week we had been royally entertained by a male blackcap (with this time – yes – a black cap) which Christina had nicknamed 'the Prince of the Quince', and as I looked into the fruit tree I immediately noticed that he'd once again taken up his usual position in the centre.

No doubt another continental blackcap, the bird had located the fat block hanging in the quince a while back, and, when not actively feeding from it himself, he spent the rest of his day defending it from as many birds as possible as if his life depended on it – which in many ways it probably did. This meant that the moment that any blue tits, great tits, robins, long-tailed tits or coal tits landed in the quince with an eye for a beakful of winter-warming fat, they were in no uncertain terms immediately sent packing. The one exception to this rule, where the bullying blackcap decided wisely to dish out a free pass instead, seemed to be the occasional blackbird that flut-tered up from the ground for a feed. Most bullies know their limita-tions, and the blackcap realised that, being only half the size and less than a quarter of the weight, this was one battle he most defi-nitely wouldn't win.

Elsewhere in the garden, the squirrels had been outmanoeuvred with the removal of their 'launch pad' from the trunk of the rowan across to the bell feeder, and had been forced to temporarily give way again to the greenfinch, but I had no doubt whatsoever that as I sat there they were probably elsewhere, planning a new way to access the feeder, and doubtless they would be back soon for another crack at glory. What was turning into a beautiful day had also prompted a few birds into full voice and in quick succession I was able to pick out my first dunnock and goldfinch song of the year, plus a distant song thrush. I'd already been listening to this particular song thrush for a few weeks now, but on this day it held much more resonance, as this had been the song that had so inspired me when I had taken on the house and garden exactly a year ago.

I couldn't believe how much had been achieved in the space of just 365 days. But it hadn't just been about the assembling of compost bins, digging a pond, constructing flowerbeds, creating a meadow, planting hedgerows, coppicing woods or building a bug hotel – it had been about creating both a home for the wildlife and also a home for Christina and me. It had been about the execution of a project for which we'd developed a joint passion and which ultimately had brought us closer together. And the best thing of all was that the journey had only just begun. We'd seen so much in the garden during the year and I could barely wait to see whether we'd be blessed with frogspawn in our pond, which other butterflies would be enticed in by the meadow, or how much higher the garden bird list would go!

After an al-fresco breakfast, we narrowed down the work to three main tasks; I would continue to tackle the pile of brash left over from coppicing the bank while Christina would be putting into practice all she'd discussed with Mark in relation to prepping the herbaceous borders for spring. The final job that I was keen for Christina to help me with was clearing out the nest boxes in readiness for the breeding season, which would be in full swing for some of our resident species all too soon.

I fired up the garden incinerator and set about reducing the pile of brash with the loppers into sufficiently small pieces for them to be easily fed into the furnace, while Christina got stuck in with the secateurs. The slightly mindless task of chopping and burning also gave me the opportunity to appreciate the *volte-face* I'd performed during the course of the year. Although I'd always loved gardens and what they represented, I'd gone from being someone who had to be

virtually dragged kicking and screaming outside to do some gardening, to a person who would be giddy with excitement at the thought
of a whole day messing around in the garden. Also, while I'd never
been the type of person capable of tackling anything *too* technically
demanding, and I certainly wouldn't be contemplating a change of
career to that of engineer any time soon, one thing I had lost was
the fear of having a go at something. After all, the compost bins
were still upright and the pond was still full of water!

As I looked up, I watched Christina throw a large worm she'd
unearthed to the girls, which resulted in a very unseemly squabble
until April finally managed to assert her dominance and come away
with the juicy item. It had not just been the chickens that had been
a revelation to me, as Christina had taken to the gardening like a
duck to water, and, like her boyfriend, she was at her happiest
amongst the plants.

As the day wore steadily on, I eventually managed to dispose of
the rest of the waste wood, meaning that at last we could see the
meadow and the beech hedge again, but with Christina still hard at
it as she mulched the flowerbeds with well-rotted manure, I could
see she was going to take some persuading to temporarily stop what
she was doing and help me with the bird boxes. 'C'mon Teens' I said
to my now stinky girlfriend, 'just give me a hand with a couple of the
boxes I can't reach without a ladder, and then I'll give you a hand
finishing off the beds.' 'They weren't used last year, so why are we
wasting our time to clean them out if they're not going to be used
this year?' she replied, before my 'humour me' remark eventually
persuaded her to stop what she was doing.

Choosing the nest box on the birch tree to clean out first, I put
the ladder up against the tree and, giving her the screwdriver,
suggested that she might like to open up the first one. I wouldn't go
as far as to say that at this point Christina had begun to get irritated
with me, but, unable to understand why this wasn't a job that could
wait for another day, she was mighty close. But to humour me, she
duly shinned up the ladder I was firmly holding at the base, before
unscrewing the lid and lifting it open. As she turned round to me,

she had a look on her face that I can only describe as that of changing from utter confusion to a state of high emotion in the second it took to realise that, while I was still holding the ladder, I was now doing so down on one knee. I must explain that inside the nest box, like a Russian doll, was another somewhat smaller box, which contained something even more precious than that of a bird's nest, as it held an engagement ring specially designed out of British oak inlaid with the beautiful grain of yew – two of our garden plants.

Have you ever noticed that at times of unbelievable pressure and emotion your voice can unexpectedly take on the sound of a choked chicken and your brain suddenly begins to mangle words? 'You will … I mean, can you … I mean, will you marry me?' I eventually managed to splutter out, and as I waited for an answer I could feel the tears from her big, beautiful green eyes plop onto my face from above, and I sensed three pairs of beady eyes watching intently from behind the electric fence.

I always knew that April, May and June were my favourite months!

ACKNOWLEDGEMENTS

First and foremost, Christina and I must sincerely thank both our families for their constant love and unstinting support, not only throughout this project, but in everything we do – they are immensely proud of us and the feeling is only too mutual. Since moving to Chew Stoke we have made firm friends with a number of village residents who have helped us feel incredibly welcome, and special mentions must go to Andy and Lorraine Isaac, Andrew Atkinson, Debbie Turner, the Barlows, the Judds, the extended Gilbert family, the Illis family, the McPhersons and all the Chalks!

I am as ever indebted to my agent Hilary Knight and her assistant Alex Wigley, who are integral to everything I do, and I am incredibly lucky to have two such wonderfully talented people 'batting on my side'. My literary agent Jane Turnbull has also been vital throughout the whole process, and has been a constant source of advice and encouragement from the book's conception through to its final delivery.

This is my fourth book and all have been published under the HarperCollins banner, so I'd like to thank the indomitable duo of Myles Archibald and Julia Koppitz for believing I have much more to offer than a voice and a face on television, and to enable Christina's fabulous artwork to get the full credit it duly deserves. I must also sincerely thank Helena Caldon for undertaking an invaluable and incredibly astute edit of this book, and the marketing team at HarperCollins for ensuring it reaches the widest possible audience. I'm also immensely grateful to Stephen Moss, my ex-boss and good friend from the BBC, who read a number of the chapters early on and came up with the genius idea of no photos!

During the conversion of the garden from that of a forgotten little corner to our pride and joy, Christina and I have been lucky enough to dip into a number of substantial wells of knowledge. We are immensely grateful to Ed Drewitt, Gary Moore and Nigel Redman for their formidable birding prowess, Graham Holvey, Mark Flowers, Ian Dorrington, Cheryle Sifontes, Chris Tovey and Terry McGovern for their horticultural/arboricultural advice and Jonathan Holvey, Ben Sexstone and Ed Miller for their practical support.

We have also been the recipients of immense generosity from CJ WildBird Foods, Simon Scarth of Chew Valley Trees and Wildlife Watching Supplies. Finally I would like to register my gratitude to Charles Church Homes, Malcolm Genge, Butterfly Conservation, Pond Conservation, Graham Appleton of the British Trust of Ornithology, Bristol Zoo, Tigress Productions and Chew Stoke Primary School for (in order) allowing us to place skips on their property, giving advice, the kind loan of equipment and the even kinder loan of children.

ABOUT THE AUTHOR

Mike Dilger is a naturalist, writer and broadcaster, best known as *The One Show*'s answer to Dr Doolittle. He spent four years as a biologist in the tropics of Ecuador, Tanzania and Vietnam and has birded, botanised and entomologised all over the world, accumulating an encyclopaedic knowledge of British and South American wildlife.